£2.99
Educ.
C14
(3)

Contemporary Perspectives in E-learning Resea

C000081558

E-learning is at an exciting point in its development; its potential in terms of research is great and its impact on institutional practices is fully recognised. *Contemporary Perspectives in E-learning Research* aims to define e-learning as a field of research, highlighting the complex issues, activities and tensions that characterise the area.

Written by a team of experienced researchers and commented upon by internationally recognised experts, this book engages researchers and practitioners in critical discussion and debate of findings emerging from the field and the associated impact on practice. Key topics examined include:

- access and inclusion;
- the socio-cultural contexts of e-learning;
- organisational structures, processes and identities;
- technical aspects of learning research – using tools and resources;
- approaches to learning and teaching practices and associated learning theories;
- designing for e-learning and the management of educational resources;
- professional roles and identities;
- the evolution of e-assessment; and
- collaboration, motivation and educational evaluation.

Contemporary Perspectives in E-learning Research provides a synthesis of research, giving a grounding in contemporary e-learning scholarship whilst identifying the debates that make it such a lively and fast-moving area. A landmark text in an evolving field, this book will prove invaluable for all researchers, practitioners, policy-makers and students engaging with e-learning.

Gráinne Conole is Professor of e-learning at the Open University, researching the use, integration and evaluation of e-learning and its impact on organisational change.

Martin Oliver is Senior Lecturer at the London Knowledge Lab, Institute of Education, where he researches the relationship between technology and higher education and leads an MA in Information and Communication Technology in Education.

Open and Flexible Learning Series

Series Editors: Fred Lockwood, A.W. (Tony) Bates and Som Naidu

Activities in Self-Instructional Texts
Fred Lockwood

Assessing Open and Distance Learners
Chris Morgan and Meg O'Reilly

Changing University Teaching
Terry Evans and Daryl Nation

The Costs and Economics of Open and Distance Learning
Greville Rumble

Delivering Digitally
Alistair Inglis, Peter Ling and Vera Joosten

Delivering Learning on the Net
The why, what and how of online education
Martin Weller

The Design and Production of Self-Instructional Materials
Fred Lockwood

Developing Innovation in Online Learning
An action research framework
Maggie McPherson and Miguel Baptista Nunes

Exploring Open and Distance Learning
Derek Rowntree

Flexible Learning in a Digital World
Betty Collis and Jef Moonen

Improving Your Students' Learning
Alistair Morgan

Innovation in Open and Distance Learning
Fred Lockwood and Anne Gooley

Integrated E-learning
Implications for pedagogy, technology and organization
Wim Jochems, Jeroen van Merriënboer and Rob Koper

Key Terms and Issues in Open and Distance Learning
Barbara Hodgson

The Knowledge Web
Learning and collaborating on the net
Marc Eisenstadt and Tom Vincent

Learning and Teaching in Distance Education
Edited by Som Naidu

Making Materials-Based Learning Work
Derek Rowntree

Managing Open Systems
Richard Freeman

Mega-Universities and Knowledge Media
John S. Daniel

Mobile Learning
A handbook for educators and trainers
Edited by Agnes Kukulska-Hulme and John Traxler

Objectives, Competencies and Learning Outcomes
Reginald F Melton

The Open Classroom
Distance learning in and out of schools
Edited by Jo Bradley

Online Education Using Learning Objects
Edited by Rory McGreal

Open and Distance Learning
Case studies from education, industry and commerce
Stephen Brown

Open and Flexible Learning in Vocational Education and Training
Judith Calder and Ann McCollum

Planning and Management in Distance Education
Santosh Panda

Preparing Materials for Open, Distance and Flexible Learning
Derek Rowntree

Programme Evaluation and Quality
Judith Calder

Reforming Open and Distance Learning
Terry Evans and Daryl Nation

Reusing Online Resources
Alison Littlejohn

Student Retention in Online, Open and Distance Learning
Ormond Simpson

Supporting Students in Online, Open and Distance Learning
Ormond Simpson

Teaching with Audio in Open and Distance Learning
Derek Rowntree

Teaching Through Projects
Jane Henry

Towards More Effective Open and Distance Learning
Perc Marland

Understanding Learners in Open and Distance Education
Terry Evans

Using Communications Media in Open and Flexible Learning
Robin Mason

The Virtual University
Steve Ryan, Bernard Scott, Howard Freeman and Daxa Patel

Contemporary Perspectives in E-learning Research

Themes, methods and impact on practice

Edited by Gráinne Conole
and Martin Oliver

Routledge
Taylor & Francis Group
LONDON AND NEW YORK

First published 2007 by Routledge
2 Park Square, Milton Park, Abingdon, Oxon OX14 4RN

Simultaneously published in the USA and Canada
by Routledge
270 Madison Avenue, New York, NY 10016

Routledge is an imprint of the Taylor & Francis Group, an informa business

© 2007 Gráinne Conole and Martin Oliver selection and editorial matter;
individual chapters, the contributors

Typeset in Times and Gill Sans by
GreenGate Publishing Services, Tonbridge, Kent
Printed and bound in Great Britain by
Cpod, Trowbridge, Wiltshire

All rights reserved. No part of this book may be reprinted or reproduced
or utilised in any form or by any electronic, mechanical, or other means,
now known or hereafter invented, including photocopying and recording,
or in any information storage or retrieval system, without permission in
writing from the publishers.

British Library Cataloguing in Publication Data
A catalogue record for this book is available from the British Library

Library of Congress Cataloging in Publication Data
Contemporary perspectives in e-learning research : themes, methods, and
impact on practice / edited by Gráinne Conole and Martin Oliver.
     p. cm. – (The open and flexible learning series)
   Includes bibliographical references and index.
     1. Education, Higher–Computer-assisted instruction–Research–Great
Britain. 2. Education, Higher–Effect of technological innovations on–Great
Britain. I. Conole, Gráinne. II. Oliver, Martin, 1973- III. Title. IV. Series: Open
& flexible learning series.

LB2395.7.C685 2006
378.1'734–dc22

                                                                 2006017345

ISBN10: 0-415-39393-0 (hbk)
ISBN10: 0-415-39394-9 (pbk)
ISBN10: 0-203-96626-0 (ebk)

ISBN13: 978-0-415-39393-5 (hbk)
ISBN13: 978-0-415-39394-2 (pbk)
ISBN13: 978-0-203-96626-6 (ebk)

Contents

Illustrations

Figures

Tables

Contributors

Helen Beetham is an independent consultant in e-learning, formerly Research Fellow at the Open University and the University of Bristol. She is principal consultant to the Joint Information Systems Committee e-learning programme (pedagogy), in which capacity she has scoped and is overseeing an extensive research programme (2004–07).

Tom Boyle is Director of the Learning Technology Research Institute at London Metropolitan University. He was Assistant Director, with responsibility for pedagogy, of the UK Subject Centre for Information and Computer Sciences from 2000 to 2005. Tom is Director of the Centre for Excellence in Teaching and Learning in Reusable Learning Objects.

Gráinne Conole is Professor of e-learning at the Open University. She was previously the Director of the Institute for Learning and Research Technology at the University of Bristol. She is editor of the *Association of Learning Technologies Journal, ALT-J.*

John Cook is Centre Manager for the Reusable Learning Objects CETL and Principal Research Fellow at the Learning Technology Research Institute, London Metropolitan University. He is President of the Association for Learning Technology and a member of the Joint Information Systems Committee 'E-learning and Pedagogy Experts Group'.

Sarah Currier is a librarian and researcher at the University of Strathclyde. From 2002 until 2004 she was Coordinator of the Centre for Educational Technology Interoperability Standards Educational Content Special Interest Group. She sits on the JISC Repositories and Preservation Advisory Group as well as the Jorum Enhancement Committee.

James Dalziel works at the interface of pedagogy and technology in e-learning, and in middleware and infrastructure in computer science. He is a recognised international contributor to next generation learning technology research and development, and to international standards for learning technology. He is Director of LAMS Foundation Ltd.

Hugh Davis runs the Learning Technology Research Group within the School of Electronics and Computer Science at the University of Southampton. He is also the University Director of Education with responsibility for e-learning strategy, and has experience of starting a spin-off company from his research into hypertext.

Frances Deepwell is an educational developer at Coventry University's Centre for Higher Education Development and Fellow of the Staff and Educational Developers' Association. She is course leader for the Postgraduate Certificate in Learning and Teaching in HE and also runs the Embedding Learning Technologies Award, a SEDA professional development course.

Sara de Freitas is a Research Fellow at the London Knowledge Lab. She is also a consultant with UK Joint Information Systems Committee E-learning Programme, founded the UK Lab Group, and edits the Network Continuum Education series of books on personalising learning aimed at practitioners, managers and policy-makers.

Maarten de Laat is a researcher at the Department of Education and Life Long Learning at Exeter University. He also works for the Centre for ICT in Education at IVLOS, University of Utrecht, The Netherlands and co-founded the software company KnowledgeWorks. He facilitates a Dutch online workshop on the foundations of communities of practice.

Charles Duncan is CEO of Intrallect Ltd and has been producing e-learning materials for 20 years. He has contributed to several books, including *Reusing Online Resources* and both 'Educational Technology' and 'From Theory into Practice' in the WMO guides for trainers.

Martin Dyke is a Senior Lecturer in Post-Compulsory Education and Training in the School of Education, University of Southampton. He has taught in schools and colleges across a range of levels and subjects and has extensive experience of working in the Learning and Skills Sector in the UK.

Isobel Falconer is a Research Fellow in Learning Technology at Dundee University. She has previously worked for 18 years as an Associate Lecturer and Research Associate at the UK Open University, teaching in the Arts, Science and Maths faculties.

Cathy Gunn is a Senior Lecturer in Academic Development specialising in computer-facilitated learning. She has contributed to organisational change at all levels within a large research university since the early 1990s. Cathy is President of The Australasian Society for Computers in Learning in Tertiary Education.

Jen Harvey is the Head of Lifelong Learning at the Dublin Institute of Technology. Prior to moving to Dublin in 1999, she was the Implementation

Support Consultant responsible for the areas of assessment and evaluation as part of the Learning and Teaching Dissemination Initiative in Scotland.

Bruce Ingraham is a Teaching Fellow at the University of Teesside and is charged with supporting the use and development of e-learning across the curriculum. He began his career as a literary semiotician and now specialises in the semiotics of multimedia and the production of online learning resources.

Kim Issroff is a Senior Lecturer at the Centre for Research in Education and Educational Technology at the Open University. Prior to this she was a Senior Lecturer at University College London in the Department of Education and Professional Development. She is on the editorial board of the *Journal of Computer Assisted Learning*.

Sanna Järvelä is a full professor of learning and educational technology and is head of the Research Unit for Educational Technology in the Faculty of Education, University of Oulu. She previously coordinated the Earli Special Interest Group, Motivation and Emotion, and has been a visiting scholar at King's College London and the UK Open University.

Ann Jones is a Senior Lecturer at the Institute of Educational Technology at the Open University and directs the Computers and Learning Research Group, part of the Centre for Research into Education and Educational Technology, where she has conducted Educational Technology research since 1978.

Christopher Jones is Reader in the Institute of Educational Technology at the Open University. He is joint editor of *Networked Learning: Perspectives and Issues* and has undertaken research for the Joint Information Systems Committee and the Scottish Higher Education Funding Council, as well as the programme-wide evaluation of the Learning and Teaching Support Network.

Peter Knight is Director of the Open University's Institute of Educational Technology. He has undertaken a wide range of consultancy and project work, as well as publishing extensively.

Diana Laurillard is Chair of Learning with Digital Technologies in the London Knowledge Media Lab, Institute of Education. Prior to this she was Head of the E-learning Strategy Unit in the Department for Education and Skills, and before that Pro-Vice-Chancellor at the Open University, She is the author of *Rethinking University Teaching*.

Philippa Levy is Academic Director of the Centre for Inquiry-based Learning in the Arts and Social Sciences, and Senior Lecturer in the Department of Information Studies, at the University of Sheffield. She is a member of the Arts and Humanities Research Council Peer Review College and serves on the editorial board of the journal *Teaching in Higher Education*.

Allison Littlejohn is Professor of Learning Technology and Director of the Caledonian Academy at the Glasgow Caledonian University. Allison edited *Reusing Online Resources* and is editing a Routledge series for practitioners, 'Designing for E-learning'. She chairs the UK Forum on Supporting Sustinable E-learning for the Higher Education Academy and received a scholarship from ASCILITE in 2005.

Patrick McAndrew is Head of the Centre for Information Technology in Education at the Open University. Current research activities are centred on the IET UserLab research group, of which he is co-Director. Patrick joined the Open University in 1999 after managing the Institute for Computer-Based Learning at Heriot-Watt University.

Claire McAvinia is a Lecturer at the National University of Ireland, Maynooth. She was previously based at University College London, where she taught on a Master's course in Learning Technology Research, and at undergraduate level on communication in digital media.

David McConnell is Professor of Education (Advanced Learning Technology) at Lancaster University and was previously Professor in the School of Education at the University of Sheffield, where he directed the Masters in Networked E-learning. He has been involved in the field since the 1970s.

Angela McFarlane holds a chair in education at the University of Bristol and is a visiting Professor at the University of Oslo. She is a director of the TEEM project, is on the steering committee of the Nesta FutureLab project, and is on the board of Teachers' TV. Angela is a writer and a columnist for the *Times Educational Supplement*.

Colleen McKenna is a Lecturer in the Department of Education and Professional Development at University College London, where she runs the Academic Communication Programme.

Carmel McNaught is Professor of Learning Enhancement in the Centre for Learning Enhancement and Research at the Chinese University of Hong Kong. Carmel has had over 30 years' experience in teaching and research in higher education, and has had appointments in eight universities in Australasia and southern Africa.

Terry Mayes was Director of Research at the Institute for Computer-Based Learning at Heriot-Watt University from its formation in 1990. He is currently a research professor in the Centre for Research in Lifelong Learning at Glasgow Caledonian University, and is chair of the steering group for the Scottish Enhancement Theme on flexible learning.

Martin Oliver is a Senior Lecturer at the London Knowledge Lab, Institute of Education, where he runs the MA in ICT in Education. He is an editor of *ALT-J*, the journal of learning technology research.

Ron Oliver is Foundation Professor of Interactive Multimedia in the School of Communications and Multimedia at Edith Cowan University and has been actively involved in the field since 1977.

Elaine Pearson is Director of the Accessibility Research Centre (ARC) and a Principal Lecturer in the School of Computing at the University of Teesside. Elaine is also a Visiting Fellow with the Educational Development and Technology Centre (EDTeC) at the University of New South Wales, Sydney, Australia.

Andrew Ravenscroft is Deputy Director of the Learning Technology Research Institute (LTRI) of London Metropolitan University. Previously he was Director of the Dialogue and Design for New Media Research Group at the UK Open University. He is an invited expert on national and international consultation groups including the EPSRC/ESRC/e-Science e-learning research group.

George Roberts is Development Director for Off-campus E-learning and a member of the Brookes Virtual Task Group at the Oxford Brookes University. George was a community-based adult education practitioner (1986–1989), then was head of corporate programmes and consultancy at the College of Petroleum and Energy Studies until 2000.

Gilly Salmon is Professor of E-learning and Learning Technologies at the University of Leicester and is head of the Beyond Distance Research Alliance. Previously, she worked for 16 years with the Open University Business School. She is the author of *E-moderating* and *E-tivities*.

Niall Sclater is Director of the Open University's Virtual Learning Environment Programme. Previously he was Head of E-learning and Assistant Director of Learning Services at the University of Strathclyde, where he led the development of the Clyde Virtual University and the EU-funded Mediterranean Virtual University.

Jane Seale is Senior Lecturer in Educational Innovation in Higher Education at the University of Southampton. She teaches on the Postgraduate Certificate Course in Academic Practice and is Learning and Teaching coordinator for the School of Education. Jane is Chair of the Association for Learning Technology and an editor of *ALT-J*.

Jane Secker is the Learning Technology Librarian at the London School of Economics and Political Science, based in the Centre for Learning Technology. She is the author of *Electronic Resources in the Virtual Learning Environment: A Guide for Librarians*, and is Chair of the HERON User Group and of ALISS.

Mike Sharples is Professor of Educational Technology at the University of Birmingham. He leads the University's Educational Technology Research

Group. He is also Director of the Centre for Educational Technology and Distance Learning (CETADL), the University's innovations centre for flexible and distance learning.

Jan Smith is a Lecturer in the Centre for Academic Practice and Learning Environment at the University of Strathclyde. Her previous post involved researching problem-based learning in electronic and electrical engineering.

Colin Tattersall worked in the telecommunications and software industries before joining The Open University of the Netherlands, where his responsibilities cover work related to innovation and standardisation in e-learning. He co-edited *Learning Design: A Handbook on Modelling and Delivering Networked Education and Training* with Rob Koper.

Melody Thompson is Assistant Professor of Education in Penn State's College of Education, project leader for the E-learning Collaborative Research Project of the Worldwide Universities Network (WUN) and Faculty Satisfaction editor for the Sloan Consortium's Effective Practices database. Dr Thompson is co-author of the McGraw-Hill *Handbook of Distance Learning*.

Bill Warbuton has 20 years' experience in developing e-learning and e-assessment applications in the public and commercial sectors. He is CAA Officer at the University of Southampton, where he has an institutional role in coordinating CAA initiatives and specific responsibilities for managing the central QuestionMark Perception CAA system.

Rupert Wegerif holds a chair at the University of Exeter. He is the author (with Lyn Dawes) of *Thinking and Learning with ICT: Raising Achievement in Primary Classrooms*. He is lead editor of the *Journal of Thinking Skills and Creativity* and a co-editor of the Elsevier book series, 'Advances in Learning and Instruction'.

Etienne Wenger is a pioneer of 'communities of practice' research, having authored and co-authored seminal articles and books on the topic, including *Situated Learning, Communities of Practice: Learning, Meaning and Identity* and *Cultivating Communities of Practice: A Guide to Managing Knowledge*.

Su White is Learning and Teaching Co-ordinator for the Faculty of Engineering and Applied Science at the University of Southampton. She is a member of the steering group for LTSN-ICS, and of the Intelligence Agents and Multimedia (IAM) research group in Electronics and Computer Science (ECS).

Denise Whitelock is a Senior Lecturer in Information Technology at the Open University's Institute of Educational Technology. Denise directs two JISC-funded e-assessment projects and is working with Robert Gordon University to develop an open source mentoring system – work that recently won an Open University teaching award for innovation.

Foreword

Fred Lockwood, Series Editor

In his book *Inside the Tornado* published by HarperBusiness (1995), Moore described the technology adoption life cycle – the succession of phases through which an innovation passes, from Innovators to the Early Adopters, on to the Early Majority, the Late Majority and finally, the Laggards. It is increasingly evident that teaching online – e-learning – is no longer the province of the Innovators and Early Adopters but that 'The Chasm' has been crossed and e-learning is now being undertaken by the Early Majority; it is becoming a mainstream activity.

This observation is reinforced when one looks for other indicators of this development. In the period 1992–9, 25 books were published in the Open and Distance Learning Series. An inspection of these books reveals that 21 books had an essentially non-Communication and Information Technology (CIT) focus; 4 clearly had a CIT focus. Between 2000 and the present, the Series published a further 20 books – with only 4 of these having a non-CIT focus; 16 were firmly in the CIT area.

Similar patterns can be observed in major academic journals. A personal review of articles published in the journal *Open Learning* from 1991 to the present revealed a clear and steady decline in non-CIT-type articles from 100 per cent in 1991, to about 25 per cent in 2005. The same period, in the same journal, witnessed a clear and steady increase in CIT-type articles from zero in 1991, to over 60 per cent in 2005. Reviews of other academic journals such as the *American Journal of Distance Education*, *Distance Education* and the *Journal of Distance Education* reveal similar trends.

If our practice and decision-making in e-learning is to be informed by evidence, there is an urgent need to review the research approaches and perspectives in this multi-faceted and growing field. As such, this book *Contemporary Perspectives in E-learning Research*, edited by Gráinne Conole and Martin Oliver, is timely. By drawing together eminent scholars in e-learning from across the world, and allowing them to work collaboratively on each of the chapters, Gráinne and Martin have assembled not only a unique collection of insights into a broad range of issues but also have made linkages within and between the various chapters. The six major themes running through the collection of chapters serve as a unifying thread in which pedagogy rather than technology is at the fore.

It is noteworthy that in their summary to Chapter 15, Gráinne and Martin state:

> The purpose of this book was not to provide simple answers. It was not intended to say how to 'do' e-learning (either as policy or practice), nor to establish any single hegemonic position on how to research it. Instead its purpose was to inform, to challenge and to sensitise. Drawing together research on this series of topics has provided a point of departure for anyone seeking to engage with e-learning. We have avoided claims of being authoritative, but have sought to be wide-ranging in this process, so that a better-informed position can be taken.

I am convinced that your study of the chapters in this book will leave you better-informed and more able to contribute to the ongoing development of e-learning.

Fred Lockwood
Yelvertoft, July 2006

Part 1

Macro dimensions of e-learning

Chapter 1

Introduction

Gráinne Conole and Martin Oliver

The impact of learning technology on education has expanded rapidly, especially in the last 15 years. This book provides an overview of these developments, identifies associated issues and reflects upon the multiple perspectives and different discourses that have come to constitute this diverse area of research and development.

E-learning technology is a multi-faceted and complex area. This book reflects this by reviewing the area from a number of different perspectives and through different theoretical lenses, highlighting different schools of thought and tensions in the area.

As a research area, e-learning is both multi- and inter-disciplinary, covers a vast range of research topics, from those that focus on technologies through to wider socio-cultural research questions, and addresses issues concerned with the impact of technologies on learning and teaching, professional roles and identities, organisational structures and associated strategy and policy. Given this diversity, the book presents a reflective and critical review of this spectrum of activity. Examples and experiences are drawn primarily from UK higher education, though reference will be made to the wider context in terms of comparison throughout the book.

Six specific themes have been woven throughout the book. These are used to frame discussion across the chapters and to bring out the creative tensions and debates in different aspects of the field:

1. *Interdisciplinarity.* The interdisciplinarity of the area will be explored both in terms of how different research perspectives influence the area and how disciplines differ in the adoption and use of learning technologies.
2. *Access and inclusion.* This will include issues around the widening participation agenda, barriers to access, equity and inclusion, and issues around the nature and extent of the digital divide.
3. *Change.* This concerns understanding the dynamics of change and its relationship to learning technologies. This theme will also explore the motivational factors associated with the use of technologies, along with the drivers and rationale for change and the subsequent consequences and impact. Finally, strategies for managing and enabling change will be considered.

4. *Commodification.* Issues of the commodification of knowledge and of technologies will be discussed, including the increase in convergence towards integrated and interoperable institutional systems and underpinning international standards.
5. *Interactivity and social interaction.* New opportunities for these will be explored, along with their impact on individual roles and identities and organisational structures.
6. *Political aspects.* The political dimensions of technologies will be considered, as well as the relationship between strategy and practice.

These themes have been drawn out as they help to define the character of e-learning as a research area and form common threads across the different topics covered here. These themes shape, not just describe, e-learning research – for example change is inherent across all aspects of research in this area. The themes are returned to in the conclusion of the book, which provides a summary of issues arising from the preceding chapters.

It is worth providing a brief note on terminology. Perhaps not surprisingly given that this is a new and emerging field, terminology is in a constant state of flux – changing according to current trends, fads and political drives and as new understanding emerges from the research findings. Even the overarching term for the area is contested. It has been referred to as educational technology, learning technology, communication and information technologies (C&IT), information and communication technologies (ICT), and e-learning, amongst other terms. In the last few weeks before submitting this manuscript, funding initiatives in the UK have attempted to introduce yet another term: technology-enhanced learning. This evolution is clearly not over.

For the purpose of this book we will use the following terms specifically.

*   E-learning is the term most commonly used to represent the broader domain of development and research activities on the application of technologies to education.
*   Information and communication technologies (ICT) refers to the broad range of technologies that are used in education.

When these are used with reference to their use in learning and teaching we tend to use the term 'learning technologies'.

A dialogic approach

Throughout the remainder of the chapters, the heart of the text is written in the conventional manner, presented as if by a single, authoritative voice. However, all of these central narratives have been co-written, so that different voices and perspectives are woven into them. In addition, each narrative has been contested by offering it up for peer review and critique. Rather than hide this process of production, dissent and re-production, the notion of separate voices, each with its own potentially productive tale to tell, is celebrated. We have attempted to follow the example of innovations in publishing academic discourse such as that of the *Journal of Interactive Media in Education*, where the dialogues that underlie the production of each published (and thus 'legitimated') article are left visible through hyperlinked discussion areas full of comment, development and asides (Buckingham, Shum and Sunner, 2001).

So, accompanying the central narrative, other researchers have been invited to comment on the text – represented as call-out boxes alongside the text. We envisaged these as marginalia, and wish them to be seen as an invitation to readers to disagree, take their own positions and then inscribe these into this text too.

We have adopted this approach as we think it the best way of encapsulating the current status of research in this area: its complexity, its multi-disciplinarity and its impact across pedagogical, technical and organisational boundaries.

Structure of the book

The book is divided into two parts. Part I – Macro dimensions of e-learning – consists of a series of chapters describing the contextual dimensions of learning technologies. Part II – Micro dimensions of e-learning – goes on to consider the use of learning technologies across different dimensions of learning and teaching, and critiques their impact on practice (Figure 1.1).

Part I – macro dimensions of e-learning

Part I contextualises the area and looks at the macro dimensions of e-learning. This chapter provides a rationale for the book and an overview of the content, introduces the cross-cutting themes in e-learning research and discusses the factors influencing the emergence of this as a research area.

The last few decades have seen a number of important changes both in the way in which society views knowledge and in universities' relationships with society. Chapter 2 provides a theoretical context for the book by considering the philosophy of knowledge in relation to e-learning, new modes of learning and the sociology of knowledge (ways of knowing, literacies, representations and knowledge engineering). The multiple perspectives and discourses are discussed in depth, providing an overview of different theoretical and methodological approaches adopted in the area and the strengths and weaknesses these different dimensions bring to the area. The chapter also provides a wider socio-cultural perspective illustrating how this new research area aligns to other related research disciplines in the social sciences and beyond. This is included because we believe that, before attempting to make sense of the relationship between the different traditions that contribute to the field of e-learning, it is worth taking a broader view of the context in which this work takes place.

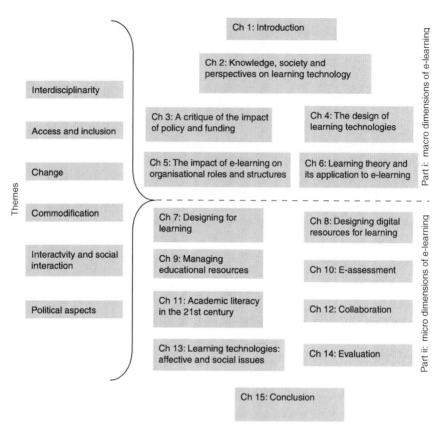

Figure 1.1 Structure of the book and cross-cutting themes

The highly political nature of e-learning research is one of its defining characteristics and has a major impact on both shaping and directing the area. This is in part because it is so inextricably tied up with practice, but also relates to the way in which policy influences and directs the area. In addition, the rhetoric that has always surrounded the area is discussed. This has raised (often unrealistic) expectations of what technologies can do, at both practitioner and senior management level. Chapter 3 gives an historical perspective on the key policies and initiatives that have influenced the emergence of this area. It provides a review of policy directives in relation to learning technologies over the past 40 years and considers their impact on practice. In particular the chapter highlights the close synergy between developments in learning technology and policy at local, national and international level. The chapter begins with a survey of some of the key areas of ICT development and provides a contextualising framework for the arena in terms of external agendas and policy drivers.

Chapter 4 is entitled 'The design of learning technologies' and focuses on the technical aspects of e-learning research. It provides an overview of tools and resources and considers the ways in which these can be organised and used to support learning and teaching. It describes different tool types and environments that have emerged in recent years, along with related standards development. The chapter considers current types of structured learning environments and resources, such as Managed and Virtual Learning Environments (MLEs and VLEs), information gateways and portals, and argues that these predefined structured environments are unlikely to be sufficient to meet the future information needs of users. Technology is not used in this chapter, or in this book, as simply meaning 'software' or 'hardware'. Rather 'technologies for learning' can be understood as the human-centred use of technology, where a priority is given to the embedding of learning into specific contexts or designing technologies that are adaptive to specific contextual behaviours of learners. The reason for putting 'technology', in this sense, at the centre of this aspect of learning technology research is twofold: first, to enable us to draw upon the theoretical resources that have become available for understanding these practices; second, to contribute to research that explores the human-centred use of technology for learning. Of course, there is a danger of being technologically driven; consequently, the chapter tries to tease out the main issues surrounding the human-centred use of learning technology. The relationship between technology and physical spaces is also questioned, looking in particular at the role of mobile devices for learning and ubiquitous mobile devices to support 'everyday learning' opportunities.

Chapter 5 considers organisational issues and the impact of e-learning on organisational structures, processes and identities. It explores the changing nature of roles and identities and the emergence of new professional groups associated with technology adoption and considers how learning technologies are beginning to have an impact on organisational structures in institutions, outlining some of the research work in the area that is concerned with the development of an integrated infrastructure, both at intra- and inter-institutional levels. This chapter provides definitions of organisational cultures, roles and identities in relation to learning technologies. It considers why organisational issues are important in the context of the implementation of learning technologies and what strategies are needed to understand and take account of them. The chapter looks at mechanisms for understanding organisational culture, identification of external drivers and articulation of the different stakeholder perspectives. It provides examples of different institutional profiles and mechanisms for identifying cultural factors and their impact.

Finally, Chapter 6 provides an overview of approaches to learning and teaching and the learning theories associated with particular practices. There are two important aspects – the way learning technologies have impacted on traditional approaches and the ways in which they can best be used for effective learning, especially when this involves new or different forms of learning. An understanding of theoretical perspectives on learning has been an active area of research across a number of subject disciplines, but particularly psychology and education. This chapter outlines some of the predominant theories and shows how these relate to e-learning; these are then mapped to different pedagogical approaches. The chapter begins by discussing characteristics of learning. This abstraction is used as an analytical tool, allowing components of learning scenarios to be described and related to appropriate theoretical approaches through the use of specific tools and resources. Our assertion is that a better articulation and mapping of different pedagogical processes, tools and techniques will provide a pedagogic approach that is more reflexive and consistent with practitioners' theoretical perspectives on learning and teaching.

Part II – micro dimensions of e-learning

Part II concentrates on 'micro' aspects of e-learning: learning and teaching practices as learning technologies relate to them, from issues of curriculum design, design and management of digital resources, through to different forms and representations of literacies and exploration of the notions of collaboration and affective issues in e-learning.

Chapter 7 introduces designing for e-learning, providing a definition of what constitutes a learning activity then going on to consider the different mechanisms that practitioners use to create pedagogically informed learning activities. It begins with a brief review of academics' curriculum design practices, locating these as social and political, before moving on to consider the various ways in which curriculum knowledge (and the role of technology) is represented. The relationship between subject, pedagogical and technological knowledge is outlined, and an attempt is made to describe media and the impact of mixing these upon teaching practice. A taxonomy for learning design is presented as a mechanism for guiding practitioners through the process of linking good pedagogy and the development of effective learning activities.

The issues that arise around designing digital resources are discussed in Chapter 8, arguing that, unlike traditional print-based technology, practitioners do not yet have a clear understanding of how to create effective e-learning resources. It focuses on three issues: designers' practices, learners' needs (particularly in relation to accessibility) and re-usability (focusing on the resource). One of the principal themes of this book is the changes to learned information associated with recent technological innovations, given the transition from print as a dominant technological medium to a situation in which a much wider range of media technologies play a significant role in the learning process. Throughout this book, authors have understood this process of change as one in which the new learning technologies provide new affordances to the conduct of educational praxis. However, it is also important to understand that all these technologies 'constrain' as well as 'afford' new opportunities. Chapter 8 involves exploring what this means for the design of specific educational resources.

Chapter 9 moves on to considering the management of educational resources, outlining the range of tools available to academics and highlighting the importance of interoperability standards. The chapter discusses the pedagogical, technical and cultural issues that may inhibit effective content management and provides insight into ways in which these challenges might be addressed. It begins by exploring the ways in which practitioners design courses and outlines a range of tools available to academics to help them manage resources. Finally, the chapter investigates pedagogical, technical and cultural issues that may inhibit effective content management and provides insights into ways in which these challenges might be addressed. In doing so, the promise of Chapter 8 – with its vision of how learning resources might benefit from economies of scale – is revisited so as to understand how re-usable resources ('learning objects') might comprise a new currency of exchange within a learning economy. However, current content management tools do not allow academics freedom and flexibility in course design to develop pedagogically effective learning activities, nor do they allow easy resource re-use or sharing. The discussion highlights how second-generation content management software might address these challenges.

Chapter 10 begins with a bold assertion that assessment is *the* catalyst for learning, considering the role that e-assessment might have in addressing the needs of students. It provides an overview of the evolution of e-assessment, as well as a summary of key criticisms of its use. Current activities are discussed, particularly developments in the design and delivery of objective tests, assessment of asynchronous and synchronous discussions, plagiarism and the automatic marking of free-text assessments. Assessment policies (at a national and institutional level) and their impact on e-assessment developments are discussed. The chapter goes on to review theory and research in assessment and discusses the extent to which generic approaches to assessment are appropriate here. It then considers the impact on practice, highlighting a broad range of issues.

Chapter 11 considers the terminology surrounding literacy in online environments and interrogates some of the conflicting views and ideological assumptions about the concept of 'literacy' in relation to e-learning. It discusses the issue of academic literacy in a modern context, giving a definition for new literacies, then commenting on the range of terms and different attempts to define and describe this area and the slipperiness of both language and concepts. Contexts in which to think about new literacies are then explored. The chapter goes on to explore issues of writing with technologies, focusing upon hypertextual, multi-modal discourse (for example, what might characterise a hypertext essay), and concludes by considering jointly constructed online discourse (such as that found in virtual learning environments), new approaches to knowledge construction and issues of power and identity.

Chapter 12 looks at collaboration and in particular provides a comparison between the terms 'cooperative' and 'collaborative' learning. It begins by examining why collaboration has emerged as such an important aspect of the potential of learning technologies to support teaching and learning, then explores the theoretical and philosophical foundations for theories of collaborative and cooperative learning and how they have been applied in relation to e-learning. The chapter explores Computer Supported Cooperative/Collaborative Learning (CSCL) and studies of cooperation/collaboration/coordination in work settings under the broad heading of Computer Supported Cooperative Work (CSCW), and concludes by considering links between collaboration and the concepts of communities of practice and social practice theories of learning.

Chapter 13 focuses on social and affective issues in learning technologies. It starts with a brief review of relevant theoretical approaches to motivation, leading to the identification of features likely to increase motivation. This chapter builds on the theme of collaboration outlined in the previous chapter by considering the social nature of collaborative learning. Informal settings are considered alongside formal ones, partly because learner engagement is often high in these contexts. Finally, the chapter is drawn together with a 'case study' example of an area where we think that learning technologies can really make a difference: mobile learning.

Chapter 14 provides an overview of evaluation and its importance in relation to understanding the nature and impact of technologies on learning. By exploring contrasting definitions of evaluation within an historical context, the complexities of this area of practice are explored. This leads to a discussion of the ethical and political dynamics of evaluation work, including the evaluator's place in such processes. Then, the practical processes of evaluation are discussed, as are issues of method, of the evaluator's role (including concepts such as bias) and of context. The chapter concludes by summarising how 'good practice' cannot be rigidly specified, but instead follows from the evaluator's own perspective on the meaning and importance of their actions.

Finally, Chapter 15 provides a reflection on the other chapters by returning to the key themes identified in this opening chapter. This is complemented by a discussion of other recurrent issues that have been raised across the chapters, along with their implications for practice. The chapter concludes by reflecting on the process of collaborating on the production of the book and how the different themes and perspectives of the area have been articulated through the dialogic approach adopted.

The ways in which the themes are explicitly drawn out across the chapters is illustrated in Table 1.1.

Introducing the field of research

E-learning is a relatively young field of research and therefore it is useful to begin by reflecting on the way in which such research areas emerge. A review of research areas that have developed in the last hundred years shows a similar pattern of emergence (Rekkedal, 1994), involving the stages outlined below:

Table 1.1 Mapping of chapters to themes

	Interdisciplinarity	Access and inclusion	Change	Commodification	Interactivity and social interaction	Political aspects
Ch 1: Introduction	✓	✓	✓	✓	✓	✓
Ch 2: Knowledge, society and perspectives on learning technology	✓		✓	✓		
Ch 3: A critique of the impact of policy and funding	✓	✓	✓	✓		✓
Ch 4: The design of learning technologies		✓	✓	✓	✓	
Ch 5: The impact of e-learning on organisational roles and structures	✓		✓			✓
Ch 6: Learning theory and its application to e-learning	✓		✓		✓	
Ch 7: Designing for learning	✓	✓	✓	✓	✓	✓
Ch 8: Designing digital resources for learning	✓	✓	✓		✓	
Ch 9: Managing educational resources		✓	✓	✓	✓	✓
Ch 10: E-assessment	✓	✓			✓	✓
Ch 11: Academic literacy in the 21st century			✓	✓		
Ch 12: Collaboration	✓	✓			✓	
Ch 13: Learning technologies: affective and social issues		✓	✓		✓	
Ch 14: Evaluation	✓	✓	✓	✓		✓
Ch 15: Conclusion	✓	✓	✓	✓	✓	✓

1. Pre-subject area – no evidence of the area or perceived need or interest.
2. Beginnings – individuals begin to research or ask new questions or issues arise that are triggered by some event or catalyst.
3. Emergence – more researchers begin to work in the area and a community begins to develop.
4. Diversification – the area starts to mature and different schools of thought emerge and the area begins to align or take place alongside more established areas.
5. Establishment – the area becomes recognised in its own right with a defined community, experts, associated journals and conferences, perceived of as 'respected' research with associated professional status, courses and career routes.

In terms of researching the use of technologies for learning, there was a marked shift around a decade ago, fuelled in part by the substantive impact of the internet on learning as well as by a number of national initiatives and policy drivers. A map of these is provided elsewhere (Conole, 2002; Conole, forthcoming). Therefore we would argue that e-learning currently falls between stages three and four since it is eclectic in nature, covering a broad church of research issues and is not as yet a rigorously defined area. But the area has not arisen in isolation and feeds on a number of cognate disciplines; research into technologies for learning per se has been an active area of interest with a long history. However, as Mason points out:

> Although e-learning builds on over 150 years of practice of distance educa-
> tion, it differs markedly from previous technological innovations and does
> not yet have an established research base. So far e-learning has not pro-
> duced a new theory of learning; in its present form it can be analysed and
> interpreted using existing theoretical models. E-learning has, however,
> defined a new paradigm for learning; a way of working, studying and prob-
> lem solving which reflects the growing connectivity of people and learning
> resources.
>
> (Mason, 2002)

Research issues

E-learning research raises a plethora of issues, which can be grouped around four main themes – pedagogical, technical, organisational, and wider socio-cultural factors (see Figure 1.2). Some of the key issues this book addresses are outlined here. The issues are considered across the chapters with reference to current research work, highlighting the dialogic tensions they raise.

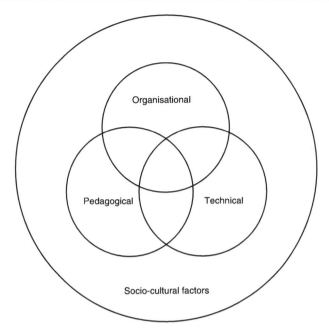

Figure 1.2 Grouping of e-learning research areas

Pedagogical research

The first of the issues is around the pedagogy of e-learning, and in particular the development of effective models for implementation, as well as the development of mechanisms for using the understanding gained from theory in the design of learning delivered through technology. These aspects are drawn out in particular in Chapters 6, 7 and 8. This area also focuses on guidelines and good practice to support the development of the e-learning skills of tutors and students, as well as understanding the nature and development of online communities and different forms of communication, forms of collaboration, the increasing flexibility and modularisation of learning opportunities and an exploration of the impact of new technologies such as games and the phenomenal growth in interest in mobile learning. These aspects are picked up in Chapters 4, 5 and 12, which consider technologies for learning, organisational issues and collaboration respectively. A key concern is how learners learn with technology and their perceptions of the use of technology; a surprisingly under-researched area, as highlighted in a recent review by Sharpe *et al.* (2005). Chapters 5 and 7 also address some of the instructional aspects such as understanding effective design principles and promulgating good practice in the development of materials, exploration of different models for online courses, understanding cultural differences in the use of online courses, identifying requirements in terms of tutor support needs and time investment, mechanisms for improving the student learning experience and improving retention rates. Of particular importance is the extent to which peda-gogical models are being used by course development teams and whether these are being made explicit; and identifying how the pedagogical model informing the design of the e-learning platform enhances or inhibits the models used by the course developers. These aspects are picked up in Chapter 6, which discusses different theoretical perspectives. The research needs to identify the most suc-cessful approaches to the development and delivery of courses and to understand what works well across different subject domains. More fundamentally, it needs to address the issue of how models of design and delivery interact and how this interaction affects the learning process.

Technical research

The second issue is research into the technology of e-learning, including the development of technical architectures to support different forms of learning and teaching, mechanisms for monitoring and tracking activity online, exploration of different types of virtual presence, consideration of the impact of wireless, mobile and smart technologies and the development of context-sensitive and flexible environments tailored to individual needs and working patterns. It is important that technological developments are continually reviewed and their implications for future developments considered. In addition, work on metadata, specifications and standards, interoperability and learning objects needs to be incorporated into the development of e-learning platforms. These issues are explored in Chapter 4.

Organisational research

The third issue concerns factors that arise at the organisational level, including effective strategies for integrating online courses within existing systems, devel-opment of organisational knowledge, new methods and processes for developing learning organisations and the seamless linking of different information processes and systems. These factors are considered in particular in Chapter 5. Additional issues include how e-learning initiatives align with other activities within institu-tions, how the experience gained from involvement in the programme is fed into strategies, the impact of these activities on roles and functions within the institu-tion, who is involved in the process, and how different institutions are dealing with these changes.

Socio-cultural factors

The fourth issue cuts across the pedagogical, technical and organisational issues, focusing on the wider context that these developments occur in, includ-ing influences ranging from policy drivers and funding steers through to current or local agendas and initiatives. In particular it is important to understand the socio-cultural context within which e-learning activities are occurring and differences in institutional approaches and cultures, which are addressed in Chapter 2. Specific examples of the impact of socio-cultural factors include the ramifications of the unintended consequences of new technologies (such as the rise of plagiarism) and the impact of new legislative requirements (such as the new disability laws in the UK). In addition, e-learning activities need to be mindful of aligning with related initiatives nationally and internationally, and this point is picked up in Chapter 3 on policy directives in this area. This area also looks at how technology mediates/plays a role in constructing identity and the power and implication of technology-supported communication of various kinds. The socio-cultural dimension is a strong theme running throughout the book; from emphasising the social and contextual aspects of learning theories discussed in Chapters 6, 7 and 12 through to the impact of new technologies used in new contexts described in Chapters 4 and 13.

Table 1.2 at the end of this chapter gives examples of some of the current research questions under each of the issues outlined above. Whilst it would be impossible in a book of this length to address all of these questions (and indeed these questions in themselves are only indicative of some of the research in this area), they demonstrate the breadth and complexity of the area. Furthermore it is increasingly evident that the questions in each of the strands are intimately interconnected; technological issues cannot be separated from pedagogical or organisational issues and vice versa.

Conclusion

This book hopes to demonstrate the complexity of e-learning as a research area, highlighting the issues and tensions that define the area. The focus of the chapters and the cross-cutting themes have been chosen to represent some of the current areas of activity in the field and to draw out these issues and tensions. We believe that this is an exciting and important point in the history of e-learning, not least because of its potential in terms of research but also because of the ramifications of e-learning developments on institutional practices and structures and associated policy at a national level. Finally, we hope the book acts as a starting point to open up the debate on e-learning, enabling us as researchers to engage in more critical discussion on the research findings that are emerging from the field and the associated impact on practice, which, we hope, will in turn lead to better clarification in the field and the development of more robust underpinning theoretical perspectives for the area.

Table 1.2 Sample e-learning research and evaluation questions

Research focus	*Research and evaluation themes and questions*
Pedagogical	Understanding the learning process
	What is effective pedagogy in terms of using learning technologies?
	Will the use of ICT result in new forms of pedagogy?
	What are students' experiences of using technologies and which do they use and for what purpose?
	What are the inherent affordances of different technologies?
	In what ways can new technologies be used to support and enhance organisational learning?
	What forms of collaborative activities were occuring and how can these be supported?
	Are current teaching and assessment activities appropriate in an e-learning context?
	How do current assessment practices enable students to demonstrate what they have learned and what is the role of e-assessment?
	Development
	What are the design and development issues associated with the production of e-learning materials?
	Who is involved in course development and what is their involvement?
	How much time do developers and practitioners spend on course development?
	What pedagogical models are course development teams using, how explicit are they and how effectively do they translate in practice?
	How are courses being designed to address different learning styles and cognate levels?
	What pedagogical models are being used and how explicit are they?
	How well do teaching and assessment methods map to the course learning aims and outcomes?
	What assessment methods are used?
	Delivery and integration
	What are the best methods of integrating ICT within the broader learning and teaching context?
	Are there pedagogical models underpinning different e-learning plat-forms and how do these influence the way these systems are used?
	How are different tools available within learning platforms being used to support learning?
	What are students' views of different learning systems?
	How useful do students find e-learning resources?
	How much do they use additional resources and the internet?

Research focus	Research and evaluation themes and questions
	What are students' experiences of online courses?
	Which aspects of learning platforms are students using and for what purposes?
	What communication mechanisms are used to support courses and for what purposes?
	What types and degree of interaction (administration, social, task related) do students have with each other and with their tutors?

Support

What new forms of literacy are emerging for students and teachers?

What effective mechanism can be used to provide support to ensure that teachers make effective use of technologies for their teaching?

What is the baseline skill set of staff needed and what staff development is there?

What is the baseline skill set of students and what support mechanisms do they need?

What support mechanisms are in place to support the development and delivery of e-learning and how effective are they?

What are the initial entry skills of students and what forms of support do they need to use e-learning?

How do students receive feedback on their progress and is this appropriate?

What e-learning expertise do tutors have?

What support do tutors get in the development of courses?

What online support is available to students?

Evaluation and quality assurance

What methods are being used to evaluate e-learning courses?

What quality assurance procedures are needed for courses incorporating e-learning?

Standards and architecture

Technical

What are the current trends in the development of underpinning standards and what are the associated interoperability issues?

How interoperable are current tools and how well do they link with institutional systems such as student records, finance, library, local VLEs and admission systems?

What research is being done into the development and testing of technical infrastructures and architectures?

Research focus	Research and evaluation themes and questions
	Tools and technologies
	What are the new and emerging technologies and how can they be used to support learning and teaching?
	What learning platforms are being used and how do they compare?
	What are the emerging new software and hardware systems and how might they be used?
	What will be the impact of emergent mobile and smart technologies?
	In what ways are in-built tracking mechanisms within e-learning systems giving rise to surveillance issues?
	Functionality and uses
	How is technology constructing new forms of identity?
	What are the new forms of power afforded by technologies and what are the implications?
	What can we learn from in-built tracking and monitoring facilities and how might this knowledge be used?
	How easy are different systems to navigate and use?
	How can we better understand the different multiple forms of representation that new media now provide?
	What functionality of different tools is being used by tutors and students and for what purposes?
	What do tutors and students think of different learning platforms and what are the perceived benefits and limitations?
	What security mechanisms are available for authentication?
	How are different forms of multimedia (images, audio, and video) being used to support learning and teaching?
	What do we know about the different characteristics of multimedia?
	How usable are different learning platforms and how easy are they to navigate around?
	Are current learning platforms able to adapt to incorporate new functionality and technologies as they emerge?
	How usable are different tools and learning environments?
	How well do different learning platforms interoperate with institutional systems and platforms?
	Users
Organisational	What is our current understanding of how stakeholders (academics, support staff, administrators, senior managers and students) work?
	What mechanisms and procedures are appropriate for developing shared knowledge banks of expertise and information?
	What are the different emerging roles and responsibilities associated with e-learning activities (management, technical, research, dissemination, evaluation, training)?

Research focus	Research and evaluation themes and questions
	What are the different views of e-learning and its role amongst academics and support staff?
	How are institutions dividing roles and responsibilities for e-learning and how much training and support are staff getting?

Structures and processes

How can we better map current institutional structures and skills and roles to capitilise on the potential use of technologies within our organisations?

What do we understand about how institutions are currently structured in relation to implementation of e-learning?

How do e-learning activities align with institutional courses and procedures?

How can we build a picture of what changes will be required to make the shift to using online learning systems to support e-learning?

How is the knowledge gained from the development and delivery of e-learning courses being used to guide e-learning practice more generally across institutions?

How is experience gained on one course being translated to other courses?

What institutional issues are arising as a result of e-learning activities?

What institutional support issues have arisen as a result of the development and what are the strategic implications?

What quality assurance methods have been developed and used?

What e-business models are being used in institutions?

Context and culture

What are the key organisational issues and challenges associated with implementing large-scale e-learning initiatives?

How do we manage the bulk of existing materials and information on university websites that have little or no coherence and consistency?

How can we ensure that different stakeholders engage with e-learning in a meaningful way?

How can we manage the transition from existing practices and processes to effective use of new systems?

What are the accessibility issues associated with new technologies and how can these be addressed?

What are the mechanisms needed to provide remote access to a variety of different users?

What are the institutional barriers and enablers to these kinds of developments?

How can e-learning be harnessed to promote lifelong learning and widening participation?

Research focus	Research and evaluation themes and questions
Socio-cultural	What are the legal and ethical issues (data protection, confidentiality etc.) associated with e-learning?
	How is plagiarism being detected and dealt with in e-learning context?
	How is accessibility being addressed?
	What are the ethical issues associated with e-learning?
	What are the specific security issues associated with different learning platforms and technologies?
	How are students being authenticated and what are the potential loopholes?
	How are different institutions dealing with the issues of copyright and ownership of material?
	What gender differences are emerging in the use of different technologies and the ways in which e-learning is being used?
	What are the cultural and linguistic issues and how are these being addressed?
	What subject discipline differences are evident in the use of the tools and the types of activities associated with different courses?
	How are the new disability laws being addressed in terms of e-learning activities?
	In what way is e-learning being used to promote widening participation?
	How are special educational needs being addressed in e-learning?
	In what ways is and might e-learning be used to support lifelong learning?
	How do our e-learning developments compare with international developments?

Chapter 2

Knowledge, society and perspectives on learning technology

Martin Oliver, George Roberts, Helen Beetham, Bruce Ingraham, Martin Dyke and Phil Levy

Introduction

The last few decades have seen a number of important changes in the way in which western societies view 'knowledge' and therefore in what is expected of the institutions for which knowledge and learning are core business. Although the terms 'knowledge society' and 'knowledge economy' (Drucker, 1994) have become a kind of journalistic shorthand for a profoundly complex shift in world-view, they nevertheless serve to encapsulate this new ideological context. The new status of knowledge in society is related in complex ways to developments in the technologies of knowledge that this book is concerned with. No attempt to understand the impact and uses of learning technologies can therefore ignore the powerful mutual influences of knowledge, society and technology in the western world.

Knowledge, society and technology

Researchers in learning technology have a particular interest in the knowledge–technology–society nexus as an *object* of investigation. For some, it is what learning technology reveals about this nexus that is one of the most interesting aspects of the field (Castells, 1999).

These changes in the relationship between people, technology and knowledge have also had important repercussions for the *methodology* and *theoretical perspectives* chosen by investigators, whether or not they focus on the knowledge society in their work. Traditionally, changes in society and institutions are studied from the perspective of specific social sciences – sociology, social psychology, business studies, etc. Changes in personal knowledge, understanding and skill are studied using the tools of psychology, personal development and educational theory. Changes in the nature of knowledge itself are studied using the tools of philosophy, linguistics, media studies, critical theory, and theories of representation that may include cultural theory and criticism. Studying the intersection of these – the relationship between people, technology and knowledge – consequently draws in all of these perspectives, as well as new disciplines such as systems theory, instructional design and a field of applied research into the use of technology in education. This bewildering array of critical and analytical tools is available to researchers in learning technologies.

An important question is whether these multiple perspectives are a source of strength or a sign of an immature discipline still struggling to define its core concerns and methodologies. Given the complexity of the phenomena under study, there is certainly a need for a wide repertoire of investigative techniques. However, the learning technology community has raided other disciplines' 'toolboxes' without always recognising the values and assumptions from which those tools have been developed.

Knowledge and knowing

From the early nineteenth until the late twentieth century, western society's relationship with knowledge was led predominantly by principles of rationality and the procedures of science. Our knowledge and understanding of the world, it was assumed, steadily increased; gradually, society was coming to know the truth about the world. Universities held a privileged position within this arrangement; they were seen as the principal sites for the generation of knowledge and, in order to ensure that this process was unfettered by politics, they were given considerable autonomy (Barnett, 1994).

However, in the middle to late twentieth century, this well-established pattern began to change. It was no longer seen as necessary, or even desirable, for the processes of generating and disseminating knowledge to take place in a separate sphere of disinterested academic endeavour; rather, they should be integrated with other social activities such as the generation of wealth, effective governance, the research needs of business and the professions, and the progress of technology.

Ideas associated with this shift include:

*   Constructivism: What are the means by which knowledge is constructed, legitimated and circulated? How do these activities reflect local values and cultures of enquiry (e.g. professional and disciplinary)?
*   Instrumentalism: How is knowledge valued? To whom is it (designed to be) useful, and how?
*   Power: Who has the authority to determine what counts as 'knowledge'? From whose point of view is knowledge constructed, and ways of knowing enacted?

This last question led philosophers such as Lyotard to observe that knowledge was seen, increasingly, as a 'thing' rather than a quality of people. It was 'exteriorised'. The traditions of atomist, 'out there' epistemologies were increasingly privileged over more holistic epistemologies. Knowledge was turned into artefacts; it was *commodified* (Lyotard, 1979). In western capitalist economies, this is aligned with a shift from the production and distribution of *things* toward the production and distribution of *knowledge* – which has implications for education.

The first implication of this [shift] is that education will become the center of the knowledge society and schooling its key institution. What knowledge mix is required for everyone? What is quality in learning and teaching? All these will, of necessity, become central concerns of the knowledge society and central political issues.

(Drucker, 1994)

This commodification of knowledge has been complemented by a shift from 'mode one' to 'mode two' knowledge: from 'is it true?' to 'what can it do?' (Giddens, 1999). Mode two knowledge has a particular affinity with the practices of design and management, which has implications for work in e-learning. Instructional designers may well ask, 'does this artefact work?' but are less likely to examine the ends for which these new systems are being developed.

Knowledge, technology and performance

Today, the postmodern consensus (such as it is) has seen the paradigm of tertiary education shift from that of the 'university' in which philosophy stood at the head of a tree of disciplines, each providing its own specialised route to the 'truth' about nature, to that of the 'polytechnic', in which it is competency and the diverse professional skills and applications of knowledge that are valued.

The impact of postmodernism has been to change the definition of being 'professional' from having knowledge to having competence. This results in, on the one hand, the standardisation of curricula and syllabi for the purpose of accrediting vocational practices, and on the other the rise of a 'constructivism' that lays claim to the cultural reproductive function and challenges the researcher's epistemologies.

Lyotard (1979) argued that computers would have a crucial role to play in supporting and extending the way in which knowledge was commodified, and that in doing so society's view of knowledge would be biased towards those things that could be represented by computers (be formally computable). In the same vein, Baker observed, 'knowledge is, or will be, what is or can be formalised in a computational way' (Baker, 2000), implicitly asking also what is or might be 'forgotten' when knowledge is digitised. Changes in what counts as knowledge, and changes in computational power, are mutually intertwined. Learning technology research should – and does – have something to say about this.

Another important contribution to the value of commodified knowledge artefacts, Lyotard argued, arises from their ability to support the generation of new pieces of knowledge. Once represented in a digital form, knowledge can be almost limitlessly disseminated and analysed, re-inscribed, re-applied and re-appropriated. The authority associated with computer-based representations is often hidden and – because of this re-writable quality – may become complicated, referring to multiple 'designers', including (in interactive systems, at least in some sense) a system's user.

McLuhan and Landow, among others, noticed the importance of context, in not only carrying but also mediating and substantially forming the 'message'

(McLuhan, 1989; Landow, 1997): that is, knowledge is instantiated in the medium – quite literally in the instruction set or logic of a central processing unit (CPU). Economically, this is made evident through the emergence of the concept of the 'knowledge economy' manifested in the artefacts of information and communication technologies (ICTs) and in the ability of people to master these forms of knowledge (understand the code).

Knowledge, society and education

One result of policies intended to realise the 'knowledge society' in a 'knowledge economy' is that learning technology becomes one of the more important features on the national and international economic, social and cultural landscape and an important battlefield of beliefs (Roberts, 2004). The social demand for computer-based information and the economic demand for computer literacy in the workforce pull education policies in two conflicting directions. On the one hand, they aim to be emancipatory and empowering for the individual: on the other, they aim to ensure a supply of compliant, appropriately skilled workers, inured to demands of flexibility (ibid.).

The relationship between material wealth and cultural wealth (Giddens, 1999) is one way of analysing the different views of knowledge and society that underlie contemporary practices in educational institutions: managerialism, massification, vocationalism, globalisation, funding/fees, consolidation in the sector and so on. Carrington and Luke, (1997) take a similar approach, exploring forms of wealth and power through Bourdieu's theory of symbolic capital.

In current education policy, however, there is a tendency to simplify the relationship between economic, social and cultural capital so that only those things that can be converted to economic capital are considered. Conversely, it is assumed that economic capital is absolutely and simply convertible to cultural and social capital. It is hardly surprising, then, that recent decades have seen repeated demands in both research and policy for universities to recognise their place as a driver for economic development.

It is worth maintaining a degree of scepticism about the idea that such changes are entirely new – Taylor, for example, points out that there were calls over a century ago for universities to feed industry and to widen access (Taylor, 1999). However, in the past decade the assumption that universities exist to provide socially (and economically) useful knowledge, and thus to equip the next generation of knowledge workers, has come to dominate public debate (Barnett, 1997).

Two contrasting positions on knowledge

Can the knower be separated from what is known? This is the fundamental question at the heart of theories of knowledge. Creating a binary divide, and either/or account, runs the risk of oversimplifying the situation. Nonetheless, one useful way of classifying epistemologies is to separate those that posit knowledge as being 'out there', as something to be sought and grasped by the knower, from those that posit knowledge as being 'in here', constructed by the knower and inseparably a part of them.

> Constructionism and realism are dominantly regarded as incompatible meta-theories. Although neither can be reduced to a homogeneous field in itself, the two positions are generally used as binary poles, which organise contemporary debates on what the social world is and how we can study it. Such debates, more often than not, exclude the possibility of a fruitful dialogue between the two positions. [...] Constructionists accuse realists of essentialism, of insisting on the illusion of some pure existence, whereas realists accuse constructionists of idealism, of the illusion that all existence is contingent on language and signification.
>
> (Chouliaraki, 2002)

These broad epistemological alignments do not map neatly on to contemporary cultural alignments: for example, 'out there' epistemologies include long traditions of religious practice and inquiry that would hold knowledge to be a property of God, separate from humanity. However, 'out there' epistemologies also include the Enlightenment tradition of rationalism and the procedures of science, which has arguably been the predominant epistemology in western education since the nineteenth century. Within the Enlightenment tradition, humanity's knowledge and understanding of the world, it is assumed, steadily increases; gradually, society is coming to know the truth about the world. 'In here' epistemologies also have long and contrasting histories, including religious trancendentalism on the one hand and much of the postmodern challenge to the Enlightenment tradition on the other.

In the following sections, we provide a brief characterisation of these two poles.

Positivism

Positivism is the 'traditional' hypothetico-deductivist view of reality as being objectively 'out there', something that can be *posited* and then investigated through our senses. This position involves constructing supposedly value-free laws to explain phenomena through deductive reasoning (from general to specific), ideally by following strict rules and procedures.

> Key aspects of the hypothetico-deductivist theory are an epistemology that asserts that knowledge consists of the truth testing of statements through a set of agreed rules of discursive procedure and an ontology that asserts that knowledge is 'about' something that is itself outside the discursive system of hypothetico deductive procedures.
>
> (Scollon, 2003: 75)

Human beings are postulated as rational individuals whose behaviour can be predicted.

There is a strong positivist legacy within research into technology and learning, building on Skinner's work within psychology that sought to explain people's behaviour. He rejected any need to account for 'minds' when studying people, arguing instead that all that was necessary was an account of how they acted, and how their actions could be influenced (Skinner, 1950). Part of his work – only part, but one element that has been strongly influential – is the idea of operant conditioning. This concerns the strengthening of desired patterns of response and the weakening of others through combinations of positive and negative feedback. Although this account of learning might seem naïve and simplistic, it is still powerful in explaining students' learning – for example, in terms of the influence of assessment on study (e.g. Biggs, 1999).

Skinner's work was built upon by theorists such as Gagné, who described a set of conditions for learning; these were taken up by the Instructional Design community, and in particular by researchers such as Merrill (2001). This produced a design protocol that advocated the decomposition of complex concepts into a hierarchical structure, enabling the diagnosis of areas of weakness and allowing tailored instruction to be provided. This formed the basis for a significant number of computer-based training programmes, and is currently being rediscovered as the basis for personalisation by researchers working in the area of learning object repositories (e.g. Lawless *et al.*, 2005).

It is worth noting that epistemologies of positivism are evolving. Popper is well known for challenging hypothetico-deductive theory from within the positivist tradition. The great fallacy of science, he argues, is the presumed assumption that because we observe something twice it must, therefore, happen a third time. We do not theorise from observation, he argues, but from a complex set of beliefs. We cannot 'purge our minds of all theories' (Popper, 1996: 86); indeed, 'all observations are theory impregnated. There is no pure, disinterested, theory-free observation' (Popper, 1996: 8). Similarly, Latour argues that in spite of assertions by some that one should not confound epistemological questions (our representation of the world) with ontological questions (what the world really is), that is 'precisely what scientists spend much of their time doing' (Latour, 1991: 93).

Popper encourages a 'new critical style' of scientific writing to counter the 'present situation in science in which high specialization is about to create an even higher Tower of Babel' (Popper, 1996: 106–7). He goes on: 'the replacement of the inductive style by something like this new critical style is one of the few ways in which mutual interest and mutual contacts between the various fields of research can be preserved' – a particularly important aim for a field such as e-learning.

The social perspective

The opposite pole to positivism can be characterised as a social perspective – although *perspectives* might be more accurate (Scollon, 1998; Goodman *et al.*, 2003). This portrays knowledge as emergent, arising from social practice, and thus constructed rather than 'found'. Consequentially, there is context-dependent variation in what is known.

Constructivism is, perhaps, the most widely recognised social position within e-learning research, having come to dominate the field over the last decades (Thorpe, 2002). However, this 'position' might be more accurately described as a cluster of related positions, some advocating learning through active experimentation (e.g. Papert, 1980), for example, whilst others emphasise the importance of social interaction (e.g. Vygotsky, 1986; Wenger, 1998) and others focus on the very personal nature of constructed knowledge (e.g. von Glaserfeld, 1993). Most constructivists, however, share an interest in the role of technology for developing knowledge, resulting in a strong historical link between this position and the antecedents of e-learning. However, it should be noted that it is common for teachers to assert constructivist credentials whilst still using behaviourist motivators (Thorpe, 2002).

A very different kind of social perspective is critical theory, which emphasises conflicting interests of social groups. Like constructivism, there are many different approaches to this, including (for example) femininst, Marxist and post-colonial theories. Each of these brings a particular focus to studies, serving to highlight issues that might otherwise be neglected. Methodologically, such positions adopt approaches such as critical discourse analysis (e.g. Fairclough, 2001), which is designed to explore how language is used to create social conditions.

Ethnomethodological approaches (Garfinkel, 1967) build from an anthropological tradition, looking for evidence of human motivation in the narratives and traces left behind in documentary evidence. In a similar vein, ethnography (Scollon, 1998) involves the researcher inhabiting the lives of those being studied so as to develop an understanding of those lives.

Other positions

The above two positions are useful as points of reference, but it should be emphasised that a large number of positions and traditions exist, including action research, activity theory, actor network theory, cognitive science, discourse analysis, grounded theory, knowledge engineering, artificial intelligence, literacy, management studies, systems theory and so on. These can be grouped in many different ways. For example, Beetham (2005) groups learning theories under four kinds:

- *Associative*, whereby people learn through basic stimulus-response conditioning, then later through the capacity to associate concepts in a chain of reasoning, or to associate steps in a chain of activity to build a composite skill. In some learners, associativity leads to accuracy of reproduction or recall.

- *Cognitive constructivist*, whereby people learn by active construction of ideas and building of skills, through exploration, experimentation, receiving feedback, and adapting themselves accordingly. Cognitive constructivity leads to integration of concepts and skills into the learner's existing conceptual or competency structures.
- *Social constructivist*, whereby people and groups learn with the support of dialogue and in the process of collaborative activity.
- *Situativist*, whereby people learn through participation in communities of practice, progressing from novice to expert through observation, reflection, mentorship and legitimate peripheral participation in community activities. Situativity leads to the development of habits, values, identities and skills that are relevant to and supported by that community.

Another approach might be to recognise positivism and the social perspective, but, in order to highlight ideologies, to contrast these with tacit communitarian or post-theoretical perspectives (Roberts and Huggins, 2004).

Bauman (2002) equates communitarianism with tribalism and asserts, 'a disturbingly thin and easy to efface line separates the lofty vision of a communitarian bliss from the practice of ethnic cleansing and ghettoization' (ibid.: 84). Tacit communitarianism is the commonsense pedagogy of normalisation that adopts forms from both the social perspective and positivism in order to reproduce a culture through its many tacit codes. The aim of designing for learning from this orientation may be to create (traceable) 'people like us'. Tacit comunitarianism is the dominant orientation of the corporate and management training sectors. Knowledge engineering and closed-systems computational approaches such as organisational learning and expert and intelligent systems characterise tacit communitarianism. From this perspective, 'truth' is forged with a common identity. Tacit communitarians are concerned with taxonomies, order and classification: defining the bounds of domains and laying off risk.

Finally, the post-theoretical or new critical approach acknowledges the disconnect in much learning and teaching practice between what teachers claim and what they do (e.g. asserting constructivist credentials yet using behaviourist extrinsic motivators). This perspective sees learners and designers in a contested social space illuminated by critical theory. The new critical approach acknowledges conflicts, be they epistemological, virtual or real: social class, gender, theoretical orientation, global economic/energy flows and balances. The approach might be characterised by project- and problem-based learning, applied and action research, and grounded and emergent theoretical approaches situated in communities of practice. Here, the emphasis is on understanding rather than 'truth', with open system models being built in order to express or test that understanding.

Our positions within this book

One of Lyotard's contributions (1979) was to call into question what he described as 'grand narratives' – which, rather than explaining some thing or experience, come to *define* it. This process of 'totalisation' limits the thing to what can be described by the theory, circumscribing what 'counts' and so excluding anything that falls outside of its explanatory power. In contrast to this stand *petits récits* – 'little stories' that provide local explanations and personal understandings rather than a single unified, objectified and hegemonic understanding that is then imposed on society.

The continued presence of the contrasting positions of positivist and social perspectives within e-learning research makes it hard to position a book such as this. On the one hand, the contribution of these different positions cannot be ignored: on the other, it is impossible to be consistent to all these positions since they are mutually opposed.

Within this book, therefore, there are two textual elements: the central narrative of each chapter, and call-out boxes positioned alongside the text that offer different (often dissenting) perspectives on what is being discussed. These additional perspectives, like marginalia, are positioned as commentaries on the text, as 'little stories' that challenge the central narrative to prevent it becoming too 'grand'.

Our primary position is to challenge the hold that 'out there' epistemologies have over the institutions of cultural reproduction, even though we do so within the form of a fairly conventional academic (scientific) text. While the text is polyvocal, however, it conforms to conventions of academic genres – and we recognise that this may undercut our intention to challenge the dominance of 'out there' epistemologies. However, a balance has to be struck between the provision of debate and establishing a coherent narrative.

This tension is of great importance within the development of learning technology research. In the quest for shared understanding and commonly valued knowledge, the various communities of researchers working in this field run the risk of producing grand narratives that close down discussion and constrain both creativity and productivity. Lisewski and Joyce (2003), for example, describe how Salmon's five-stage model of e-moderating (Salmon, 2000) arose as an explanation of experiences within one particular course, but now threatens to supplant other conceptions of what it means to learn collaboratively online. At the same time, there is the feeling that little, local stories are not enough – that we need to share knowledge and beliefs if we are to prevent the society of researchers fragmenting.

Our primary focus is on the relationships between learning, identity and action: relationships that are ongoing positionings carried out through mediated social action. The mediated social action with which we are concerned is education – however construed – particularly education through, by, with and about learning technologies.

Methodology

The different epistemological positions outlined above have profound implications for how e-learning should be studied. This is often explained in terms of
the 'paradigm debate', and framed as a contrast between qualitative and quantitative methods. This, however, is an unhelpful over-simplification
(Hammersley, 1997). Qualitative data such as interviews can be treated in a positivistic way (versions of grounded theory do this, for example Glaser, 2002),
and quantifications can be interpreted, for example by exploring the rhetorical
effects of a model of a phenomenon.

Instead, we need to consider how different philosophical positions would interpret the kinds of data generated by particular empirical methods. 'Methodology'
describes this relationship, and must be understood separately from 'methods',
which are the techniques used to collect and analyse data (this will include things
like interviews, questionnaires and observation). Methodology determines
whether the implementation of particular methods is successful or credible.
Indeed, according to Agger, 'methodologies can't solve intellectual problems but
are simply ways of making arguments for what we already know or suspect to be
true' (Agger, 2004: 77). To do this, methodology codifies beliefs about the world,
reflecting 'out there' or 'in here' positions.

> The view that knowledge is hard, objective and tangible will demand of
> researchers an observer role, together with an allegiance to methods of nat-
> ural science; to see knowledge as personal, subjective and unique, however,
> imposes on researchers an involvement with their subjects and a rejection of
> the ways of the natural scientist. To subscribe to the former is to be positivist;
> to the latter, anti-positivist.
>
> (Cohen, Manion and Morrison, 2000: 6)

Such commitments and interests arise from historical, cultural and political influences, which collectively shape traditions of research that provide the context for
current work (e.g. Conole, 2003). These have profound implications for the topics
that people study and the kinds of conclusions they are willing to draw.

In Chapter 1, a list of research questions was presented, and each was classified as pedagogical, technical, organisational or contextual. A simple assertion
that some methods are better suited than others to addressing particular topics
from this list would hide these parallel positions on knowledge. For example, documents could be used when researching practices and organisational structures. If
it is assumed that these documents reveal practice – that they correspond with patterns of behaviour in some comprehensible way – this might reflect a positivistic
perspective. A contrasting social perspective would be that these documents are
accounts that are created to explain (or predict, or influence) what people do. The
conclusions that could be drawn would then be interpretations about how the
claims made are justified, and thus how some people seek to influence others'

practices. Both the focus and the nature of these two sets of conclusions are different, even if the source data are the same.

Importantly, some methodologies protect certain kinds of knowledge by hiding, rather than making explicit, the rules and assumptions through which knowledge is legitimated. Not all methodologies are open about their assumptions. For example, feminism is explicit in its assumption that gender is an important category for attention and analysis. By contrast, positivism hides the assumption that its theories correspond to systems and patterns in the natural world by 'naturalising' it – it does not need to be stated, since the alternative position (relativism, in which such theories are treated simply as accounts) is attacked as unreliable and thus invalid.

A consequence of this is that it is impossible to talk about e-learning in a research context without reference to methodology, since any claim about e-learning rests on data collected and interpreted in accordance with some methodological position. That methodology might not be named, or even shared with others; in many cases, it may be a naïve position. This criticism can certainly be levelled at much of the work that describes itself as evaluation (Conole, 2003).

For researchers, this is a problem, since no conclusions can be drawn about the plausibility of interpretations when the process of inference remains implicit, hidden from critique. Consequently, we can define one aspect of 'good' research as an openness about the assumptions made and the processes through which claims are legitimated.

How e-learning influences research methods

The kinds of data that are available to e-learning researchers may suggest particular kinds of interpretation. As an illustration, early research into the use of online discussion fora focused on analysis of the content of the threaded messages. There was a naïve assumption that this was enough to capture the whole event, without an understanding of the context within which the discussion took place (Jones, 1998a). However, the meaning of such data may change entirely when viewed as part of a wider context. For example, one of the cases Jones discusses shows how a well-constructed exchange as part of an assessed piece of online discussion was revealed to be a 'fake', which had been constructed in order to guarantee good marks by four students using scripts and notes, seated around a table within a computer room. This illustrates a more general problem for researchers: that the meaning of data has to be inferred, largely on the basis of preconceptions or guesswork, since much of the context of use will be remote, private or otherwise inaccessible (Oliver, 2001).

In an edited collection Jones provides a critique of internet research and the methodological issues that arise (Jones, 1999), emphasising the danger of misinterpreting online interactions. Using multiple methodologies can be one way of addressing this. For example, De Laat *et al.* (2005) combine the use of social network analysis with content analysis and critical event recall in a study of an online Masters course in education. Social network analysis is used to visualise the social structures and dynamics of the course, content analysis is used to identify the learning and teaching processes, and critical event recall is used to elicit teachers' experiences and perceptions.

Different perspectives on learning technology

Given the complexity of this research context, in this section different positions are described in relation to one fictional case. This illustrates how different theoretical perspectives would explain this situation differently, and how each can contribute to our understanding of this field.

A fictional case

Adam has just been appointed as a lecturer and has inherited a first-year foundation course, SO 101: an introduction to sociology. Adam is concerned about the size of the course; there are about 130 students in each cohort. Assessment is a particular worry, since each student produces three 3,000 word essays under exam conditions. Finally, there has always been a split in grades: most of the students get a 2:1 or a first but the remainder fail outright.

Assessment isn't Adam's only worry. He was able to sit in on some teaching this year to prepare for the handover. The memory of one seminar in particular stays with him: it degenerated into a heated argument between a student who demanded to know why the course totally ignored black, feminist or post-colonial sociology and another who dismissed such approaches out of hand, saying that the course was already worrying him because it didn't seem to do much for his career prospects anyway, and that diluting it further would only compound the problem. Adam was also struck by the fact that both combatants had been young, middle-class white men, although he isn't altogether sure why he thinks this might be important.

His other anxiety is about technology. Last year, the course introduced a Virtual Learning Environment, mainly for course announcements and managing online readings. It was popular with the students and gained support from senior management, all of whom seem keen for the institution to move into distance learning (and international student fees). The Vice Chancellor has asked the head of department to make sure that Adam develops this further.

What should he do? He knows there are some researchers in a number of different departments across Cottlesham University who study this whole area; should he ask them for advice, or even to work with him, he wonders? Or should he just bid for some support from the Learning and Teaching Development Unit, where he gathers there are some full-time Instructional Designers and media specialists?

Would moving the seminars online tone down some of these confrontational out-bursts and allow others within the group to speak up? And could he replace the exams (or at least some of the credit for them) with the online quizzes he's heard academics from the medical school talking about? He doesn't feel ready, and isn't at all sure that he wants to get caught up with online learning. His job is precarious enough as it is, without his main function (teaching this module) being taken over by web pages. What will all this mean for him?

An action research perspective

Action research in educational settings involves practitioners researching their own educational situations and practices, as a means of improving these. The classic action research spiral entails at least two cycles of action-planning, implementation, monitoring, critical reflection and then application of what is learned through this process to a new iteration of the cycle. However, different perspectives on action research reflect different epistemological and political commitments. Three broad perspectives can be identified (Melrose, 1996) as follows:

- 'Technical' action research reflects an instrumentalist view of educational provision and professional competence, becoming a vehicle for developing practitioner knowledge and expertise through applying established models of best practice to a situation and evaluating impact in relation to pre-specified educational objectives. From this point of view, Adam could opt to hand over the re-design of his course to an expert in instructional design and test the effectiveness of his running of it over a couple of implementations, making adjustments to his practice where appropriate and focusing on whether or not key performance indicators were being achieved.
- 'Practical' action research assumes that, while theories and models may pro-vide useful guidance, educational practice is contested and professionals must take responsibility for developing their own understanding and prac-tices. Professional competence from this perspective therefore emphasises the capacity to exercise informed, practical judgements in response to com-plex situations in which there are choices to be made. Action research is seen as a way of developing this capacity by involving educators in critical reflec-tion on the assumptions and values that they bring to their work, and by exploring the impact of their practice on the learning experiences of their stu-dents. In Adam's case, this would be re-designing his course with advice and support from the Learning and Teaching Development Unit and researcher colleagues as appropriate, to address problems and issues that are of personal concern. The study would involve exploring students' experiences through techniques such as observation and focus-group feedback, but would also involve systematic personal reflection on aspects of his own practice. Two or

more iterations of the action research cycle would provide an opportunity to develop further the practical, 'living' theory of his personal professional practice (McNiff *et al.*, 1996; Levy, 2003).

- 'Emancipatory' action research extends the practical tradition by adding a normative political dimension: establishing more egalitarian, democratic forms of educational practice (Carr and Kemmis, 1986). From the perspective of critical theory, which informs this view, it is essential that educators recognise and engage with the structural constraints on their practice and with the role of power in educational relations. Action research is seen as a way of identifying the systemic changes, as well as the changes to individual practice, that need to be made in order to improve specific educational situations. Adam's concern about group dynamics might focus his action research on finding ways of encouraging participatory and inclusive dialogue, including an exploration of how the online elements relate to this. He would explicitly situate this exploration within wider social and political contexts, identifying structural constraints in institutional culture that need to be challenged.

Finally, both practical and emancipatory perspectives on action research emphasise the importance of sharing the knowledge that is produced in this way across the wider educational community.

A behaviourist perspective

Behaviourism is primarily a perspective on learning (Skinner, 1950) rather than a pedagogy, although the principles of operant conditioning (reinforcing desired behaviours through rewards, diminishing others through punishment) have been used to guide instructional materials for decades, as discussed earlier.

Adam's situation, as described here, is well suited to the adoption of a behaviourist approach. The move online aids this. Replacing one of the essays with a series of shorter computer-based multiple-choice tests would reduce the assessment burden, so long as the tests could be re-used each year and no one asked too many questions about verifying student identities. The sequential nature of these should reinforce students' mastery of basic concepts and should prompt failing students to improve from an early stage.

Another assignment could be cut by formally assessing participation in online discussions. Quiet students could be encouraged to participate by giving marks for postings; unwanted contributions (conflict, perhaps described as 'flaming') could be penalised through having marks deducted; and the student could identify (say) three constructive contributions to discussions to be read and marked (this would also save the tutor having to read the entire discussion – which could be difficult, given the number of students involved).

The research would lend itself to a quasi-experimental design, comparing the performance of cohorts over time. The change in assessment might complicate this but retention of one of the three exam essays could provide a point of reference to ensure that standards had not slipped.

An activity theoretic perspective

Activity theory builds on the work of Vygotsky (1986), particularly the idea that learning is a social activity and that all human action is mediated through the use of tools (which might be conceptual, symbolic or physical). These ideas were developed to form activity theory (Kuutti, 1996). This theory proposes that individuals' activities involve them using tools to achieve their 'object' (in the sense of their objective), and that this takes place within the context of a community that has its own conventions and division of labour. This interest in the social context of tool use makes the theory an obvious one to use in studying e-learning.

Activity theory is particularly useful for analysing situations in order to highlight why problems have arisen. In this case, analysis would reveal (for example) that the introduction of new technology has caused conflicts within the system. The introduction of online learning has changed the way in which teaching materials are produced, altering the division of labour within the community by adding new tasks. Who should take these on? Adam's suggestion that this could be passed to the Central Learning and Teaching Development Unit would resolve the conflict between the division of labour and achieving the object of the system, but may cause further problems. The central unit may want to change the unwritten rules of materials production so that, for example, it has plenty of time to implement and test what it produces – whereas Adam might well want to defer decisions about what to teach until just before the course, to ensure the material is current (and because other concerns take priority).

Used like this, activity theory allows researchers to analyse systems and to focus on particular problems within them; this may allow solutions to be proposed. It is important to recognise, however, that the theory itself does not propose these solutions.

A perspective on power

A sociologist of technology might consider how *power* is being manifested and understood in several dimensions of this situation. Locally, Adam may well experience himself as *dis*empowered, both in relation to the curriculum and technologies to help manage and deliver it. He designed neither the curriculum nor the assessments his students must pass if they (and by extension he) are to 'succeed', but is responsible for making them work. He has even less power to adapt the virtual learning environment he is being urged to adopt, and rightly suspects it will change his teaching practice and relationships with students. Because of the department's aim to draw in distance learners, Adam must consider how to translate existing course materials and activities to an online environment in which – even without the challenges of unfamiliarity – he will find his teaching practice more exposed. If his position were more secure, he might welcome this as an opportunity for self-evaluation and reflection, but as things stand he has much to fear, including student criticism and management disappointment.

Adam's students are clearly experiencing their own different relationships to power as manifested in the learning/teaching situation. Adam is right to suspect that moving discussions online will shift these relationships. The online environment is less obviously a public space than the classroom, and discussants have more time to consider their comments, both of which tend to favour contributions from less socially confident individuals and groups. However, new inequalities will be introduced, including confidence with the technologies involved, access to computer time and preferences for social 'presence' over mediated forms of communication.

At the institutional level, the virtual learning environment he is expected to adopt may have contributed to the lack of flexibility Adam is experiencing. This is likely to have been chosen by IT managers on the basis of an institution-wide cost–benefit analysis, rather than taking into account local learning and teaching practices such as the strong focus in sociology on dialogue, argumentation, and critique of sources. Adam may well find these activities poorly supported.

A socio-cultural perspective on Adam's situation would involve investigating the meanings attached to these different manifestations of power by the participants, and relating these to a wider tradition of representing and discussing power – such as standard texts on the sociology of technology, or on the cultures of online discussion. While such investigations would not offer easy answers, they would identify the implications of different courses of action in this complex socio-cultural situation.

Conclusions

This chapter has provided a context within which to situate the chapters that follow. The themes identified in the first chapter are easily visible here. The inter-disciplinary nature of research in e-learning has formed the central theme throughout the chapter, looking at the ways in which different perspectives both shape and interpret what it is that is being studied. The conflicts – and some complementarities – between these have been highlighted, not least because this reveals another theme: politics. The dominance of different traditions sets a political frame for research in this area that researchers will either need to align with or deliberately challenge. These linked themes explain the stylistic approach adopted in the rest of this book of a central narrative commented on through marginal comments.

The plurality of perspectives on this context is, in itself, a reflection of inclusivity towards researchers of this area; access and inclusion in teaching is further foregrounded by particular perspectives such as the critical traditions of feminism or post-colonial theory.

The wider discussion of knowledge and society demonstrates why commodification is such a concern for this area, since technology is thoroughly implicated in the commodification of knowledge.

Finally, issues of change, interactivity and social interaction have been identified as primary topics for e-learning research.

By exploring the connections between changes in society, positions on knowledge and research methods a fundamental issue has been identified. In a complex, contested area such as this, clarity about the researcher's position is a necessary condition for establishing the credibility of research findings. This charitable interpretation in terms of internal consistency can then be complemented by critical interpretations of the work (was this the right question to ask in the first place?). Such sensitivity is a necessary condition when researchers who have adopted different positions attempt to work with each other or share research findings.

Chapter 3

A critique of the impact of policy and funding

Gráinne Conole, Janice Smith and Su White

Introduction

In this chapter we outline the relationship between policy directives and practice. Higher education (HE) has changed dramatically in the last thirty years through policy drivers such as widening participation, lifelong learning and increased quality assurance. The sector has expanded and diversified, leading to a context that shapes policy directives and has a direct impact on e-learning practice. We consider these structures and trace the growth in the use of learning technologies and associated research.

One side-effect of rapid technological progress and the rhetoric that dominates policy is the continuing but elusive suggestion that technology can 'transform the ways we teach and learn' (DfES, 2005). This can lead to unfortunate decisions. The most publicly visible example in recent years is the demise of the much promoted and publicised UK e-Universities Worldwide Limited (UKeU). At its launch the then Secretary of State proudly announced, 'it is clear that virtual learning is an industry which is striding forward all around us' (Blunkett, 2000). When the UKeU collapsed only five years later, Sheerman suggested the investment had been 'a disgraceful waste of public money' (Sheerman, 2005). Conole *et al.* (2006) undertook a detailed evaluation of the UKeU, highlighting a

For me the clue to the eventual sad demise of the UKeU is the 'industry' bit in the Secretary of State's original announcement. It's likely that the industrial nature is at the root of lots of unfortunate failures of recent big collaborations in the e-world. Claiming 'it's a disgrace' (presumably signed 'Outraged of Cyberspace'), is an inadequate response. In the commercial world, the goals, timescales, focus of direction and yes, even collective accountability, are very different from the reflective, diverse, messy, aspirational and pseudo-democratic culture of higher education. It needs some clever science to mix that chalk and cheese.

Gilly Salmon

direct relationship between policy (and associated rhetoric) and its impact on practice. The findings echo many of the arguments cited in this chapter: the need for a more measured and reflective approach to e-learning policy, the need to account for organisational context and in particular to deal with clashes between different cultural perspectives, and the importance of the human aspects of implementing e-learning rather than a focus on technological developments.

Whilst this chapter will focus on issues in e-learning since the advent of the internet, a brief review of the history of e-learning is given to situate and contextualise policy and practice. Then we consider the relationship between e-learning development, policies and funding to illustrate an increasing politicisation. In critiquing the policy agenda we suggest there are lessons from the past forty years that could be applied to policy-making today.

Context

White (2006) suggests that change in HE may be driven by a wide range of factors and illustrates the relationship between these (Figure 3.1), showing the complexity of the area. There are many types of potential perturbations of change, of which the application of e-learning is only one.

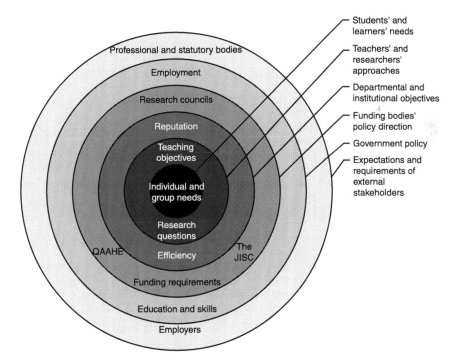

Figure 3.1 Factors impacting on higher education

Any snapshot of change within an institution will be complex, with factors being co-dependent and inter-related. Policy-makers need to have an understanding of the nature of each of these and the relationships amongst them. Examples in the current climate include the quality assurance agenda, widening participation, life-long learning, accessibility, skills and employability, the drive for research excellence and the development of enterprise activities. At a national level strategic directives are driven through policy and more tangibly through targeted funding. In the UK, e-learning has had significant funding ring-fenced to increase its impact and promote innovation. There is a strong political rhetoric around e-learning but this is in many ways naïve, containing unrealistic expectations about its potential (Carr-Chellman, 2005). Decision-making is often based on ill-informed perspectives of what is achievable. Instead, there needs to be a close inter-relationship between the nature of education, technology and sector-wide/institutional models or structures.

Widening participation illustrates the relationship between e-learning and other policy directives particularly clearly, but leads to paradoxes on at least two levels. First, e-learning is often seen as a way of supporting increasing diversity, but it may be that non-traditional learners do not have suitable preparation to work in online environments, exacerbating inequality. Second, even amongst the traditional student population, claims about sophisticated use of technologies tend to derive from personal and gaming technologies, rather than those that support learning. Whilst widening participation stands as a policy goal for higher education generally, the increased use of e-learning is often suggested as a means to achieve this goal – for instance where spatial and temporal factors are important variables in the learning and teaching environment – but to be successful, this may entail additional support.

A further two important dimensions concern the relationship between e-learning and quality assurance, and increasing accreditation needs (Beaty, 2006; Oliver, 2005a). The way in which e-learning exposes the process of curriculum development has led many institutions to adopt a closer scrutiny of course developments to ensure evidence of the quality of such courses. This is mirrored at a national level through bodies such as the Quality Assurance Agency (QAA) that have developed precepts and guidelines specifically for e-learning, and the spread of professional development courses in e-learning (Oliver, 2003a).

A chronology of technology policy

Whilst technologies change rapidly, the management of them does so more slowly. There have been a number of specific reports and committees over the past forty years focusing on technologies (Flowers Committee, 1965; Barnard, 1970; CBURC, 1968–1991; HEFCE, 1998; JISC, 2001; Nelson, 1983; NCIHE, 1997, and others), but we are conscious that models of institutional policy for learning technology integration are in their infancy (Salmon, 2005). In the early days, such reports focused on planning and funding (Barnard, 1970; CBURC,

1968–1991) but changes in funding arrangements – such as the introduction of the Minor Facilities Grant in 1983 – shifted the focus to concerns about deployment, access and take-up (Nelson, 1983). The change in technologies from highly specialised tools to more generic applications (Smith, 2005) again elicited a perspective shift, from managing, costing and designing computer-assisted learning (CAL) production (NDPCAL, 1973) to Booth's (1998) expectation of the use of learning technologies as another 'tool of the trade' for HE staff.

Smith (2005) traces the emergence of information and communication technologies (ICT) from the mid-1960s, highlighting key technical developments alongside pertinent policies and initiatives. She categorises technologies into four timeframes: 1965–1979, 1980–1989, 1990–1999 and 2000 to the present (Table 3.1). The first timeframe is characterised by centralised mainframe systems, with time-shared resources and expert operators. The period from the beginning of the 1980s marks a shift towards stand-alone computers and the emergence of distributed resources and experimentation by early adopters. The 1990s were dominated by the impact of the internet and the development of networked technologies with a focus on increased collaboration and communication. Since 2000 a more coherent and joined-up approach to the application of technologies has emerged, with more evidence of large-scale e-learning programmes with overarching themes, for example, the Joint Information Systems Committee's (JISC's) e-pedagogy programme and e-framework initiative, and alignment with strategy, for example the HEFCE (2005a) and DfES (2005) e-learning strategies. We note two distinct shifts in perspective: from a focus on using technology as an individualised, instructional tool to a more discursive and communicative medium, and from niche-based software environments to overarching organising systems.

It has been argued (Conole, 2002) that there are difficulties in retaining and applying the lessons learned from earlier eras to current technological and

Reading this chapter made me realise how diverse this so-called connected world is. It was not only the acronyms that felt strange; it was the underlying assumption that governments are deeply involved in e-learning policy in universities. In this part of the world, that is not the case. In Hong Kong only 16 per cent of school leavers get a university place inside Hong Kong. Universities are thus elite organisations and the society at large (a fairly conservative force) exerts significant influence on the shape of internal university policy. Universities are reliant on government funding and there is now some performance-related (and hence competitive) funding. Teaching and learning quality is very important but 'e' or 'not e' is not a government matter. It is up to individual universities to decide how to use technology to enhance students' experience. This is a theme I will return to in Chapter 5.

Carmel McNaught

policy developments. To illustrate this, Table 3.1 provides a chronological map of the relationship between tools, policies and funding initiatives that have characterised learning technology research and development in UK HE. It explores the kinds of learning and teaching approaches and issues that technologies are used to address. We have selected only those macro-level initiatives that we believe are of particular importance in relation to the development of e-learning.

Phase one: 1965–1979

The Flowers Report (1965) gave one of the first indications of the impending importance of technology in education. It notes the predominance of the use of computers for physical science research but foresaw growing demand in other disciplines. The following year saw the establishment of the Computer Board for Universities and Research Councils (CBURC) (a precursor of today's JISC), whose remit was to advise on the use of computers for research. At the schools-level, in 1967 the Council for Educational Technology was established, differentiating between 'computing for education' and 'education about computing'. The first reference to the role of computing for teaching came with the Barnard Report (1970), which concluded that all undergraduates should study computing. In particular it noted that introductory instruction in computing would lead to 'major new demands … from students using computers in their own primary disciplines'. This was followed in 1973 by the establishment of funding by the National Development Programme in Computer Assisted Learning (NDPCAL). A decade later a study was commissioned by CBURC to explore the potential of computing to support teaching. The report identified fourteen ways in which technology could be used, including the use of standard application packages, communication via email and simulations/modelling (Nelson, 1983). Darby (2001) highlights the significance of this report and argues that it raised awareness of the need to make provision for networked computers to be used by students to support their studies. The report recommended that a national staff development programme 'be initiated as a matter of urgency to create a higher level of awareness of the uses of information technology in teaching'.

The focus in this phase was very much on the application of computers in a scientific context primarily for research purposes; mainframes operated by computer specialists dominated the discourse although there were hints of the potential wider application of computers across institutions.

Phase two: 1980–1989

In 1984, the £10-million Computers in Teaching Initiative (CTI) was established, providing funding for 139 subject-specific software development projects. This was followed in 1989 by the establishment of 24 CTI subject centres to promote the use of technology within subject disciplines (Darby, 2001). This was later consolidated by the creation of the Learning and Teaching Support Network, the setting up of the

Table 3.1 E-learning timeline

Time	Technologies	Reports	Initiatives	Characteristics	Impact on practice
Phase one, 1965–1979: Mainframe systems					
1965	Mainframes, batch processing, machine code	Flowers		Provision of computers for research; central planning for regional consortia	Predominant pedagogical emphasis is instructional, behaviourist. Research is concerned with navigational issues
1966			Establishment of Computer Board for Universities and Research Councils (CBURC)		
1970		Barnard		All students to be taught programming; proposal to develop CAL system to teach programming	
1973			National Development Programme for Computer Assisted Learning (NDPCAL)		CAL in the disciplines: exploratory use, planned use, service use
1979	Microprocessors				
Phase two, 1980–1989: Stand-alone systems					
1981	Desktop PCs			Shifting costs from centre to periphery; early service developments such as the Resource Discovery Network	
1983		Nelson		Move from computing to IT; emphasis on teaching requirements; suggested national staff development programme	Increased activity in terms of multimedia functionality but still content driven and focused on the interactive tutorial paradigm

Year	Technology	Report/Author	Initiative	Development activity	Commentary
1984			Computer Teaching Initiative (CTI)	139 subject-specific development projects	
1987	Graphical interfaces				
1989			CTI centres	Promoting software use	

Phase three, 1990–2000: Networking technologies

Year	Technology	Report/Author	Initiative	Development activity	Commentary
1990	Janet launched				
1991	The web				
1992			Teaching and Learning Technology Programme (TLTP)	Collaborative software development projects	Beginning to see more emphasis on the wider contextual issues (skills, strategy, importance of embedding and integration). Also a shift away from the emphasis on the individual to the concept of situated learning
1993	Internet browsers	McFarlane	Establishment of Joint Information Systems Committee (JISC)	Beginnings of network use by non-technical disciplines	
		Kennedy			
1995		JISC 'Guidelines for developing an information strategy'	JISC electronic libraries (e-Lib) programme	Beginnings of digitisation/ preservation projects	
1997	Commercial Virtual Learning Environments (VLEs) appear	Dearing		Increased use of ICTs; open access to facilities for all students	A move to more holistic and joined-up thinking. Evidence of more linking of development to strategy and policy
1998		Booth	TLTP3	ICTs use 'tool of the trade' for HE lecturers; strategies for integrating ICTs in the curriculum	

Time	Technologies	Reports	Initiatives	Characteristics	Impact on practice
1999	Managed Learning Environments (MLEs) begin to appear		Learning and Teaching strategies JISC Distributed National Electronic Resource (DNER) programme JISC Managed Learning Environment (MLE) programme Institute for Learning and Teaching (ILT) launched	ICTs in support of non-traditional/off-campus learners; staff development, accreditation	

Phase four, 2000 to the present: Politicisation and systematisation

Time	Technologies	Reports	Initiatives	Characteristics	Impact on practice
2000	XML/CMS		Learning and Teaching Support Network (LTSN) launched Human resource strategies	Repositories, services, portals, re-usable learning objects	Pedagogy shifted away from individual learner to collaboration, communication and the notion of communities of practice
2000	Mobile and wireless technologies become more prevalent	Government White Paper on HE			
2004		DfES and HEFCE e-learning strategies	Closure of the UKeU Launch of HE Academy		

Institute for Learning and Teaching, and the subsequent merging of these into the HE Academy. The JISC, through initiatives such as its Technology Application Programme (JTAP) and the Electronic Libraries (e-Lib) programme, focused more on technological aspects. A range of research and development centres emerged during this period (e.g. IET at the Open University, ICBL at Heriot-Watt and ILRT at Bristol). To complement the more development-focused initiatives outlined above, the research councils launched related research programmes, such as the Economic and Social Research Council's *Virtual Society?* programme and the Engineering and Physical Sciences Research Council's focus on emerging technologies that might impact on learning and teaching innovations.

What is evident from initiatives in this phase is that they were characterised by two things: the exploration of the potential of technologies through the 'let a thousand flowers bloom' approach and the emergence of a complementary dissemination mechanism through the establishment of CTI. Also the emergence of the desktop PC enabled the wider uptake of computers and exploration of their potential for teaching and learning.

Phase three: 1990–1999

Following the establishment of the CTIs, the government invested further in the area through the launch of the £100 million Teaching and Learning Technology Programme (TLTP) in 1992. This complemented the work of CTI by providing investment for technical development and implementation. Evaluation studies of these initiatives were mixed. On the one hand it seemed technologies were leading to a change in practice, such as a shift from lecture-based to tutorial-based teaching (White, 2006). On the other hand, external evaluation (Coopers and Lybrand, 1996) found little evidence of large-scale take up or a shift into mainstream teaching beyond the early innovators, although the latter phase of funding prioritised embedding technologies and institutional strategies. Institutional-TLTP projects (White, 2006) identified a set of successful activities to achieve the integration of learning technologies and by implication institutional change within HE. Approaches were characterised by achieving a high degree of ownership of that change by the departments, faculties or schools that were directly responsible for teaching. White notes that, as well as the ongoing TLTP projects, there were a large number of technology-related initiatives designed to influence the processes of learning and teaching which, over that period, amounted to more than 100 projects and tens of millions of pounds of investment.

The CBURC was replaced by the JISC in 1993, which aimed to 'promote the innovative application and use of information systems and information technology'. The JISC operates through a series of committees made up of representative stakeholders from the community and funds a number of initiatives and developments to take forward this overarching aim.

The Fund for the Development of Teaching and Learning (FDTL) was also of particular note (HEFCE, 1997; HEFCE, 1998) as it was led by educational objectives, demonstrating a maturing of the funding approach with the realisation of the importance of applying learning technologies in a teaching and learning context.

One of the most influential policy reports of this time was the Dearing report (NCIHE, 1997). This was the culmination of a systematic review of higher education, and included at least fifteen recommendations that make explicit reference to ICT. These significantly influenced the focus and direction of many of the resultant ICT projects (Conole, 2002). Similar effects arose as a result of the Kennedy (1998), Fryer (NAGCELL, 1997), and Booth (1998) reports, and associated papers on lifelong learning (DfEE, 1998).

One of the most prominent features of the impact of technology on teaching and learning is the way in which it acts as a catalyst for debating wider learning and teaching issues (Littlejohn and Cameron, 1999). This relationship became evident as institutions began to develop interlinked strategies (in areas such as Information, Learning and Teaching, and Human Resources). Taken together, these strategies were an attempt to ensure that technologies were effectively implemented and embedded (McNaught and Kennedy, 2000) and they opened up the debate on the impact of ICT-scale-up, infrastructure and associated staff and student training needs.

During this time the National Grid for Learning (NGfL) and the University for Industry (UfI) sought to increase the base level of ICT skills and provide a solid technological infrastructure for education from primary through to tertiary level. Throughout the 1990s a range of online products, services and resources emerged to support learning and teaching (such as virtual learning environments; digital libraries, gateways and portals; resources and tools for learning; and underpinning architecture and standards development).

This indicates that, during this period, learning technologies were moving from being peripheral innovations and developments to affecting all aspects of learning and teaching, although probably at this stage this was still more at the strategic rather than the operational level. Institutions were beginning to understand that the 'ICT debate' could no longer be addressed in isolation, but needed to be considered across both institutional and national strategies and policies. There was the start of evidence of better consolidation nationally with more coherent programmes. The funding also enabled the growth of individuals with expertise in this area and the emergence of associated research centres (see Chapter 5). The web, of course, was the most significant trigger in terms of raising the profile of learning technologies and increasing use. Virtual learning environments (VLEs) were also significant later in the 1990s in terms of acting as a catalyst for increasing uptake beyond the early adopters.

Phase four: 2000 to the present

An increased emphasis on support for learning and teaching is evident in funding calls since 1999. Examples include programmes supporting the development of Managed Learning Environments, sharable resources and digital repositories and recently the JISC's articulation of an e-framework for learning, research and administration. Institutional issues are being addressed through projects supported through the JISC Organisational Support Committee, such as IT skills needs of students and staff, the cost of networked learning, auditing of the type and scope of new learning technology professionals and the changing nature of organisations. The main focus in terms of e-learning has come out of the JISC's e-pedagogy programme, which is looking at both practitioner and student experiences of e-learning.

There appears to be more coherence emerging at a national level with both the HEFCE (2005a) and the DfES (2005) developing e-learning strategies and a working group has been established across the funding bodies to develop a multi-disciplinary cross-funding-body programme on e-learning research (Taylor, 2004). Together this strategic and funding coherence shows evidence that the area is maturing and that there is better dialogue between policy-makers, funders and practitioners, but that national strategies keep it in a political domain. How effective this will be in the future and what impact it will have on the area only time will tell.

Factors emerging from the inter-relationship between policy and practice

A number of factors influence whether policy is translated into practice and whether e-learning initiatives are successful. Having provided a chronological overview, this section will consider themes that emerge from this review.

Short-term funding

Funding for e-learning has traditionally been short-term. This provides opportunities for practitioners to experiment with the development and use of e-learning

The chapter betrays an impatience with progress in research and policy. This is understandable, but we also have to remember that, historically, technological innovation follows a remorseless trajectory from misguided use (e.g. telephones for broadcasting music, programmed learning) to incremental improvements to current practice (e.g. horseless carriages, film as theatre, lecture notes on the web), to, eventually, radical reconfiguration, but only after a long period of expert development, risk-taking and exploration. It will take us a while yet to learn how to use new technology properly in education. Yes, we do have to demonstrate its effectiveness, but it's a bit like asking for evidence of the value for money of a motor car in about 1925. We scarcely have the infrastructure, the training, the habits, or the access to new technology, to be optimising its use just yet. The new focus on leadership in our e-learning strategies places responsibility for changing practice where it needs to be.

Diana Laurillard

but prevents against long-term sustainability, embedding or reflection on impact. Hence there is no opportunity for a longitudinal perspective, which many believe is essential for understanding how to successfully embed technologies.

The interpretation of policy is necessarily subjective. Few can quibble, however, that the most distinctive feature of policy and funding in learning technologies – successive short-term initiatives – dictate not only what can be achieved, but also what can be promised within such timescales and who can undertake the work (Oliver and Conole, 2003). The implications for learning technology are clear: an important external representation of success will be the size and power of whatever institutional structure is developed to support the deployment of learning technologies. Internal cohesiveness and collegiality, necessary for successful embedding of e-learning, is not favoured by the short-term approach. This prohibits the development of longer-term and more reflective research.

The management of change and the catalytic nature of e-learning

Lewin's (1952) force-field analysis developed the notion of equilibrium in a system that can readily be applied to change in educational systems. Lewin suggested that there were three key phases to embedding changes – unfreezing the current system, a change period, and refreezing the system – suggesting that not addressing all of these would result in failure. This work has been drawn on by Elton (1999), who has developed a framework for managing change in relation to pedagogical developments. Elton outlined a ten-point model that can often not be addressed in short-term learning technology projects. One lesson learned from the wealth of learning technology projects funded over the last forty years is that the associated change is both complex and time-consuming. These issues are explored further in the following section.

The evaluation of the teaching quality enhancement funding (TQEF) is a good illustrative case of UK policy – it sought to address many of these issues by providing funding at three levels (national, institutional and individual), has now changed the criteria for the nationally recognised Teaching Fellow scheme and has extended, almost grudgingly, the institutional funding strand (HEFCE, 2005b) with the caveat that a further three years' funding will be the last before the funds available are reallocated within a core grant. The point made by those with the remit to oversee utilisation of these funds – that special funding denotes that an activity is valued – is virtually dismissed in the report. It does seem clear that those who make funding decisions (or those who evaluate the outcomes of such decisions) do not fully appreciate the importance of policy-level recognition, and that the development of models of managing change in general, and in e-learning specifically, is an area that still requires more research and development.

Complexity and collaboration

E-learning developments, whether small- or large-scale, are complex, having a raft of implicit and explicit consequences across an institution. Many believe that because of this e-learning initiatives need to be undertaken by multi-disciplinary teams, drawn from across the institution (educationalists, technologists, subject specialists and support staff). At the heart of the success of such teams is the adoption and management of a collaborative approach; however, successful collaboration is notoriously difficult.

The complex nature and importance of collaboration are key features of learning technology work that have long been recognised. Introducing yet more complexity in an already complex environment (McNay, 1995) inadvertently sets up problems to be overcome that never feature in bids for funding. In many instances new agglomerations of staff have been created, or the remit of existing centres has been widened (Gosling, 2001), often with a view to operationally focused tasks and little consideration of their strategic importance. Without this higher-level work, as explored by Elton (1999), achievement may be less than planned. The wide variety of contextual variables can also preclude the widespread adoption of those developments that are admired and supported.

Practitioners are comfortable teaching in a face-to-face context and have a good deal of control over how to do this. In contrast, the rules and norms in an e-learning environment are unfamiliar. Most practitioners do not possess the technical knowledge to be able to introduce learning technologies without at least some support. If for no other reason than this, we return to the initial point in this section: the introduction of today's technologies suggests at least a competent web editor or server administrator, with whom to negotiate any kind of substantial learning technology project. The demarcation of roles due to funding arrangements can often see the locus of control of any such project dispersed. Despite policy rhetoric, e-learning is automatically both more visible and more subject to evaluation than traditional approaches to teaching and learning, even where comparable structures or information is lacking. Work is at least underway to develop frameworks in relation to e-learning, even if the current policy focus suggests that fair comparisons to conventional techniques are not a high priority (Nicol and Coen, 2003; Bacsich *et al.*, 2001).

Risks and unintended consequences

It is evident from the literature and from the reflective review outlined here that there is a raft of risks associated with e-learning developments. There is a risk that the speed and pace of information change militates against reflection: 'It leaves no space for contemplation and considered judgement, and promotes a more pragmatic, reflexive immediate response to new information' (Conole and Dyke, 2004). Moreover, technologies have not necessarily been taken up or used in the ways originally intended. For example, the increase in the volume of

The use of the term 'unintended consequences' suggests that someone somewhere knew what the upshot of all this would be. But, for me, no one did know, and no one is still sure. It's creative and dead scary.

'If you can look into the seeds of time, and say which grain will grow and which will not, Speak then to me, who neither beg nor fear, Your favours nor your hate' Shakespeare, *Macbeth* 1.3.58–61 (Banquo to the witches).

Could we use the term emergent consequences or outcomes? Thinking of it all in this way suggests we need policy and funding that accounts not only for creative and evolving pathways but also allows for grand visions and small baby steps towards achievements.

Gilly Salmon

information available on the web has led to new forms of plagiarism. Ubiquitous use of email has resulted in increasing commercial exploitation and unwelcome mail. There are risks and levels of uncertainty associated with a dependence and reliance on the instantaneous provision of information and communication. The intensification of work (Pollert, 1991) and need for immediacy associated with the 'flexibility' presented by information and communication technologies can result in levels of dependence whereby an individual's success or failure in meeting commitments hangs by a tenuous digital thread (Conole and Dyke, 2004).

Conole and Dyke (2004) also argue that new technologies present new Foucauldian means by which those with power can secure greater knowledge and control over others (Foucault 1979). There is increasing concern about potential infringements on individuals that the infiltration of technological applications makes possible. Land and Bayne (2005), for example, have critiqued the increased default inclusion of monitoring tools within VLEs, giving teachers the power to monitor student activities more closely than ever before. Practitioners can also be surveyed and/or made to comply with institutional norms, which raises issues about the nature of professional roles/identities and trust relationships with institutions. Similar concerns are being voiced about many of the new 'smart' devices and personal tags that are being included in commercial products which enable providers to target and personalise products more accurately. There are concerns about how these tracking devices might be used for other purposes (such as surveillance) or by other agents.

Visibility and accessibility

Another aspect that impacts on how successful an e-learning initiative is, or is perceived to be, is the degree to which it is visible and accessible to relevant stakeholders. It is encouraging to note that funders are more aware now of the importance of ongoing strategically directed dissemination of project outcomes. Many repurpose research outputs to target the findings for particular audiences, for example the JISC's recent effective practice and innovative guides (JISC, 2005a & b) or the ESRC TLRP briefing papers (available at http://www.tlrp.org/ pub/research.html). Similarly, extensive use is now made of specialised mailing lists, online conferences and workshops, and interactive toolkits to provide guidance and support.

Conclusion

It is interesting to reflect on the hype that ICT has purported to offer society and to consider what actually happened. This is important because, as outlined in Chapter 1, the political aspect of e-learning is a core characteristic of this area, and rhetorical mantras have found their way into policy directives that are having a direct impact on practice. However, many of these 'dreams' are little more than

Are we limiting our ability to reach aspired goals by our own terminology, one that effectively obscures many of the elements that desperately need to be addressed by policy? Whereas education is by definition a multi-faceted activity understood to involve a variety of players and activities – teachers and teaching; students and studying; institutions and structures; information, knowledge and, it is hoped, learning – e-learning is a term comprising one letter representing a physical property of technology (e for electronic) and the *hoped-for* outcome (learning) for one participant in the interaction. Given the power of language to constrain our thinking, is our current circumscribed terminology making it increasingly difficult to keep in mind and focus on elements of this expanding activity that, while not readily apparent in the term 'e-learning' itself, must be understood and included when establishing policy and researching the phenomenon? In the US a number of public and private organisations have addressed quality issues through the development of guidelines relating to design, instruction, student support, faculty devlopment, etc. At the same time that US educational researchers are expanding their repertoire of methodological tools for studying an increasingly multi-faceted educational environment, many funders of research – most notably the federal government, but others as well – are narrowing their focus to 'scientific research', which can answer some questions very well but many questions poorly. Although presumably done with the best of intentions in the name of 'accountability', this trend has the potential to greatly hamper e-learning research efforts by excluding many of the methods best suited to answering the important questions associated with this incredibly complex phenomenon.

Melody Thompson

that and often lead to failure. Technological initiatives are frequently criticised for not achieving unrealistic goals. Promises included the notion of 'universal on-demand access to education'. This is a benefit that has been repeated for each new technological advance (Mayes, 1995) – radio, television, the internet, and so on – but is a dream that is still only partially met; indeed one could argue that it is further away than ever with the increasing digital divide between the 'haves' and 'have nots' of society; 'home working' (working patterns have shifted but the social dimensions of being part of an organisation are now recognised and many prefer to work in a mixed-modal way); and the shift from teacher as expert to facilitator of learning mediated online. However, some aspects of technology are fundamentally changing practice, both in education and in society as a whole. These include most importantly the rise of the internet, the ubiquitous uptake of mobile technologies and the impact of gaming in terms of shaping the next generation's cognitive skills and e-literacies.

The labels and boundaries described in the last two sections share common features. For example the persistence of a gatekeeper role is evident. Although the focus of this role shifted from guarding access to the mainframe to administering the VLE, the issue remains the same: there is a delicate power relation that needs to be developed and maintained in order to make e-learning feasible. Another disquieting trend is investment in repositories or virtual workspaces to support community building. A lack of demonstrable success with such projects reflects earlier niche-based CAL development that rarely spread beyond their initiators. It seems few of the lessons learned from TLTP, reported at length by Coopers and Lybrand (1996), have been fully integrated into today's policy and funding decisions, as is indicated by the evaluation undertaken of the UKeU (Conole *et al.*, 2006).

In reviewing policy and funding arrangements, one thing has crystallised: research has a tendency to follow policy directives and technological developments, rather than informing them. For example, the Networked Learning movement, which is so visible as a productive avenue of research, did not exist until internet developments supported asynchronous communications. Equally, the concept of re-usable learning objects was of little interest until controlled vocabularies and information architectures arose from the technical end of learning technology work, but are now seen as a vehicle with which to develop learning repositories (Littlejohn, 2003). However, these developments take little notice of the socio-cultural elements that, in recent years, have proved to be crucial in terms of creating learning communities. Similarly, the establishment of large-scale e-learning funding programmes (such as CTI and TLTP) enabled practitioners to experiment with the use of technologies and gave rise to a wealth of new centres focusing on e-learning as a research area and the emergence of specialised professions to support the implementation of e-learning (such as learning technologists and e-assessment officers). Aspects of this are discussed further in Chapter 5. Research in this area seems pragmatically derived from the tools at our disposal; it is predominantly responsive, with little in the way of vision or research informing tool design. However, research can also be used to appropriate tools or subvert policies, even laying claim to technologies that were never developed for the HE sector.

One of the key lessons that emerges from this review is that policy (particularly with funding) fundamentally and radically impacts on practice. Time shows that sadly there has been too much evidence of knee-jerk policy, which does not take account of evidence emerging from research. The demise of the UKeU is the most publicly visible example of this. Another key lesson is the importance of setting in place formative evaluation mechanisms alongside initiatives so that individuals and the sector as a whole can reflect on initiatives and distil recommendations for future directions. Most funding calls now have evaluation as a standard requirement of the workplan and many also put in place overarching external evaluations to draw out cross-programme lessons.

This chapter has demonstrated that there is a close relationship between policy and practice which is in turn driven by broader educational and technological drivers. Numerous initiatives and funding programmes over the last two decades have focused on the development and use of learning technologies, resulting in significant changes within HE institutions; increased uptake and use of learning technologies impact on policy and strategy within institutions, as well as impacting on organisational structures and roles (see Chapter 5). However, despite this, the increased use of technologies has raised many new questions and issues. One of the most fundamental is: Given the interconnection of policy directions and the subsequent impact on practice, what factors need to be taken into account to make appropriately informed policy decisions? This question surely is central if we are to see a better and more strategic and targeted use of technologies in the future.

What I think is missing here is how everyone in HE is struggling with the tensions between the essential nature of collaborating to produce change through ICT and the daily impact of increased competition at all levels from individual to institution. In my view, in such tensions, in the boundaries between sharing and achieving, the most creative and exciting work happens. But I can't see such understanding being built into policy, funding, or anything much actually.

Gilly Salmon

Chapter 4

The design of learning technologies

John Cook, Su White, Mike Sharples, Niall Sclater and Hugh Davis

Introduction

Technology is not used in this chapter as meaning 'software' or 'hardware'; we argue that 'technologies for learning' should be understood as the human-centred design and use of technology, where a priority is given to the embedding of learning into specific contexts or designing technologies that are adaptive to specific contextual behaviours of learners. In order to understand the future potential of technologies, we need to have an awareness of the historical context of the development of technologies, therefore we begin by examining key technological events and briefly explore the consequences that these innovations had on the field of learning technology. The chapter then examines some current trends in technologies for learning.

Chapter 6 provides an overview of learning theories and critiques their relevance to and use in e-learning. Here we focus in on the set of 'buzz words' that tend to be associated with learning technologies and which say something about the particular nature of experience that technologies might provide. Clusters of closely related words or phrases of particular pertinence which are widely used in relation to e-learning and the typical technologies that support them include:

1. *Independent, flexible, self-directed, blended, open, online, resource-based and distance learning* – reusable learning objects, virtual learning environments, managed learning environments, learning design
2. *Group and team work, computer-supported collaborative learning* – social software, asynchronous learning networks
3. *Assessment, drill and practice* – computer-assisted assessment, item banks, automatic text analysis
4. *Motivation and engagement* – multimedia, virtual reality
5. *Discovery learning* – hypermedia, simulations, games
6. *Personalisation* – adaptive learning environments, portfolio systems
7. *Informal learning* – mobile learning, ubiquitous computing

We acknowledge that there are many other approaches to examining the design and development of learning technologies. And, whilst we note the limitations of these clusters, they provide a useful framework for discussion and in this chapter we will focus in particular on the 'design' of the learning environment perspective. We will conclude the chapter by examining two large-scale initiatives that cut across the above clusters: the Open Source software initiative and the UK Joint Information Systems Committee (JISC) e-learning framework.

Papert – learning-by-making

All too often the use of learning technologies means little more than putting lecture notes on the web; as Chapter 6 asserts there is a predominance of didactic/behaviourist modes of delivery, focusing on transmission of knowledge. Such approaches focus on content, with the consequence that the learner's primary experience of technology is to be presented with information, rather than use of the technologies to promote more active learning. Our argument, which echoes that made in Chapter 6, is that we need to design for learning and not content transmission. Indeed, our exploration of learning technologies in this chapter draws on a view that sees learning as being socially mediated by new tools, in a manner similar to that articulated by Papert (1980) when discussing Samba Schools as a community of craft and practice in his seminal work *Mindstorms*.

Papert comes from the 'cognitive' school of thought; he was heavily influenced by the work of Piaget and described his own work as constructionist, i.e. 'learning-by-making'. However, although his work has been influential on school teachers, many constructivists do not appear to formally acknowledge the importance of his work. Indeed, we would suggest that Papert would be quite

---

Case study: Seymour Papert

Thinking seriously about a world without schools calls for elaborated models of the nonschool activities in which children would engage ... I recently found an excellent model during a summer spent in Brazil. For example, at the core of the famous carnival in Rio de Janeiro is a twelve-hour-long, procession of song, dance, and street theatre ... The level of technical achievement is professional, the effect breathtaking ... [However, the] processions are not spontaneous. Preparing them as well as performing in them are important parts of Brazilian life. Each group prepares separately – and competitively – in its own learning environment, which is called a samba school. These are not schools as we know them; they are social clubs with memberships that may range from a few hundred to many thousands ... Members of the school range in age from children to grandparents and in ability from novice to professional. But they all dance together and as they dance everyone is learning and teaching as well as dancing. Even the stars are there to learn their difficult parts.

(Papert, 1980: 178)

glad not to be labelled as a 'constructivist'. Learning by tool-making isn't the same as learning by knowledge construction.

Learning by tool-making is an attempt to put the user of technologies at the centre of the tool design process. As such, the following question arises: Why put humans at the centre of the design of new learning technologies? The answer is that we cannot assume that we know how to design systems that match the cognitive capacities of users or indeed that align smoothly within the social and organisational settings in which the system will be used. Evidence that this is problematic can be seen in that many current implementations of technologies have not been successful because these factors have not been incorporated in their design (Landauer, 1995). More research is needed that attempts to better match systems development with user needs. This research also needs to feed back into the evaluation and design of more effective educational systems and products (Cook, 2002). In the next section we briefly examine key historical events from a design of technology perspective and explore the consequences that these innovations have had on learning and theory. The remainder of this chapter then goes on to examine some of the major trends in the design of technologies for learning.

History

In order to articulate the influence that particular technologies have had on learning over the past few decades, Table 4.1 summarises selective historical events and highlights related designing for learning consequences.

Using computer technologies for teaching and learning is not new, it began soon after the first modern stored program computers came into use in the 1940s. Hardware and software developments can be seen as a function of a number of different factors but primarily reflect available technology (computers, programming languages, terminals, networks), educational models or objectives (training, hypertext) and available resources (finances, programming time, technical support). The earliest application of technologies for learning focused on delivery of content, primarily applying behaviourist models using early mainframes in the late 1950s and 1960s (Skinner in Table 4.1).

Clusters of technologies and their impact on learning

In the introduction to this chapter, clusters of types of learning and the technologies used to promote these were highlighted. This section picks up on this by describing specific types of 'technologies' for learning, illustrating how each type is being used to promote different aspects of learning. The broader issues listed under cluster one are addressed in Chapters 7, 8 and 9; e-assessment is addressed in Chapter 10; and computer supported cooperative/collaborative learning (CSCL) is discussed in Chapter 12. Here we focus in particular on clusters four to seven.

Table 4.1 Technologies for learning: selective historical 'design' events and related consequences

1945	In the paper 'As We May Think' (Bush, 1945), Bush provided the first description of a system with hypertext-like capability: Memex. This was one of those 'big' ideas that influenced a lot that came later.
1954	Skinner developed the 'Teaching Machine' and his 'Programmed Learning Theory' (Skinner, 1954). His model is still important today, especially from the perspective of motivating learners.
1956	SAKI – the first commercial adaptive tutoring system – was developed by Pask in 1956, based on cybernetic, rather than behaviourist principles (see Scott, 1996; Mallen, 2005).
1960	PLATO was one of the earliest multi-user, timesharing systems, which introduced what are now tools for collaborative learning; e.g. email, file sharing, bug reporting (see Woolley, 1994 for an overview). Its TUTOR authoring language enabled the development of a wide variety of learning software, including dynamic simulations.
1960	Nelson coined the term 'hypertext' in the early 1960s, which he defined as 'non-sequential writing' in *Literary Machines* (Nelson, 1982). Hypertext was to be the organising idea for the early web.
1969	ARPANET, the precursor to the internet, was established by the US Department of Defence. The internet, as we know it, appeared on 1 January 1983 when a standard networking protocol (TCP/IP) was adopted by all ARPANET users. Scholar was developed by Carbonell (1970) as the first intelligent tutoring system, or ITS. This technology has remained a research tool for exploring the links between technology and pedagogy.
1972	The Xerox Dynabook project. When Microsoft came up with its tablet PC, Kay was quoted as saying 'Microsoft's Tablet PC, the first Dynabook-like computer good enough to criticize', a comment he had earlier applied to the Apple Macintosh. Kay wanted the Dynabook concept to embody the learning theories of Bruner and some of what Papert was proposing (http://en.wikipedia.org/wiki/Dynabook, accessed 20 November 2005). See Kay (1972) for the seminal paper.
1982	Yeager of Stanford University produced a Motorola 68000-based router. Routers make possible the incredible networks comprising the modern internet.
1987	Atkinson developed HyperCard, which was distributed freely with Apples. It became widely used in schools and as a consequence started the move towards rich multimedia/hypertext environments that made use of Piagetian notions of learning environments.
1988	Macromind (now Macromedia/Adobe) released Director, a multimedia authoring tool. Director allowed people to communicate ideas on diskette, CD-ROM and eventually on the internet.
1989	The World Wide Web (WWW or W3) began life in CERN, the European Laboratory for Particle Physics in Geneva, Switzerland. The web enabled more constructivist and distributed notions of learning to emerge.
1993	Mosaic became the 'easy to use' face of the internet, spawning browsers like Navigator and Internet Explorer. The internet became more user friendly.
1990s 2000s	We end the timeline here by stating that technology is getting faster and smaller; and search engines such as Google are affecting many areas of learning in unpredictable ways.

Multimedia, hypermedia, simulation and games

Multimedia refers to the orchestrated combination of text, graphic art, sound, animation and video elements. Multimedia authoring is the design and creation of multimedia artefacts. Interactive multimedia is where the user is able to control the material being presented to them, an example being interactive CD-ROMS (Vaughan, 1998). Alternatively, hypermedia is where a structured set of linked elements is provided through which a user can navigate (for example web pages). Hypermedia has various advantages and disadvantages; the non-linear navigation possible with hypermedia is powerful in terms of potentially promoting discovery learning. However, it is easy to get lost in 'hyperspace' when following hyperlinks (Nielsen, 1990); a learner may tend to become disoriented in terms of the goals of their original query and the relevance to the query of the information they are currently browsing. This problem is often referred to as the 'navigation problem' (Levene and Loizou, 2003).

Hypertext supports a social constructivist view of active learning in two distinct ways. Learners who navigate and explore a corpus of information are making choices and decisions at every point. As they do this they are experimenting with their understanding of the space and building their knowledge; the interactivity allows them to quickly retrack and build new paths until their understanding is complete. But perhaps an even more powerful tool for learning is the *construction* of hypertexts. The earliest users of hypertext in teaching (e.g. see Landow, 1992) observed that the people who understood the most about any particular topic were the graduate students they employed to build the learning materials. Innovative teachers now exploit this idea by requiring students to work, sometimes in teams, to construct hyperspaces and blogs.

Related concepts of relevance to learning from interactive multimedia communications are the notions of 'modalities' and 'channels' (Elsom-Cook, 2001). There are five modalities: touch, taste, sight, hearing and smell. Many channels of communication can exist for a single modality. So, for example, the modality of hearing can have different channels for receiving spoken language, listening to music or hearing noise. Being aware of and taking account of these issues is important in effectively designing for learning.

Multimedia software is used across a range of subjects to support learning. For example, the creation of a virtual chemistry lab might require the bringing together of images, sound, maps, video and animation, controlled through user interaction. Other examples of where multimedia applications are used to facilitate learning include their use in languages and visually based subjects. Simulation is a way of using multimedia in a project-based context, engaging learners in solving particular problems. Simulations may take many forms, such as scenario-based simulations, knowledge- or model-based simulations or multi-platform/multi-user synthetic environments enabling cooperative and adaptive immersion learning.

Facer *et al.* (2003) have pointed out that the use of games can allow learners the opportunity to imaginatively inhabit alternative realities in which they can test out ideas and take control and that this may lead to the development of new cognitive abilities and literacies. An interesting question for learning technology research is: Why are games motivating? Facer *et al.* (2003: 72) suggest that learners are 'personally responsible for the outcome ... The role of challenge in engaging and motivating games players is already well recognised and has been identified as an experience of a "flow" state'.

However, it is not easy to get tasks at the right level in gaming environments. Games do not offer true interactivity and are in essence a very structured experience where 'semiotic links to reality are merged with action without real world consequences that seems to be enjoyed, as in the ever popular Grand Theft Auto games' (Facer *et al.* 2003: 73). Another factor is that there are no real consequences associated with games (e.g. the frequently reported activity of intentionally opposing the supposed aims of the game, such as refusing to take over any worlds in the game Risk). Thus in games there exists the opportunity to inhabit alternate reality and see what it is like to take control.

There are links here to the work of Malone and Lepper (1987) on motivation, an issue that is discussed in more depth in Chapter 13. They identified four major factors in relation to motivation – challenge, curiosity, control, and fantasy – arguing that these are what make a learning environment (such as a gaming activity) intrinsically motivating. So to be challenging, activities should be kept continuously at an optimal level of difficulty to keep the learner from being either bored or frustrated. To elicit sensory or cognitive curiosity in activities one can use audiovisual devices or present information that makes the learner believe that their current knowledge structure is incomplete, inconsistent or unparsimonious. Activities should also promote a sense of control on the part of the learner, that is, a feeling that learning outcomes are determined by their own actions. Finally, one can engage the learner in make-believe activities (or fantasy contexts) to allow the learner to experience situations not actually present.

Elsom-Cook (2001) points out that we are seeing a shift towards multi-modal communication abilities and literacies. However, Facer *et al.* (2003) point out that being 'literate' in a digital age is more than information seeking and handling. It operates on three dimensions: operational (use of the computer), cultural (participation in authentic forms of social practice and meaning) and critical (ability to critique resources and use them against the grain, to appropriate or even redesign them). In addition, Rieber (2001) points out that play is an important component of promoting learning.

Virtual reality, visualisation and virtual labs

Virtual reality (VR) is an example of technology that provides near real experiences. Approaches include immersive systems, non-immersive systems and shared VR systems (Pakstas and Komiya, 2002). Heim (1998) identifies three 'I's with reference to VR: immersion, interactivity and information intensity.

What learning can be guaranteed from open-ended environments? Whilst it is possible to identify and describe a myriad of potential learning opportunities arising from technologies and systems that provide open-ended environments that support and encourage informal and non-formal learning, for example interactive multimedia, simulations, virtual reality and gaming environments etc., such learning settings can also be extremely problematic for many teachers. With such settings it is often very difficult to deliver particular and targeted learning outcomes amongst a cohort of learners. The very aspects that provide the motivation and contexts for learning, for example information richness, learner choice, and diversity of activity, also make it very difficult for such settings to deliver guaranteed learning outcomes. Different learners will learn different things from such settings but often teachers are intending similar learning outcomes being achieved by all. Is this a problem? What strategies can be used to deal with it?

Ron Oliver

Immersion makes a person feel transported to another place. Interaction, for Heim, derives from the ability of fast computers to change a scene's point of view in such a way that matches a human's ability to alter their physical position and perspective. Information intensity is the notion that a virtual world can offer special qualities such as telepresence and artificial entities, such as avatars, that show a certain degree of intelligent behaviour.

Communication tools, adapativity and personalisation

Rheingold (2002) in his book *Smart Mobs: The Next Social Revolution* conveys how mobile phones, pagers and personal digital assistants (PDAs) are shaping modern culture. Rheingold says techno-hipsters can congregate in 'Wi-Fi' areas that interact with their wireless devices to let them participate in a virtual social scene (see also mobile learning and ubiquitous computing below).

Adaptive-intelligent systems are based on ITS research, which is often funded by big research grants in the US. The field made extravagant claims in the early days about its ability to provide personalised tutoring. The following positive claims can be made for ITS. There now appears to be a long list of ITS that have been used and evaluated on a large scale in classroom teaching and which have been proven to facilitate learning. See for example the papers by Koedinger (http://pact.cs.cmu.edu/koedinger.html). Collaboration is dicussed in more detail in Chapter 12.

Mobile learning

The importance of mobile learning has increased dramatically in recent years, as more and more sophisticated mobile devices have appeared (Kukulska-Hulme and Traxler, 2005). Until recently, most mobile technology provided a single function: phone, handheld computer, PDA, digital camera, Sony PSP, etc. Now these are converging into single devices that offer a range of functions. They provide new opportunities for both personal and informal learning. Furthermore, mobile learning (or m-learning) can extend classroom teaching and it can also allow people to learn in their own time and space. The affective issues of mobile learning are discussed in Chapter 13.

Some schools have equipped all students with wireless networked laptop computers. As a result they are beginning to develop new patterns of learning, with students working on shared projects, critiquing each other's work, carrying out research through the internet and continuing classwork at home. Djanogly City Academy's 11–14 Centre (Djanogly, 2005) is the first school to have been built from new to support mobile and lifelong learning.

A range of projects, particularly through the Palm Education Pioneers scheme in the US (http://www.palmgrants.sri.com/), have also explored the use of PDAs in classrooms and successful uses include classroom response systems (e.g. see Draper and Brown, 2004), where students use handhelds to give answers to questions that can then be displayed to the whole class. They are also being used for data gathering for experiments and for collaborative simulations. An example of this is where students have used wireless-linked PDAs to simulate the spread of disease. A project at the University of Santiago has developed a system running on wireless PDA to support small-group collaborative learning. Each learner first attempts to solve a problem on the handheld computer. The system compares the individual answers and if they differ, encourages the group of students to discuss their work and come up with an agreed answer. The teacher can monitor the work of individuals and groups, walking round the class to intervene when needed or presenting the results of the groups for full-class

What forms of learning technologies do learners prefer? Given that so much of the learning we do is outside of the classroom, why is it that the bulk of this learning is supported by low technology applications? The most common learning technologies used for everyday learning include television, books, videos and increasingly the World Wide Web. There are no interactive technologies firmly in this suite of resources, although for formal education purposes, interactive technologies are the prime choice of many learning resource developers. Is there a difference in what learners prefer and what formal education provides them?

Ron Oliver

discussion. The system has been tested with positive results in four schools across Chile and also with trainee teachers (Cortez *et al.*, 2005).

It is important to remember that most learning occurs beyond the classroom. We learn throughout our lives – at home, with friends, outdoors. The average person carries out around eight major learning projects a year, such as learning a foreign language, a sport or a new skill (Livingstone, 2000). Bookshops and television schedules are filled with advice on gardening, cooking or home repairs – yet very little of this informal learning is currently supported by computer technology and provides fertile ground and possibilities for new innovations and application of technologies.

The goal of lifelong mobile learning can be stated as being to provide learning services to people on the move (ranging from complete courses to expert advice) and to help people to manage their personal learning projects and informal learning activities. Two major European projects have investigated learning outside the classroom with mobile technology. The MOBIlearn project (www.mobilearn.org) developed new mobile technology and services for learning outside the classroom. Field trials covered learning on a work based MBA course, learning in museums and galleries, and learning first aid skills. The m-Learning (www.m-learning.org) project was aimed at young learners at risk of social exclusion. It developed software on mobile phones to provide advice (e.g. on teenage pregnancy) and teach basic skills in literacy and numeracy.

Mobile technology offers new opportunities for access to learning support. Developing countries in Africa, South America and the former Soviet Union are rapidly adopting mobile technology. In Kenya, for example, the government has a programme to provide universal primary education. This requires training thousands of teachers across the country. Many rural areas have no fixed phone lines or internet connections, but they do now have mobile phone networks. A project funded by the UK Department for International Development is using SMS messaging to coordinate distance training of teachers, providing reminders of coursework, outlines, summaries, feedback and student support (Traxler, 2005).

A longer-term vision with mobile learning is to make buildings and outdoor locations 'learning enabled', so that they can help visitors to learn about the location itself and its surroundings. Some museums, such as the Tate Modern in London, already provide visitors with multimedia guides, and projects such as Caerus at the University of Birmingham are developing location-based audio and video guides to botanic gardens and historic sites (Naismith *et al.*, 2005). In the future, cities' public spaces may offer a combination of handheld guides and walk-up-and-use displays to teach about their history or architecture or enable communication and collaboration between learners. A hotel lobby or airport, for example, may offer services such as video-conference links to experts, or support for just-in-time distance learning.

Ubiquitous computing

Many of the issues raised above about mobile learning are echoed in the context of ubiquitous computing. Cook and Wade, in their section to be found in Roberts *et al.* (2005), suggest the following set of issues about informal learning and ubiquitous computing. They argue that, although people are now averaging about 15 hours a week on informal learning activities (Livingstone, 2000), very little of this informal learning is supported by e-learning or ubiquitous computing. Informal learning may harness ubiquitous computing environments of the future by providing 'learning services' to people in formal, non-formal and informal learning settings, and by helping people to manage their personal learning goals, projects and informal learning activities. There is real potential to empower learners with the new learning services provided by ubiquitous computing. They suggest that the central theme of ubiquitous computing is the interconnection of the devices to support user goals or activities and furthermore that ubiquitous computing and computing devices challenge the control of the tutor and put more control in the hands of the learner. Cook and Wade (in Roberts *et al.*, 2005) go on to state that, although truly ubiquitous computing is a long way off, adaptive devices (wireless/mobile) are here now, although cautioning that there are big trust issues in ubiquitous computing, and concluding that if ubiquitous computing is to be a friend it is necessary to focus not on technology but on learning needs.

Informal learning occurs when a learner is motivated to follow some self-directed learning. It is important to note that there appears to be great variation in the literature on 'informal' and 'non-formal' learning regarding definitional and theoretical issues. The context of such learning seems crucial and we would expect to see attributes of informality and formality present in all learning situations. Attributes of formal and informal learning can typically be described in terms of location/setting, process, purpose and content (Colley *et al.*, 2002). It may be useful

When is ubiquitous computing truly ubiquitous? Teachers need to have confidence when they rely on ubiquitous computing resources that all students in their classes will have access to them. Until teachers can be confident that all students can access the ubiquitous resources, they cannot plan these as formal elements in learning environments. Planning learning settings tends to be all about catering for the lowest common denominator. Until teachers have assurances about universal access to external resources, they will never rely on them as integrated and important elements in their learning settings. Such approaches whilst equitable and laudable can be wasteful of many opportunities and possibilities. Will we ever see the day when ubiquitous computing is ubiquitous to the point where teachers can assume universal accessibility?

Ron Oliver

to think of non-formal learning as being something the tutor knows about and informal learning as either being carried out under the radar of a tutor or something carried out individually by a self-motivated learner (or group of learners).

Ubiquitous computing envisages environments that have computers embedded in everyday objects as well as more traditional computing devices, e.g. laptops, desktops, palm-held devices, mobile communication devices, etc. One of the central themes of ubiquitous computing is the interconnection of the devices to support user goals or activities, e.g. the smart living room, smart building, etc. In such environments, the computing is performed both explicitly by the user and, where appropriate, implicitly in anticipation or as a reaction to activities of the user. The vision of e-learning in ubiquitous computing environments raises the idea that the environment, and the devices in that environment, can be coordinated to help support the learner's activities or collaboration. Although we have not achieved such environments, different aspects of such environments are being tested and explored. Simple examples of such ideas can be seen in the coordinated use of mobile handsets, traditional laptops and collaboration tools to support learning.

Within the UK the terms 'pervasive' and 'ubiquitous' computing are more prevalent than the European version of ambient intelligence (which means the same as ubiquitous computing), but the vision features strongly in a number of recent reports on the future of learning technology in the UK.

Current large-scale technology initiatives

To give an indication of some of the major directions in technological research in this area, two case study examples are given here: the open source software initiative and the JISC's e-learning framework.

Open source software

Open source software is a general term that refers to practices in production and development of software where the source code is made publicly available. The open source movement has had a significant impact on industries where online services are part of the core business. Linux, for example, is used as the operating system for 29 per cent of web servers, while Apache is the clear market leader in web server software (Abel, 2005). MySQL and its more scalable counterpart Postgres are robust database systems, while PHP is an increasingly used scripting language enabling the easy integration of data from these databases within web pages.

Higher education has been as quick to implement these technologies as many other industries. There are now also educational open source products available that appear to provide real alternatives to commercial systems. Prominent in this arena is Moodle, the most widespread open source virtual learning environment, recently adopted by the UK's Open University amongst other big players. Another initiative,

SAKAI, led by several top-ranking US institutions, is developing a suite of e-learning tools and the associated architecture. Efforts have also been successful in linking U-Portal, an open source portal, with both SAKAI and Moodle.

Objections to open source products are that they are usually poorly documented and relatively anarchic in their development and therefore subject to 'feature creep' in a way that their commercial counterparts are not. There is no doubt that open source development culture is very different from what universities' systems departments are used to and they need to develop better ways of engaging with the open source communities if they are to influence the products. Far from being chaotic though, successful open source projects are run by exceptional leaders who combine technical skills with organisational and communicational abilities and 'manage' their dispersed communities effectively (Woods and Guliani, 2005). It is not yet clear if more controlled projects such as the e-Framework (see below) and SAKAI will develop the necessary leadership and culture where enthusiasts work together voluntarily around the globe to develop sustainable open source software.

E-learning frameworks

Whether you refer to them as course management systems, virtual learning environments or managed learning environments, they have in reality only been around since the late 1990s (e.g. WebCT was established as a company in 1986 and Blackboard in 1987). Initially they provided tools to allow teachers who were not necessarily IT literate to upload and manage content on the web; they then provided coherent and integrated tools for managing and communicating with and between groups, and more recently they have focused on the interface with enterprise systems such as student information systems. In just a few years such systems have moved from being esoteric tools for early adopters to becoming mainstream; nearly every university supports at least one such environment, and thus a significant majority of HE courses have a web presence of some kind.

In spite of this enormous success there are many criticisms and shortcomings of what, after all, is the first generation of large-scale web-based learning systems. These systems are monolithic, may not use standard representations for their content, may not be open at the service/API (applications program interface) level and are typically commercial rather than open source, so interoperability (the ability of one system to communicate with another) is a serious issue. The SCORM (sharable content object reference model) approach of many learning management systems also tends to support a particular pedagogical viewpoint, which more often aligns with commercial training requirements than academic education (Wirski *et al.*, 2004).

Current thinking is that the next generation of e-learning environments will be modular; they will allow the creation of bespoke systems sewn together from appropriate modules that will interoperate to create the whole. These systems will be developed by communities (including software vendors) rather than single suppliers and they will be content and communication standards compliant, ensuring interoperability. This technical solution should enable teachers to specify learning tools and environments appropriate to their pedagogical purposes, rather than as dictated by the features provided by a particular technology. At the same time institutions should benefit financially, as not only are they sharing in the cost of development, but also the cost of deployment of new functionality is much reduced, involving maybe only the addition or replacement of a module rather than waiting for and deploying a full system upgrade.

There are a number of such tool frameworks under development. Probably the most mature is that developed by the SAKAI Project (mentioned on the previous page (http://www.sakaiproject.org)). SAKAI is a consortium of around 80 members developing an environment for collaboration, learning and research. The framework is intended to allow applications, not necessarily originally written for use in the framework, to be integrated to provide a coherent experience for the user. Necessarily, the original releases of this software featured a fairly coarse integration of a number of tools such as a portal, a quiz and test tool, a discussion tool and a drop box tool, all hailing from different code bases which then had been integrated. However, this software exists and is in use. It is being developed by a version of open source called the Community Source Development Model, which gives defined roles to community members, who are then funded from the community membership to carry out their responsibilities.

Another important consortium is the E-learning Framework or ELF (http://www.elframework.org), being developed by JISC-CETIS in the UK, Australia's Department of Education, Science and Training (DEST) and Industry Canada (IC) in collaboration with the SAKAI Project and Carnegie-Mellon University's Learning Systems Architecture Laboratory. This framework is being implemented as a service-oriented architecture (SOA) where each of the services is intended to factor a discreet component of behaviour. Workflows then orchestrate the services to provide the composite functionality. There are numerous advantages claimed for this approach (Wilson *et al.*, 2004) but as yet there is little evidence to support the hype, and there are still those who doubt the efficiency and scalability of the webservice approach.

Perhaps the most interesting feature of the ELF is the 'top down and bottom up' approach that is being taken by the funders to its specification and development. Unlike the SAKAI approach, which is centrally specified and coordinated, the ELF

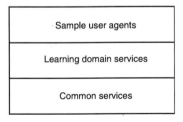

Figure 4.1 The layers of the ELF

architects have imposed on the community only the most conceptual of designs, in the form of a diagram known within the community as the 'wall'; it consists of a number of 'bricks' representing each of the services, organised in three layers (Figure 4.1).

User agents, such as VLEs, portals and assessment engines, provide the user interface to the services. Learning domain services include functionality such as course management, sequencing, assessment and e-Portfolios. Common services provide the underlying infrastructure such as email, messaging, calendaring, metadata management and security. The funders are approaching the specification of the system in two ways. Toolkit developments are being funded to produce components of the system without any de facto specification of their interface – encouraging bottom-up emergent specification. At the same time 'Reference Model' projects are defining the scope, functionality and interfaces to functionality of various domains (such as Learning Design, Assessment, e-Portfolio), encouraging community top-down specification of the product.

This is an exciting moment in the development of technologies to support learning and at the time of writing discussions are underway amongst the ELF partners and others to create a unified framework encompassing e-learning, research, digital libraries, and administration.

Conclusions

Interestingly, Papert's emphasis on 'informal learning' in samba schools, described in the introduction and which cropped up under m-learning and ubiquitous computing, has also been identified as a key research theme in a workshop called 'Realising the Potential of E-learning'. The workshop was held in May 2003 and sponsored by DFES, EPSRC, ESRC, eScience Programme and JISC (see EPSRC, 2003). Specifically, the workshop identified the following as one of nine key research issues: 'Understanding the needs of learners both inside and outside formal learning environments and methods for capturing their achievements'.

Research to address this type of issue would clearly be interdisciplinary and would need to employ the human-centred approach articulated in the introduction to this chapter. In addition, in this chapter we have explored the notion of how game playing, a core element of Papert's samba schools, can help motivate learners. Finally, Papert's work raises an interesting question that we feel needs further work: How can we design technologies that enable learners to strike a useful balance between competition and cooperation within a community of formal and informal learning?

Chapter 5

The impact of e-learning on organisational roles and structures

Gráinne Conole, Su White and Martin Oliver

Introduction

Large-scale technological implementations are commonplace in the business sector (for example, with online banking and shopping). In contrast, despite a long tradition of distance education, educational institutions have been slower to take advantage of the potential of new technologies to support their teaching, research and administrative procedures (Jochems *et al.*, 2004). This chapter considers the impact of e-learning on institutional change, particularly changes to roles and organisational structure.

The chapter begins with a categorisation of the types of organisations that exist in HE and their different characteristics. A critique of the factors that shape and define institutions is then provided, considering these in relation to current thinking on the context of education in modern society. Chapter 2 provides more detail about current epistemelogical perspectives. This chapter also considers research on organisational change and different forms of representation that can be used to describe the complexity of organisations – such as the use of metaphors. It then considers the different types of interventions that occur in organisations, grouping these into educational, technical and organisational. It goes on to discuss the changing roles that have arisen as a result of the impact of technology, focusing in particular on the rise of learning technologists as a distinct professional group.

Understanding organisations

Types of organisations

Every institution has its own particular culture, which is in part sector-specific, but is also influenced by local context, institutional mission and strategic priorities. This cultural context shapes the way in which the institution is organised. McNay (1995) identifies and characterises four organisational types (Figure 5.1). Although these are clearly generic, idealised types, understanding which of these an institution most closely fits can help in formulating appropriate strategies for successful e-learning implementation.

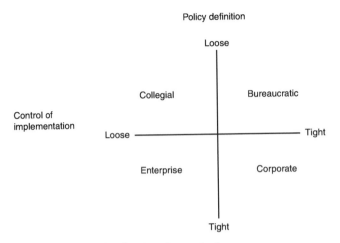

Figure 5.1 McNay's classification of organisations

The first category describes 'collegial' organisations, typified by research-led institutions. There is a clear divide between academic and support roles and structures, with decision-making through a complex structure of committees. Reporting lines tend to be poor and there are usually strong local cultures and agendas, with an allegiance to subject disciplines rather than the institution. Academic status is valued over support functions. The second category describes 'bureaucratic' organisations, characterised by strong central management and top-down decision-making, with clearly defined roles and career progression paths. These are commonly found in further education colleges and new universities. The third category describes 'corporate' institutions, with tight policy definition and control over implementation. The fourth category describes 'enterprise' institutions, which are more closely aligned to business organisations, being driven by financial objectives and responsive to external opportunities. They have traditional management roles and structures with clear demarcation of responsibilities and hierarchical decision-making processes. These are more common in America, particularly in those organisations focusing on distance education.

Organisational context

Organisations are complex and multi-faceted, and this has a direct impact on the degree to which learning technologies are successfully taken up. An organisation's profile includes its structure, culture (at different levels), mission and business needs.

Institutions are influenced by a range of drivers. External drivers include current national policy and funding opportunities (see Chapter 3), accessibility (see Chapter 8) and widening participation (DfES, 2003). E-learning is seen by many as one means of supporting these and as an essential element in delivering higher education efficiently and effectively to a diverse, mass audience. This is in part driven by economic imperatives but is also because of the current government's roots in social democratisation (Simpson, 2005: 91). This, coupled with the growth of globalisation, means that institutions have become increasingly interested in exploring international alliances (such as the Universitas 21 – http://www.universitas21.com/ and WUN networks – http://www.wun.ac.uk/) and different business models for distance learning (Guri-Rosenbilt, 2005).

Giddens (1999) argues that we live in an unpredictable, constantly changing world of globalisation where the increasing impact of technologies results in unintended consequences. This links to Beck's notion of a risk society, and particularly the notion of 'manufactured risks' (Beck, 1992). Beck (1992), Giddens (2000), Castells (1996) and others suggest that nothing is certain and that we live in an increasingly culturally rich and complex society with changing norms and values. The impact of ICT across all aspects of our lives is one of the key features of this, and we are only just beginning to understand some of the ways in which technologies are changing our practice. For example, as Giddens notes (1999), 'instantaneous electronic communication isn't just a way in which news or information is conveyed more quickly. Its existence alters the very texture of our lives' (available online at http://www.bbc.co.uk/radio4/reith1999/lecture1.shtml).

Coupled with external drivers, an institution is defined by its organisational culture, which is in part instantiated or reified in institutional strategies and policies. An organisation consists of a variety of stakeholders, with differing, often conflicting agendas. Part of understanding organisational culture is about clarifying the needs of stakeholders (academics, support staff, librarians and senior managers), critiquing changes in associated roles and exploring the impact of technology on practice.

Organisational change

Approaches to and critiques of achieving organisational change by harnessing the potential of technologies abound. Some focus on the impact of learning technologies (Beetham et al., 2001; Timmis, 2003); some describe the role of developing coherent intuitional strategies to change (McNaught and Kennedy, 2000; Salmon, 2005); others focus on associated support and staff development issues (Smith and Oliver, 2000; Oliver and Dempster, 2003); whilst others still offer models or means of representing and understanding organisational contexts and change management (Morgan, 1986; Mumford, 2003). White (2006) provides a review of the theories of innovation and change, citing Rogers' (1995) ideas on motivation, uptake and the implementation of new methods and Moore's (1991) bell-curve graphical categorisation of the users of new technologies into 'early adopters', 'early majority', 'pragmatists', 'conservatives', 'late majority' and 'laggards'. Moore identifies a chasm between early adopters and early majority and contends that successful implementation results where there are mechanisms to bridge this gap.

In the context of e-learning a number of frameworks have been developed to provide guidance about managing change. The book of TALENT (available

online at http://www.le.ac.uk/talent/) focuses on managing organisations, especially concerning changes to learning and teaching, whilst the ELTI (embedding
learning technologies institutionally) project includes an audit designed to inform
embedding, assist in developing institutional structures, culture and expertise and
encourage cross-boundary collaboration and groupings (ELTI, 2003). In terms of
understanding the development of institution-wide IT systems (often referred to
as Managed Learning Environments – MLEs), a recent study provides an
overview of MLE activities (Social Science Research Unit, 2003), whilst
Holyfield has critiqued models for describing MLEs (Holyfield, 2002) and
Britain has developed a pedagogical model for understanding their use in teaching (Britain, 2004). In addition, a number of reports have also synthesised lessons
learned from these institution-wide implementations (Boys, 2002a; Boys, 2002b;
Condron and Sutherland, 2002), reiterating the need to take account of the organisational and human factors in implementing large-scale e-learning initiatives.

Representations of organisations

As discussed in Chapter 1, part of the difficulty of understanding and implementing e-learning is that there is no one unique description for 'e-learning'; terms and
conflicting definitions abound – ICT, learning technologies and e-learning are all
terms that have been described to cover aspects of this area. As discussed in
Chapter 7, even the term for resources – 'learning objects' – is highly contested
(Polsani, 2003; Koper and Olivier, 2004; Wiley, 2000). Nowhere is this lack of
definition more evident than in the discourse around the development of integrated learning environments. For example, in relation to the term MLE,
Holyfield (2002) concluded that no one representation alone provided a complete
description of the domain. This complexity suggests that viewing and articulating
the nature of the artefacts and processes involved in e-learning from multiple perspectives is necessary. This section describes some of the representations that can
be used to understand the nature of organisations, focusing on modelling and the
use of metaphors as examples.

Modelling is increasingly being used as a tool for understanding organisational
change. The unifying modelling language (UML) can be used to produce a highly
structured model of the operational and functional processes of an institution
(Wilcox *et al.*, 2005). The benefit of this systems thinking is that it encourages both
stakeholders and designers to think in loops and develop a shared understanding of
the problem domain. It particular it allows them to develop a clearer understanding
of the nature and intended function of an e-learning development within their institutional context and the perceived benefits. UML helps produce a highly structured
model of a business process, from which a technical specification can be produced
without having to question whether the original business process made sense.
Modelling at this relatively abstract level allows clearer thinking about what the
intended function of an e-learning development is within the organisation and how
linking two systems together will benefit a particular organisational operation.

Morgan describes a series of metaphorical models, each of which facilitates different ways of thinking about an organisation and highlights different characteristics, which combined help to build a rich picture of the overall organisational context, priorities and agendas (Morgan, 1986). Five examples are discussed here in the context of their relevance to the understanding of e-learning. These metaphors can be used either as a means of understanding and highlighting different aspects of organisations or as a basis for structuring organisations.

The 'machine' metaphor highlights the structural aspects of organisations. Institutions that adopt this approach tend to have clear work allocation, management structure and division of labour. This approach is useful when the environment is stable and relatively easy to define, but new issues tend to be dealt with piecemeal through *ad hoc* groups and reactions tend to be slow with a lack of coordination.

The 'organism' metaphor considers an organisation as a living system existing within a wider environment on which it depends, consisting of different species each adapted to particular conditions. This draws out the concept of different life cycles within organisations and focuses on relationships between different inter-related species/sub-units. This approach favours a project-based matrix structure, with flexible jobs and roles developed through individual expertise. The advantage of this approach is that it helps to breaks down barriers and allows members from different functional specialisms to fuse their expertise by focusing on a shared problem – leading to increased adaptability, coordination and good use of human resources.

The 'brain' metaphor is based on the idea of organisations as information processing systems capable of learning. This highlights that systems need to have the capacity to sense and monitor their environment, be able to detect changes and initiate corrective action. It encourages an open and reflective approach acknowledging that situations are complex and changing and encourages the exploration of different viewpoints.

The 'culture' metaphor views organisations as mini-societies with their own distinctive patterns of culture and sub-culture. Organisations are viewed as socially constructed realities and different professional groups have distinct views of the world, each with their own language and set of favoured concepts (see also Chapters 2 and 14). It can be used to develop shared meaning and understanding and as a means of creating organisational activity by influencing language, norms, local values and beliefs.

Finally, the 'political' metaphor highlights the relationship between interests, conflicts and power. It focuses on understanding that people think and act differently from one another, viewing organisations as loose networks of people with divergent interests. It emphasises the pluralist nature that shapes organisations and highlights that all organisational activity is interest-based.

Each of these metaphors focuses on different aspects of an organisation and hence can be useful in providing a rich picture of the institutional context within which e-learning occurs. They can also be used as a basis for undertaking research in this area – highlighting different aspects of organisations, including the tensions and differing agendas of the stakeholders involved.

Having worked in both corporate (RMIT University in Australia) and collegial (Chinese University of Hong Kong, CUHK) universities, I can attest to the differences in culture in different contexts. Implementing Blackboard at RMIT was like taking a horse to water when she wasn't thirsty! The University had decided it would be used and so it was rolled out. After that experience, the approach we adopted here at CUHK was to create interest first and then provide support for a demonstrated demand. There are several legacy systems here that have not been removed by force, staff development is largely within individual departments or faculties, and evaluation support is an integral part of the service. Academics respond well to an evidence-based approach to changing their teaching practices. Staff developers who demonstrate scholarship in their own teaching ('with' and 'of' staff) are more likely to engender it in their colleagues.

Carmel Mcnaught

Interventions in organisations

E-learning is often described as a catalyst for change, precisely because it cuts across institutional structures and impacts on all aspects of practice. Furthermore it makes existing practice, and in particular poor practice, more explicit. Some of the interventions associated with the increased impact of e-learning concentrate on the technical or educational aspects, whilst others focus on policy developments, staff developments and changing organisational structures. A selection of commonly used examples is discussed below.

Educational interventions

These include interventions that primarily concern the development of innovative approaches to teaching and learning. Many institutions, for example, have set up funds to enable practitioners to experiment with the use of technologies and report back their evaluation findings. Initiatives about staff development also fall into this category; examples include the development of support materials or workshops for effective use of technologies, institutional 'show and tell' conferences or themed learning and teaching semesters to promote dissemination of activities across an institution. One of the most common types of educational intervention involves providing small grants to enable practitioners to explore the use of learning technologies in their teaching. White (2006) notes that many institutions are engaged in this type of small-scale experimentation, whereas large-scale systematic interventions are less common.

Technological interventions

Technological interventions are those that are primarily driven by either the development or implementation of technologies. Examples include the increased interest across the sector in the past decade in the use of virtual learning environments (VLEs) – although it should be noted that the scope of what constitutes a VLE

Case study: The JISC MLE programme

In the late 1990s the JISC instigated a programme exploring the development of institutional MLEs. This case study summarises the lessons learned from this initiative (further information is available in an online infokit – JISCInfoNet, 2003). It echoes many of the arguments made in this chapter: namely that organisations are complex and multi-faceted; successful e-learning implementation is dependent on context; and that human and organisational issues, rather than technological ones, are usually the main barriers to success. The key findings were:

- Knowledge about organisations is tacit and therefore difficult to capture.
- The environmental context within which UK institutions work has changed dramatically in recent years. Previously the environment was relatively stable, with standard and established teaching and administrative processes.
- Technologies are now having a major impact on organisational structures, roles and identities and are prompting new forms of learning and teaching innovation.
- Stakeholder perspectives should be identified and expectations managed.
- Institutions still have fairly traditional divisions between academic, administrative and learning support staff. Power remains within the academic departments, especially in terms of influencing decision-making.
- There is often a mismatch between central vision and understanding at departmental level. For example, senior management may have signed up to the concept of e-learning, but often this is not adequately communicated with staff in support services and academic departments, who will be responsible for implementing, supporting and using it.
- Cultural change needs time to be managed.
- E-learning developments inherently demand a high level of cross-institutional collaboration and commitment.
- There is a conflict between maintaining existing modes of working and adapting or moving to new systems, processes and models.
- Technical issues are overshadowed by institutional and human issues.
- There are significant difficulties in trying to integrate existing legacy systems that have been badly designed and in dealing with inaccurate data.
- Institutions know little about existing data flows or organisational processes.
- Institutions lack cost–benefit models for evaluating the effectiveness of both traditional educational and e-learning processes.

varies dramatically from use of commercial all-in-one software packages through to integrated MLEs. A number of institutions invested significantly in this area, instigating campus-wide initiatives, for example Sheffield and Coventry Universities' adoption of webCT and Durham's adoption of Blackboard. Most institutions, however, adopted a more cautious approach to the introduction of VLEs, usually letting practitioners decide the extent to which they wanted to use the VLE in their teaching. Some institutions concentrated on particular types of technological use, for example Loughborough and Luton's institution-wide use of computer-assisted assessment (CAA) and exploration of the potential of CAA for summative assessment. Recently activities have shifted to the implementation of institution-wide MLEs (see case study), as well as the use of open source approaches (see also Chapter 4). For example, the Open University is currently integrating an open source VLE with its existing administrative and e-learning systems, with the aim of providing a fully integrated online learning experience for the student.

Organisational interventions

These include top-down interventions, either directed through the formulation and implementation of strategies (such as e-learning, teaching and learning or

There is a general misconception that technology drove the large-scale implementation of a virtual learning environment at Coventry University. This is not the case. The pedagogical and practical teaching and learning requirements were the key to this development. Technology was more the vehicle. Pedagogy was the engine. The origin of the implementation was a strategic decision at senior level, in response to the national agenda set by the Dearing Inquiry and our own self-analysis, to enhance the students' learning experience, through ICT where appropriate. This was set out in the Learning and Teaching Strategy of 1997. Investment followed the strategy – investment in a critical mass of academic and learner support colleagues who were seconded to the University's Teaching, Learning and Assessment Taskforce. These members of the Taskforce worked independently on their own innovation projects but significantly also worked together, across disciplinary and functional boundaries and under the leadership of educational developers, to identify blocks in teaching and learning developments. The most tangible, early outcome of this work was the major roll-out of the virtual and semi-managed learning environment in 1999, available to all students in all modules and designed around a common template which fulfilled the learning and teaching criteria for the use of technology that had been identified by members of the Taskforce.

Frances Deepwell

information strategies) or in response to external requirements (such as quality assurance). Often strategic interventions follow a top-down/bottom-up mixed-mode approach of the type described by McNaught and Kennedy (2000). Salmon (2005) describes an institution-wide implementation that draws on the development and use of an appropriate e-learning strategic framework. Using the metaphor of flight, she suggests that in terms of e-learning, 'the introduction of ICT into the world of learning and teaching in universities is now in transition from "flapping" to mass take off'. She goes on to describe the approach adopted at Leicester University, which consists of a four-quadrant framework that takes account of the integration of both mainstream and peripheral technologies.

Quality assurance is an important example of an externally imposed intervention. Oliver (2005a) provides a comparison of quality assurance activities in the UK and Australia and contends that there are two main ways in which the quality of a process or activity can be assessed: through benchmarking or by the specification of standards. Quality assurance in essence has acted as a driver for change by requiring institutions to examine their existing practice and demonstrate the ways in which they support learning and excellence in teaching.

Changing roles

One of the most evident indicators of the impact of technology is the way in which professional roles are changing. This includes the emergence of new roles as a consequence of the development and implementation of learning technologies, as well as changes to existing roles.

A review of the impact of tools (Conole, 2006) demonstrates how even common applications such as Word have had a dramatic impact on practice. The most obvious example of this is the demise of the secretary as there is now no longer a need for dictating and typing. Traditional roles are changing in both support services and academia (Conole, 2006). Job titles and structural units within support services have been in a constant state of flux in the last few decades as institutions struggle to keep up with the impact of changing technologies and try to introduce appropriate structures and roles to provide support for teaching and research activities within the institution (see Gosling, 2001 for a review of the rise and impact of these types of units). The nineties saw the emergence of new units to provide support to staff on using learning technologies. However, there was no consistency in terms of either the location or the status of such units – some were located in central information services, others in educational development centres, whilst others still were located in academic departments; additionally, institutional 'learning technologists' ranged in status from senior management positions through to low-level support service roles.

In addition, an academic's focus of work is now different from two decades ago; in particular, there is a much greater emphasis on managerial work than there used to be (Henkel, 2000). Academics are less likely to view themselves simply as researchers, but are instead required to undertake a multi-functional role with an emphasis on research, teaching and attracting external funding through grants or consultancy. The modern academic is also expected to work more closely with staff in support services. There has also been a noticeable rise in the role and importance of support and administrative staff as the nature of universities has become more complex and multi-faceted.

A review carried out by Price *et al.* (2005) shows how academics internation-ally are increasingly expected to work in teams (especially when developing curricula), are positioned as part of a more industrialised process of teaching and are forced to re-think their teaching approaches. It would be over-simplistic to say that technology has 'caused' all this, but it is certainly implicated – the promotion of teaching approaches using new technology is often seen as a way to achieve these wider changes.

As well as these changes to the balance of academics' roles (teacher, researcher, administrator, etc.) and the division of labour between them and related support staff, there have also been changes to their role as a teacher. These echo the wider debate about whether or not changing media has an effect on communication –

Case study: The invisible transformation of teaching

In a study of how academics' teaching changed when they started to use virtual learning environments (Oliver *et al.*, 2005), one participant described the support he gave to learners as being no different whether through the technology or face to face. 'I'm looking for some kind of contribution, any contribution, and if I don't get that then I know there's probably something wrong. It's when people are chip-ping in their bits and then all of a sudden it goes quiet. That's the danger sign. You do pick up on odd stuff like that – it's just transferring what you normally do in normal situations to a virtual environment.'

Closer analysis showed that at the strategic level there was no significant change: the overall aim is still that the tutor provides support to their student, looking for signs of disinterest, unhappiness etc. This remains the tutor's responsibility, and the tools used (watching for symbolic events such as non-participation) are the same. However, at a more fine-grained level, differences emerge. Although the tutor still looks for signs of non-participation, the way these are noticed changes. Rather than glancing around a room, student monitoring functions within the virtual envi-ronment are used.

At an even finer level, everything looks different. Instead of operations such as 'scan the room', 'listen for things to go quiet', etc., the steps would consist of things like, 'click this link to generate a list of contributors', 'click this link to reveal students' patterns of reading the online materials', and so on. At this level of analysis, the role of the teacher is almost entirely different online than face to face. This is how teaching online and face to face can be both the same and completely different simultaneously.

whether 'the medium is the message', as McLuhan (1989) claimed, or simply a neutral vehicle for 'delivering' content (Clark, 1983). Analysis suggests that teaching both changes *and* stays the same – the purposes and values endure, or at least change very slowly, whereas the techniques used to implement these might be totally different depending on the technology involved.

The emergence of learning technologists

Perhaps the biggest change has been the emergence of a new professional group, learning technologists, who provide a bridge between the technologies and the ways in which they can be used to support learning and teaching (Beetham, 2002a; Beetham, 2002b) and who help academics harness the potential of new technologies, often acting at both a strategic and a local level.

The emergence of educational/learning technologists began over a quarter of a century ago (e.g. Lawless and Kirkwood, 1974). However, their identification as a distinct group became clear about a decade ago. This was in part due to the substantive impact of the internet on learning but was fuelled by a number of national initiatives and policy drivers (Conole, 2002). This provided opportunities to experiment using developmental funding and led to an increased interest in the role of technology across education, as well as better senior management engagement and consequential change in strategy. There was an influx of researchers from related domains (such as computer science, education, psychology, general social science, business studies, mathematical modelling and linguistics) as well as academic practitioners with an interest in pedagogy.

This first generation of learning technologists tended to adopt multi-faceted roles; often combining e-learning research with support for practitioners in terms of the use of technologies, and input at institutional level in terms of strategy and policy. There was no clear location for these pioneers: some were located in central units such as educational development units, learning support or computer services; others were located within specific departments or at faculty level. The level of 'prestige' and gravitas of the roles also ranged dramatically from very high-level professorial equivalent or senior lecturer level appointment to low-level support grades. This was linked to the kinds of work the support staff were involved in, either involving formal research or else being restricted to applied curriculum development projects (Oliver, 2002). There was also a growth of new 'centres', such as the Institute of Computer Based Learning at Heriot-Watt (created as a direct consequence of national policy directives at the time, in particular the McFarlane Report (1992)) and the Interactive Learning Centre at Southampton. A decade on, many institutions now have clearly defined centres of this kind, ranging from some that specialise in research to those who have an institution-wide support brief.

Beetham *et al.* carried out a detailed survey of learning technologists (2001) and found that this first generation of learning technologists shared a set of common characteristics. They tended to come from a wide range of professional backgrounds and acted as brokers across institutional silos. They acted as change agents, adopting multi-faceted roles, and were often involved in the entire process of development, support and use. Often they occupied a pivotal institutional role in terms of negotiation, liaison and facilitation of change. A major concern of this first generation was the perceived status of their roles and the academic legitimacy of their specialism. Motivations cited for taking up the role included: excitement of working in an emergent field; intellectual rewards; helping students to learn more effectively; working with academic staff; and personal enjoyment. Disincentives included: lack of time and overwork; job security; concerns about status and financial reward; no obvious career progression; and the difficulty of keeping up in a rapidly changing area.

The current, second generation of learning technologists do not have such a holistic role and tend to orientate towards either researching e-learning or providing a support function for those using learning technologies. This dictates their location; the former in dedicated research centres or academic departments, the latter in support services. Newcomers to the area often have Masters-level learning technology qualifications and may not perceive themselves to be pioneers in the same way as their predecessors.

This division between researchers and practitioners can be classified according to Chartrand's notion of science and arts (1989); with the researchers veering towards the scientific end of the spectrum and the practitioners towards the arts. This suggests that researchers are focused on developing and advancing knowledge about learning technologies, whilst support staff are focused on practical applications. Researchers are motivated by traditional research drivers (peer-reviewed publication and reward through funded research grants), whereas support staff tend to be concerned with providing support on the effective use of ICT and are often embroiled with institutional politics, including battles to establish the relevance of their role and their 'position' within the institution. Researchers tend to network primarily with other researchers in the field as well as those from allied fields such as education, psychology and computer science, whereas support staff primarily network with other local support staff such as staff developers, quality assurance officers and IT/library staff. As e-learning becomes a more credible and recognised field, the associated career path for researchers is beginning to follow that of other subject disciplines (lecturer, reader and chair), whereas there is still no established career pathway for support staff in this area (Oliver, 2003a).

As noted, one characteristic of the original learning technology pioneers was that they were engaged in multiple roles and hence could see the interconnection between research outputs, support, staff development, and strategy and policy initiatives. Separating out these functions within the second generation raises the question of whether this higher level interconnection has been lost. Is there a danger that the research will become more and more esoteric and removed from practice? Equally, will the more practitioner-focused learning technologist be in danger of becoming remote from current research findings and hence out of date in terms of informing practice? There is also a danger of an insidious hierarchy emerging, with learning technology researchers being considered more privileged than their practically oriented peers.

Coupled with the different agendas of those engaged in research and those providing support roles, there is a tension between the needs of policy-makers/senior managers and learning technologists. The former are frequently concerned with efficiency gains and cost effectiveness, wanting to see evidence-based practice establishing the benefits of new technologies over existing teaching and learning methods, whilst the latter are concerned with how the technologies can be used to improve the student learning experience.

Conclusion

This chapter has attempted to articulate the complexity of organisations and to highlight the importance of taking organisational context into account when considering e-learning. It has shown that e-learning has had, and is continuing to have, a significant impact on both organisational structures and professional roles. As discussed in Chapter 3, many early e-learning innovations failed precisely because they did not take account of pedagogical and organisational issues, concentrating too much on the technical aspects. The complex and contested nature of organisations, which is well illustrated by Morgan's (1986) use of metaphors, aligns well with one of the central themes of this book – complexity. The future is unknown but what is certain is that technologies will continue to develop and continue to have a significant impact; we need to develop sophisticated methods and theories to take account of this and ensure that the impact is beneficial not detrimental, and avoid what Beck (1992) refers to as unintended consequences.

Chapter 6

Learning theory and its application to e-learning

Martin Dyke, Gráinne Conole, Andrew Ravenscroft and Sara de Freitas

Introduction

This chapter explores approaches to learning that we argue best reflect a constantly changing, dynamic environment as reflected in current thinking (Giddens, 1999; Beck, 1992; Castells, 1996). We acknowledge that there are many different schools of thought in terms of learning theories, but we will focus here on those we believe are most relevant and applicable to e-learning. This will include a discussion of the following: a critique of behaviourist approaches and their impact, advocacy of the application of experiential/reflective, social constructivist and socio-cultural approaches, and the argument that effective e-learning usually requires, or involves, high-quality educational discourse (Ravenscroft, 2004a) combined with an experiential and reflective approach (Conole *et al.*, 2004; Mayes and de Freitas, 2004).

Philosophical foundations

The chapter seeks to explore those approaches to learning that we argue have had an impact on the field of e-learning. In doing so, we have tried to adopt a practice orientation towards learning theory that is reminiscent of Aristotle's emphasis on praxis. He argued: 'thought by itself, however, moves nothing; what moves us is thought aiming at some goal and concerned with action' (Irwin 1985: 150). Aristotle would also appear to be an early advocate of another theme promoted in this chapter – that of transformative activity that turns information into knowledge. The chapter in part adopts a conceptualisation of learning as the *transformation of experience*, a theme that is evident from Aristotle through to Kant (1781) and Dewey (1949) and articulated by Jarvis, who argued, 'human learning is the combination of processes whereby whole persons construct experiences of situation and transform them into knowledge, skills, attitudes, values, emotions and the senses, and integrate the outcomes into their own biographies' (2004: 111). This emphasis on learning as the transformation of experience echoes the socially constructive perspective argued for in Chapter 2. As Laurillard argued, 'knowledge is information already transformed: selected, analyzed, interpreted, integrated, articulated, tested, evaluated' (1993: 123), a view that corresponds with the perspective of reflective learning theorists (Jarvis, 2004: 111).

The information revolution is an important marker of shifts in the nature of modernity noted by social theorists (e.g. Castells, 1996; Kumar, 1995). The information revolution has produced vast amounts of new and often contradictory information that forces people to reflect on experience and make decisions (Dyke, 2001). Changing information can present a challenge to the very ontological security provided by everyday living. As the media networks feed us the latest information on everything from the global to the local, people are forced to think again about their actions and accept or reject a need for change. Giddens described this process as a 'reflexive monitoring of the self' (1991: 244). At one level this is individualised, evident in the way people reflexively develop a level of lifestyle expertise and seek to actively reconstruct their personae. However, there is potential for more collective action with the world; Beck acknowledges that reflection may be a consequence of reflexive modernisation, which 'necessitates self-reflection on the foundations of social cohesion and the examination of prevailing conventions and formations of rationality' (1992: 8).

Whether individualised or collective in form, reflexivity in the social world is part of the stream in which e-learning flows. The speed and scope of information change, and the need to transform this information into knowledge and learning is particularly pertinent to the network society. This connects with the concept that we learn through reflection, experience and engagement with others. We argue in this chapter that these dimensions are the central tenets of learning in late modernity and we believe this focus provides a framework for e-learning.

It has been argued that socio-economic changes have required greater creativity, innovation and adaptability in work (Lash and Urry 1994). This in turn has produced demands for 'permanent creativity in education' (Forrester *et al.*, 1995: 150) and reflective approaches to learning (Dyke, 2001). It is the transformation of experience, the essence of reflective learning (Jarvis, 2004: 111), that can help turn the information revolution into a knowledge revolution.

Theoretical approaches

One approach to summarising and capturing the various theoretical approaches has been given by Conole *et al.* (2004). Table 6.1 provides an overview of the main learning theory perspectives along with an indication of the kinds of e-learning practice they most obviously support.

In this chapter we do not intend to provide a review of these different perspectives. Wider reviews of learning theories are provided elsewhere, although a previous account by Ravenscroft (2004a) that links learning-pedagogical theory to specific examples of e-learning innovation are drawn on throughout this chapter. Also, it is useful to briefly summarise that Mayes and de Freitas' (2004) group learning theories into three categories: *associative* (learning as activity through structured tasks), *cognitive* (learning through understanding) and *situative* (learning

Learning theories are often presented as being alternative accounts of the same phenomena, rather than perfectly compatible accounts of very different phenomena. The term 'learning' is very broad indeed, covering as it does a range of processes which stretches from acquiring the physical coordination to throw a javelin, through to the sensitivities involved in marriage guidance. One class of theory deals with a description of learning a perceptual-motor skill, another with building a framework of knowledge, while a third theoretical perspective essentially deals with why people should want to learn something in the first place, and why they should be motivated to carry on learning it. In principle these can be joined up as compatible sub-theories. Perhaps we should differentiate more carefully what is being explained: it might then be clearer why the theories themselves draw on different assumptions.

Terry Mayes

as social practice). They suggest that theories of learning provide 'empirically-based accounts of the variables which influence the learning process, and explanations of the ways in which that influence occurs'.

The nature of learning, and what characterises it, has been the subject of intense research for centuries. As a result various schools of thought have arisen that emphasise particular aspects of learning – such as learning by doing and through reflection, either individually or in a social context. These can be grouped into a number of broad educational approaches depending upon which learning characteristics they foreground (reflection, dialogue, etc.). More recently, numerous models for learning have been proposed, such as Kolb's experiential learning cycle (Kolb, 1984), Jarvis's model of reflection and learning (Jarvis, 1987), Laurillard's conversational framework (Laurillard, 1993) and Wenger's community of practice (Wenger, 1998). Despite these rich theoretical seams, these models are rarely applied to the creation of e-learning activities (Lisewski and Joyce, 2003; Beetham *et al.*, 2001; Clegg *et al.*, 2003; Oliver, 2002).

Arguably what is missing is a metaview of the key themes that emerge across these different positions, with specific reference to e-learning. There have been attempts to provide a more holistic approach to identify key elements of learning, such as a model proposed by Dyke (2001) that includes elements of 'learning with others', 'reflection', 'knowledge' and 'practice'. Conole *et al.* (2004) provide a map of learning theories against three axes: individual – social; reflection – non-reflection; information – experience. We argue here that e-learning developments could be improved if they were orientated around three core elements of learning:

* through thinking and reflection
* from experience and activity
* through conversation and interaction.

Table 6.1 Learning theories and potential e-learning applications

Theories	Approach	Main characteristics	Potential e-learning applications
Behaviourist	• Behaviourism • Instructional design • Intelligent tutoring • Didactic • Training needs analysis	• Focuses on behaviour modification via stimulus-response pairs, controlled and adaptive response and observable outcomes • Trial and error learning • Learning through association and reinforcement	• Much of current e-learning development represents little more than transfer of didactic approaches online, the 'web page turning mentality' linked directly to assessment and feedback
Cognitive	• Reflective practitioner • Learner-centred	• Focus on internal cognitive structures; views learning as transformations in these cognitive structures • Pedagogical focus is on the processing and transmission of information through communication, explanation, recombination, contrast, inference and problem solving • Useful for designing sequences of conceptual material that build on existing information structures	• Salomon's notion of distributed cognition (Salomon, 1993) could lead to a more shared knowledge structure between individual and surrounding information-rich environment of resources and contacts • Development of intelligent and learning systems, and the notion of developmental personalised agents
Cognitive constructivism	• Active learning • Enquiry-led • Problem-based • Goal-based • Cognitive-apprenticeship • Constructivist-based design	• Focus on the processes by which learners build their own mental structures when interacting with an environment • Task-orientated, favour hands-on, self-directed activities orientated towards design and discovery	• Useful for structured learning environments, such as simulated worlds; construction of conceptual structures through engagement in self-directed tasks • The concept of toolkits and other support systems that guide and inform users through a process of activities could be used to good effect to embed and enable constructivist principles

			Access to resources and expertise offers the potential to develop more engaging and student-centred, active and authentic learning environments
Social constructivism	• Dialogic • Argumentation	• Emphasis on interpersonal relationships involving imitation and modelling • Language as a tool for learning and the joint construction of knowledge; as a communicative or cultural tool, used for sharing and jointly developing knowledge and as a psychological tool for organising our individual thoughts, for reasoning, planning, and reviewing	• Multiple forms of asynchronous and synchronous communication offer the potential for more diverse and richer forms of dialogue and interaction between students and tutors and amongst peers, as well as the use of archive materials and resources for vicarious forms of learning • Different online communication tools and learning environments and social fora offer the potential for new forms of communities of practice or facilities to support and enhance existing communities
Experiential	• Experiential learning • Action-based • Problem-based • Enquiry-led	• Experience as foundation for learning • Learning as the transformation of experience into knowledge, skill, attitudes, values and emotions • Reflection as a means of transforming experience • Problem-based learning a focus • Experience: problem situation, identification and definition • Theory formation and test in practice	• Asynchronous communication offers new forms of discourse, which are not time-bound and hence offer increased opportunity for reflection • Archive and multiple forms of representation of different communications and experiences offer opportunities for reflection

Theories	Approach	Main characteristics	Potential e-learning applications
Activity-based	• Activity-based • Systems thinking	• Focus on the structures of activities as historically constituted entities • Action through mediating artefacts within a framework of activity within a wider socio-cultural context of rules and community • Pedagogical focus is on bridging the gap between historical state of an activity and the developmental stage of a person with respect to that activity • Focus on organisational learning, or on modelling the development of learners in response to feedback	• New forms of distribution and storage, archiving and retrieval offer the potential for development of shared knowledge banks across organisations and forms of organisational distributed cognition • Adaptation in response to both discursive and active feedback
Situated learning	• Collaborative learning • Reciprocal teaching • Vicarious learning	• Take social interactions into account and learning as social participation • Knowledge is a matter of competences with respect to valued enterprise; participating in the pursuit of this, i.e. active engagement	• Shift from a focus on the individual and information-focused learning to an emphasis on social learning and communication/collaboration Networking capabilities of the web enable more diverse access to different forms of expertise and the potential for the development of different types of communities • Online communication tools and learning environments offer the potential for new forms of communities of practice or can facilitate and enhance existing communities

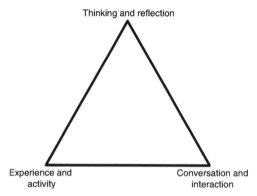

Figure 6.1 E-learning framework

These three aspects are interweaved across many of the commonly used categorisations of learning approaches outlined in the reviews mentioned above. In the following sections, they will be used to structure a summary of theoretical perspectives on e-learning.

An archaeology of e-learning

Before exploring the three core elements outlined above, we will provide a critique of some of the historically significant e-learning developments against their predominate theoretical positions, summarising a previous account provided by Ravenscroft (2004a).

Arguably, early applications of technology for learning were characterised by the adoption of behaviourist ideas about the development of 'teaching machines', using Skinner's (1954) notions of operant conditioning and programmed instruction. Skinner believed that behaviour was shaped by reinforcing consequences in response to actions made by subjects. Therefore, the emphasis was on designing an environment that shaped behaviour through learner-system interactions. Typically, small chunks of information were presented, followed by questions and feedback that positively reinforced correct responses.

There are a number of problems with this approach. Although correct behaviour was reinforced, incorrect responses, and even minor errors, such as misspellings or incorrect semantic substitutions, could not be dealt with because no diagnostic, explanatory or learner support strategies existed in such systems. In addition, this approach took no account of the role of cognition in learning. For example, there was no opportunity for reflection and intervention on the part of the student that deviated from the prescribed learning tracks. Finally, focusing on observed behaviours does not reflect the complex dimensions of the processes of learning, such as aspects of learning that may be latent (i.e. learning does not necessarily always manifest itself as an observable behaviour).

Despite these criticisms, elements of behaviourist approaches can inform and improve learning; for example there are times when learning through association and positive reinforcement has a role, such as drill and practice scenarios, revision, or memory recall. This type of learning maps well to Bloom's (1956) lower-level cognitive skills and is particularly evident in subjects where rote learning is essential as a building block to higher-level learning (for example languages and aspects of sciences). What is problematic is where this becomes the dominant paradigm or where the inherent architecture of the learning environment is geared solely towards this particular pedagogical approach. Many early computer-based training materials consisted of electronic page turning peppered with behaviourist reinforcement schedules. Aspects of this approach are visible today in mainstream software help systems. Another example of a content-driven didactic orientation is evident in the development of standards, such as the Advanced Distributed Learning Shareable Content Object Reference Model (SCORM) (2004) metadata schema. Lukasiak *et al.* (2005) state that SCORM is based on 'the premise that learning context can be decomposed into discrete entities that are context independent', and argue that SCORM is not pedagogically neutral but is based on a content-driven, individual, self-paced approach to learning with a focus on tracking learners' progress through the content. There has been significant criticism about commercial virtual learning environments (VLEs) that foster a content-driven approach which promotes and therefore limits learning to a didactic approach (O'Shea and Scanlon, 1997; Britain and Liber, 2004; Lisewski and Joyce, 2003; Conole *et al.*, 2004).

It follows from this work that e-learning design needs to be extended beyond behaviourist principles; to nurture initiative, students should be provided with opportunities for experimentation, dialogue, reflection, 'higher level' conceptual thinking and reasoning. These processes align with our arguments throughout this book, which echo the point made by Ravenscroft, that: 'Learners are not *tabula rasa* and they are all different. So the knowledge and processes they bring to an educational interaction has a significant bearing on what and how they learn from these interchanges' (Ravenscroft, 2004a: 6). Or, putting the implications of this more broadly, students are heterogenous with different prior experiences, and so may learn quite differently from similarly designed learning activities.

Learning through thinking and reflection

It is the aptitude for higher-level thinking that is the hallmark of human learning. E-learning needs to nurture this ability to think, reflect, deliberate and anticipate the possible consequences of our actions. In 'How We Think' Dewey (1938) contrasts reflective thought with reliance on instruction and the mere transmission of received wisdoms. He defines reflection as: '[A] better way of thinking that … is called reflective thinking: the kind of thinking that consists of turning a subject over in the mind and giving it serious and consecutive thought' (Dewey, 1938: 113).

Our technological age, which Giddens refers to as a 'run away world' (1999), is characterised by rapid change that forces people to respond and reflect on new information that guides their actions. Such transformation of information is the juncture at which learning flourishes; it can pick up where there is disjuncture, a breach of understanding, where we experience something different, something new. Dewey, somewhat optimistically, argued: 'The function of reflective thought is therefore to transform a situation in which there is experienced obscurity, doubt, conflict, disturbance of some sort, into a situation that is clear, coherent, settled, harmonious', (Dewey, 1933: 195).

It is open to question whether settled harmony is the outcome in a world of change. Perhaps when confronted with constant change we need to become accustomed to our knowledge being more short-term, contingent and open to revision in the light of new information and experience. Bauman talks of living with uncertainty, ambivalence and risk as features of our age and 'liquid modernity' (2000). The key issue is that learning environments must nurture opportunities for reflection and the ability of individuals to make more knowledgeable decisions. That is to facilitate the intellectual processes which enable the transformation of information and experience into knowledge and learning.

It is also worth noting that the centrality of reflective thought is implicit in many of the accounts explored below. It is a central element in both experiential learning and activity theory, it underpins theories that emphasise the dialogic and conversational aspects of learning and is acknowledged by Lave and Wenger (1991) as a feature of situated learning and communities of practice. An example of e-learning that aimed to encourage reflection on experience, engagement with others and the construction of practitioner knowledge is the emergence of online toolkits. These are designed to be easy to use and encourage reflection, so that the user can build their knowledge over time and adapt their thinking. An example is the DialogPlus online toolkit, which can be used to create more pedagogically informed learning activities, providing a bridge between learning theories and effective use of ICT tools (Conole and Fill, 2005).

Learning through experience and activity

Kolb's learning cycle is perhaps one of the best known models for learning (Kolb, 1984). Building on the work of Dewey, Lewin and others, it presents an action-based or 'learning by doing' approach to learning through a four-stage cyclical model (experience, reflection, abstraction and experimentation).

This emphasis on learner-centred and activity-oriented cognitive processes for knowledge assimilation, creation and construction are typical features of the *constructivist* paradigm, which has been developed by a number of researchers (e.g. Papert and Harel, 1991; Fosnot, 1996; Jonassen *et al.*, 1993: see Duffy *et al.*, 1993 for a review) who have been influenced by the work of Piaget (1971; 1973). The articulation of this approach in the context of LOGO and its evaluation, that has been presented by Ravenscroft (2004a), is summarised below.

According to Piaget, the child acts on the world, with expectations about consequent changes, and when these are not met they enter into a state of cognitive conflict or disequilibrium. Thus, they seek to retain an equilibrium state and so accommodate unexpected data or experience into their understanding of the context under exploration. In a sense, the child is conceived of as a scientist (Driver, 1983), setting hypotheses and testing them by actively interacting with the world.

Ravenscroft (2004a) also argued that probably the most engaging application of this theoretical stance within e-learning was delivered by Papert (1980) in his book *Mindstorms* and with the LOGO programming language that he developed. Although this work was aimed at understanding and developing intellectual development in children, arguably the work carries broader significance, in that it focuses on processes and mechanisms (such as experimentation, reflection and abstraction) that are also prevalent and important in 'adult' learning. The LOGO language allowed learners to create and explore their own mental models and programmed microworlds and thus create individual meaning for themselves. It was designed to prompt a purely learner-centred interaction in which the student 'told the computer what to do' and observed its response. It was a curriculum innovation, fostering 'learning by discovery', and allowing students to develop their own knowledge and understanding in a principled manner through devising their own curriculum of activities.

An important finding from evaluation studies of LOGO (Sutherland, 1983; Hoyles and Noss, 1992) was that teachers who had used LOGO were sceptical about the value of *pure* discovery learning, because they needed to support the interactions directly through guided discussions, or indirectly by providing worksheets. So, it had to be grounded in authentic discursive activity. In defence of LOGO, Papert argued that most of the studies were flawed in their philosophy, measuring outcomes instead of examining the richness of the interactions and the learning process. But another critical question, considering the particularity of the language in relation to issues of transfer, remained unanswered. Was LOGO an effective cognitive tool supporting conceptual development and learning? Or, was it the case that students learned to think in a 'LOGO way' only about LOGO itself?

Other examples of environments that are built explicitly on constructivist principles include knowledge building communities (Scardamalia and Bereiter, 1996), communities of learning (Seely-Brown *et al.*, 1989) and cognitive apprenticeship (Collins *et al.*, 1989). Jonassen has developed a model that encapsulates the factors which need to be taken into account when constructing a learning environment which promotes a constructivist approach (http://www.coe.missouri.edu/%7Ejonassen/courses/CLE/index.html). He goes on to argue that 'technologies should be used to keep students active, constructive, collaborative, intentional, complex, contextual, conversational, and reflective'. By articulating what is necessary to support a constructivist approach, he argues that it is then easier to consider the ways in which technologies can be used to support or promote these.

A theoretical perspective that takes account of both the social dynamics of learning and the wider context within which this occurs is activity theory. This builds on Vygotsky's work and starts from the premise that activities occur within a context and that this needs to be taken into account if we are to make meaning of the situation and appropriate interpretation of the results. Engeström et al. argue that there is a need for a new unit of analysis.

> Activity theory provides a strong candidate for such a unit of analysis in the concept of *object orientation, collected,* and *culturally mediated human activity* or *activity system*. Minimum elements of this system include the object, the subject, mediating artefacts (signs and tools), rules, community, and division of labour.
>
> (Engeström *et al.*,1999: 9)

Activity theory therefore enables conceptualisation of both individual and collective practices in the wider socio-cultural context within which they occur. Ravenscroft (2004b) has emphasised how this is essentially a development of Vygotsky's (1978) work that provides a framework for learning which accepts that meaning arises and evolves during interactions that are influenced by the social relations within a community of practice. Or, as Nardi suggests, that 'you are what you do' (Nardi, 1996: 7) in a natural context that is influenced by history and culture. Hence, human practices are conceived as developmental processes 'with both individual and social levels interlinked at the same time' (Kuutti, 1996: 25). So activity theory emphasises the relationships between interactions, processes and outcomes and the relevance of social conditions, such as a shared enterprise and the need for mutual engagement of conceptualisations. Mwanza (2002) has applied the concept of activity theory by describing a model for activity consisting of eight parameters: activity of interest; objective; subjects; tools; rules and regulations; divisions of labour; community; and outcome. However, Issroff and Scanlon (2001) suggest activity theory is useful as a framework for describing and communicating findings, but less effective as a framework for uncovering 'further insights' into designing and interpreting collaborative learning activities. Similarly, although Baker *et al.* (1999) have used it to analyse and examine different forms of grounding in collaborative learning, and Lewis (1997) has employed it in researching interdependent parameters in distributed communities, Ravenscroft (2004b) has pointed out that its value as a prescriptive design paradigm for e-learning remains limited, although he accepts that it has forced us to focus on the necessity to conceptualise the relationship between dialogical activity and the learning communities in which it occurs.

Another aspect of this is the situated, authentic aspects of learning through experience and activity. The requirement for authentic learning in social settings is a central tenet of situated learning and communities of practice (Seely-Brown *et al.*, 1989; Lave and Wenger, 1991). Pea and Seely-Brown (1996) advocate that learning in social situations is a key aspect of learning; it is social activity mediated by cultural tools. Wertsch and others also describe the concept of mediational means or artefacts (Conole, 2005). Wertsch argues that there is an irreducible inter-linking between the individual and their mediational means (Wertsch, 1991). He also talks about collective memory in terms of considering to what extent mental functions are mediated by socio-historically evolved (i.e. collective) tools. Pea and Seely-Brown argue that cognitive theories of learning focus on the individual and neglect the importance of social relationships to learning. This argument is also made by Dyke (2006) who has emphasised the importance of the role of the Other in experiential learning. Pea and Seely-Brown suggest that 'in changing situations of knowledge acquisition and use, the new interactive technologies redefine – in ways yet to be determined – what it means to know and understand, and what it means to become a 'literate' or educated citizen' (Pea and Seely-Brown, 1996: vii).

Although Ravenscoft (2004a) has pointed out that some 'hard situationists' might question whether computer simulations are truly representative of real situ-ations, he argues that simulations can be used to foster 'experiential learning' and 'learning by doing', which map to the central principles of situated learning (see Hartley *et al.*, 1992). However, he points out that some studies have illustrated that simulations are more effective when both the description of the conceptions underpinning interaction with the system and reflection on the consequent output are guided and elaborated during a dialogue with a tutor (Hartley, 1998; Pilkington and Parker-Jones, 1996).

These socio-cultural perspectives present a difficulty for designing e-learning, if design is considered as a top-down, production-led and prescriptive approach, which is primarily content driven. Building in the social dimensions of learning in

I find it interesting that this chapter hesitates to articulate the design implications of social learning theory for e-learning. I believe that social learning theory has profound implications for the design of pedagogical e-learning environments but it is true that we have only started to understand how to harness the design affordances of emerg-ing technologies from this perspective. Yet for e-learning there is perhaps an even more profound lesson to derive from social learning theory – a theory, by the way, that does not so much recommend any specific pedagogy as it invites us to explore the ways in which our engagement in the social world, by ourselves or in direct inter-action with others, does or does not constitute an act of learning. Rather than focusing solely on the design of self-contained learning environments, this view sug-gests that e-learning also explores the learning potential of emerging technologies, that is, the ways in which these technologies amplify (or curtail) the learning opportu-nities inherent in the world.

Etienne Wenger

an e-learning context is difficult (see, for example, Lisewski and Joyce's criticism of the inappropriate adaptation of Salmon's (2000) e-moderating framework). Similarly we doubt whether or not it is possible to technically design and 'manufacture' into an e-learning environment Wenger's concept of Communities of Practice. In contrast we believe that designers and practitioners should aspire to provide an enabling framework to foster Communities of Practice. Designing e-learning environments that orchestrate these more social and communicative dimensions of learning is difficult precisely because they are more organic and unpredictable. Social patterns of communication are dynamic, constantly changing depending on the context and the people involved in the process. In contrast there may be a tendency for designers to focus at the content level precisely because it is simpler; content is relatively fixed and the outcomes are generally predetermined. Along with others (Laurillard, 2003), we suggest that a more organic approach to the development of e-learning environments is required. The adoption of the principles of the open source movement might lead to a better model for evolution of e-learning. There is some evidence that this is beginning to occur, for example with the way in which the e-learning community, and practitioners more generally, are now using software such as blogs and wikis to share practice and ideas.

Learning through conversation and interaction

Closely aligned with the situated learning perspective is the notion of the development of Communities of Practice (Wenger, 1998). According to Preece (2000: xii) 'the internet has given rise to a new community model of communication'. Currently, however, as Ravenscroft (2004b) points out, there is little agreement on what this model actually is, how we can conceptualise it, or how it can be operationalised and exploited for educational purposes. Preece (2000) herself argues for community-centred development (CCD), community development and maintenance, putting the 'community' firmly at the centre of the design process. Within this scheme she points out that we need to support the evolution of communities, design for usability and plan for sociability. This approach seems to hold that learning should be conceived as a social process, but raises a crucial question about whether we can actually build online communities that truly satisfy the necessary social conditions for effective, and often dialectical, discourse interactions. As Ravenscroft (2004a) questions: 'Can we be sufficiently social online to have meaningful conversations, discussions and arguments that lead to conceptual change and development?' (Ravenscroft, 2004a: 11).

Wenger's (1998) work on Communities of Practice considers meaning, along with learning and identity, as important features in the educative process and holds that: 'engagement in social practice is the fundamental process by which we learn and so become who we are'. Central to this notion is that these communities have knowledge about practice embedded within them, and therefore learning occurs through legitimate participation within the community: 'Learning is a process that takes place within a participation framework, not an individual mind' (Lave and Wenger, 1991: 15). Wenger (1998) defines Communities of Practice as characterised by the concepts of *mutual engagement, joint enterprise,* a *shared repertoire* and the *negotiation of meaning in practice.*

Whilst this approach, like situated cognition, provides a useful analytic framework, this descriptive emphasis means that it is not easily applicable to the problem of designing for e-learning, a point that is emphasised by Wenger (1998) himself. The challenge is to stimulate and promote engagement in social practice that in turn leads to the formation of a Community of Practice for learning. There is also a problem mapping some of Wenger's features to desired discourse practices in educational contexts. Ravenscroft (2004b) argues that one reason why it is not yet clear how to design, develop and maintain a Community of Practice supporting and engaging e-learning discourse is because in educational settings it is often unclear what the 'practice' actually is. In such contexts a greater emphasis should be given to cooperative and collaborative tasks rather than being driven by knowledge-based and conceptual activities.

Another tradition that has emphasised the importance of dialogue can be traced back (like activity theory) to the work of Vygotsky. The necessity for providing a 'scaffold' between the learner and a tutor was the focus of Vygotsky's (1978) theory of the development of higher mental processes. His approach makes a substantial contribution by linking activity situated 'in the social' to higher-order thinking and reasoning. A central tenet of his account is that learning occurs through *internalising* dialogical activity and its signification systems (i.e. languages) that occur in the social. So, for example he would argue that we develop critical reasoning skills through internalising the process and content of dialogical argumentation.

This primacy of language in learning and the requirement to adapt interaction to individual learners was reflected in a number of intelligent tutoring systems (ITS) initiatives (see, for example, Wenger, 1987) that modelled and maintained

Emphasising the importance of dialogue in learning has played an important role in counterbalancing the tendency to see learning technology as a vehicle for delivering content. However, the distinction becomes slightly blurred when we consider whether the dialogues generated by other learners might themselves be valuable learning resources. This is the idea behind recent work on 'vicarious learning': learning through observing others learning (Mayes *et al.*, 2001). The key research issue is to identify what might lead new learners to identify closely enough with the discussions and questions of previous learners that they will derive at least some of the benefits of dialogue enjoyed by the original participants. This question becomes increasingly interesting with the rapid growth of 'social software' on the internet.

Terry Mayes

instructional dialogues. A number of early ITSs aimed to teach the learner using a 'Socratic dialogue' derived from discourse analysis of human tutoring, such as SCHOLAR (Carbonell, 1970) and WHY (Collins, 1977). However, although these systems had good semantic and syntactic natural language properties, they had limited or shallow strategic knowledge. Later work by Clancey (1987) on a system called GUIDON attempted to address this through a separation of domain and pedagogical knowledge, but the strategic knowledge that guided the dialogue was still too shallow. McCalla (1993) and Ravenscroft and Pilkington (2000) have emphasised that this is only part of the problem. They hold that pragmatic or contextual dialogue features, such as the goals and relative roles of interlocutors, the strategies they adopt and the types of speech act (Searle, 1969) they may perform, are neglected by much of this work, yet they have to be carefully considered in designing educational dialogue.

Other studies (e.g. Maudet and Moore, 2000; Ravenscroft and Pilkington, 2000) have started to reconcile this difficulty through focusing on pragmatic level dialogue features, including the roles and goals of interlocutors, the types of speech act they may perform and rules for legitimate educational dialogue. Specifically, some of these approaches have integrated domain knowledge within a dialogue game approach that specifies explicit dialogue strategies and tactics, with rules of initiative taking and the transfer of commitment through the types of utterances that are made (Ravenscroft and Hartley, 1999; Ravenscroft, 2001). Ravenscroft (1997) developed a computer-based pedagogy and approach to inter-action design called 'learning as knowledge refinement' that is based on a Vygotskian approach to dialogue and empirical studies of collaborative argumen-tation (Hartley, 1998). Through generalising this approach to system development, Ravenscroft and Pilkington (2000) proposed a methodology of 'investigation by design' (IBD) that is currently being used to develop a number of dialogical cognitive tools (Ravenscroft, 2001) and games-based approaches (Ravenscroft and McAlister, 2006) that emphasise dialectical interaction.

Conclusions

Our contemporary risk society (Beck, 1992) produces a reflexive response to rapidly changing information, reflective learning, by doing and in the company of others that may therefore be a key to transforming that information into knowl-edge and providing informed judgements to guide action. E-learning offers the potential to facilitate reflective learning to extend what Usher and Bryant refer to as the 'captive triangle' (1989) of theory, practice and research. The triangle can-not simply be 'captive' as Usher and Bryant note, but must be responsive to a diverse and changing context, to be open to knowledge and experience. The cen-tral tenet argued in this chapter is that fossilisation of learning theories into a set of prescriptions for practice is unhelpful. Rather we argue that learning is com-plex and multi-faceted and that it is more important to distil out the key characteristics of learning as we have done in our framework at the beginning of the chapter; namely learning can be nurtured by fostering *thinking and reflection, experience and activity, conversation and interaction*. We offer this as an enabling framework that we invite practitioners and designers to use as they see fit and to apply, or adapt, to work in their own context.

We believe that there is an inherent risk of e-learning adopting an almost positivistic perspective that claims to apply particular theoretical positions to designing for learning; in other words a naïve over-prescription of the domain. Such an approach would suggest that a practitioner takes an e-learning 'model' as a true representation of the world and then believes they can simply apply it to practice and that – hey presto! – this will bring about the intended learning approach implicit in the model. We believe that a more holistic, organic approach is needed, taking theoretical positions as a starting point from which designs can then be developed, applied, reflected on and adapted in the context of a wider community of practice, with the result that the 'lived' model applied may look significantly different from the one the practitioner started with.

There may be parallels to what we are advocating here as an approach to learning theory and its application to e-learning to the open source movement. We believe that application of the principles developed in the open source movement have immense potential in terms of developing more effective and innovative e-learning design and adaptation/evolution of e-learning environments that can help to promote both individual and collective creativity, and innovation in learning. We propose that this approach should be built on the e-learning framework that we introduce in this chapter, foregrounding what we believe are the key principles of effective learning – reflection, experience and interaction. We need to develop an approach to e-learning that nurtures reflection, dialogue and an approach that seeks to transform and extend our experience, one that fuels the fire of learning.

Part II

Micro dimensions
of e-learning

Chapter 7

Designing for learning

Gráinne Conole, Martin Oliver, Isobel Falconer,
Allison Littlejohn and Jen Harvey

Practitioners have a multitude of learning theories that guide the development of learning activities (Chapter 6). In addition, as discussed in Chapter 4, there is a rich variety of ICT tools that can be used to support the implementation of these. Despite this, the actual range of learning activities that demonstrate specific pedagogic approaches (such as constructivism, dialogic learning, case- or problem-based scenarios, or socially situated learning) and innovative use of ICT tools is limited, suggesting that practitioners are overwhelmed by the plethora of choices and may lack the necessary skills to make informed choices about how to use these theories.

This chapter explores the issues surrounding designing for learning. It starts by considering this in the context of curriculum design, before looking at learning activities, educational vocabularies, and the tools and resources that are increasingly being used to support informed judgements in designing learning activities. It will reflect on the complexity of designing for learning and the tension between an atomistic, component-based approach to design (such as advocated by the use of controlled vocabularies and the Learning Design specification) discussed in this chapter and a more holistic, practice-focused approach, considering how each approach can or is being used in the context of e-learning.

Designing for learning: the creation of curricula

'Designing for learning' involves the intentional creation of learning activities that are intended to influence what others understand or can do (JISC, 2005b). Such designs are effectively curricula – although it must be recognised that many designs will not be formalised as curriculum documents, or even used within formal education. Nonetheless, it is useful to use curriculum design as a point of reference here.

As outlined in Chapter 2, different philosophical traditions have shaped research in this field; they have also had a profound effect on the design of curricula. In relation to technology, curriculum planning has traditionally focused on how best to organise and present content (an 'out there' perspective – see Chapter 2). Building on Gagné's work on the conditions of learning, Merrill (2001) describes a scientific approach to the decomposition of learning tasks into components that can then be sequenced, suitable for delivery in an automated way.

A radically different approach was taken by constructivists (e.g. Jonassen *et al.*, 1993). This model emphasises learners' creative activity, social negotiation of knowledge and the contextuality of understanding. Unsurprisingly, constructivist curricula tend to be more open-ended, emergent and negotiable as a consequence.

However, these positions are primarily concerned with the immediate context of teaching – what might be understood as pedagogy. This is only one of several 'layers' of curriculum planning that teachers in higher education identify (Oliver, 2003b):

- Curriculum as 'content' (syllabus)
- Curriculum as plan (either at the level of lesson or course)
- The curriculum as planned process (pedagogy)
- The hidden curriculum (political or value-based influences that remain unstated).

These can be seen as nested, with each new level containing the earlier ones; however, the academics from this study also spoke of 'the lived curriculum', the performance that emerges from interactions with specific students in an improvisatory manner – i.e. in terms of both the way students make their own meaning of the curriculum and the way in which teachers adapt to specific teaching situations. This marked a discontinuity with the planned, intentional layers, revealing how designs – no matter how thorough – are only part of the story, albeit an important part.

The creation of curricula in higher education is both social and political; the selection of reading lists reflects personal values and loyalties (Millen, 1997), and the approval of courses rests on meeting the expectations of colleagues (who may be conservative) and managerial processes (Oliver, 2003b). This context, so important to the hidden curriculum, is often ignored in the literature on technology and learning.

One commonplace managerial requirement for formal curricula is the specification of learning outcomes. These are often qualified as 'intended' or 'desired' since, although the curriculum provides a context for learning, it is not a simplistically causal one. These specified outcomes are usually explicitly linked to assessment – the single greatest influence on learner behaviour in formal settings, because of the 'backwash effect' whereby learners choose to spend their time focusing on what will earn them marks (Biggs, 1999).

This makes the role of technology in designing for learning particularly complicated. A particular artefact can be treated as a mechanism for delivery or a means of expression; as a resource or as an indicator of personal beliefs and loyalties; and as part of pedagogy or of administrative management. Clearly, technology can have an important role to play, but quite what it is remains problematic.

A recurrent theme throughout this book is the issue of 'commodification'. 'Standardisation' is being taken further through the increased uptake in the creation of nationally and internationally agreed frameworks. A good example of this is the proposed European Qualification Framework (Bologna Working Group on Qualification Frameworks, 2005), which seeks to ensure that the outcomes of learning achieved within various contexts are properly valued and aims to help clarify different programme access, progression and transfer routes. The aim is to better accredit both formal and informal learning to support the concept of life-long learning as a cumulative process taking place over a period of time and in a combination of different kinds of learning. While the potential recognition of different kinds of learning would support an increasingly diverse student population, systems (even nationally recognised systems operated on a voluntary basis) will, however, remain heavily dependent upon the cooperation of the various key stake-holders working at appropriate strategic levels.

Social and economic developments and a current shift towards more of a knowledge-based economy have at the same time increased the pressure on education providers to be able to support different kinds of learning opportunities, in particular within the workplace. At the same time as different kinds of learning in different educational, professional or social contexts are being formally recognised within national qualifications frameworks, technology is being increasingly viewed as a way to provide opportunities through which such learning can occur. The creation of virtual learning environments and new learning communities has become common as effective strategies to enable knowledge sharing and to encourage learning embedded in real-work tasks and activities. In addition, trends towards the utilisation of curriculum design models that are problem-based, project-orientated or collaborative have become more widespread in order to simulate real-life situations within institutional contexts. Many educators consider both social context and social processes as an integral part of learning activities: 'Learning is located in the interplay between culture and individuals, and it implies the transformation of individuals and collectives in terms of the nature of the task they master' (Säljö, 1999).

The potential versus the reality of e-learning

Boud *et al.* (1993: 9) argue that 'the job of the teacher is to create imaginative ideas that make the learning engaging and meet the needs of learners', going on to state that 'the teacher creates an event which the learner experiences and may learn from'. Clearly technologies offer new opportunities to enhance the learning experience, but usually these opportunities are not being realised.

Coupled with the gap between the potential and actual use of technologies is a failure to apply effectively the range of learning theories that have emerged in recent years, in particular those centred around more socio-cultural and constructivist perspectives which emphasise learning by doing and collaboration. Therefore, although there is now a wealth of knowledge about what makes for good and effective learning, there is still a predominance of didactic/behaviourist applications in e-learning, with a focus on transmission of knowledge.

This second failure is not necessarily dependent on the first – it is quite possible to employ constructivist methods in a traditional face-to-face situation, for example, or to adapt a virtual learning environment (VLE) that is designed to promote a transmission mode of learning to foster more socially orientated learning. However, it does make the task of creating pedagogically innovative learning activities that promote a range of theoretical perspectives more difficult. This suggests that more is needed in terms of mechanisms for supporting the creation of such effective learning activities that bridge the gap between potential and actual practice.

Learning objects and activities

Partly driven by the tantalising promise of the potential re-use and re-purposing of learning materials (Littlejohn, 2003; Littlejohn, 2004), a considerable body of research has accumulated on the development of two key concepts: learning objects and learning design. Learning objects in relation to managing educational resources are discussed in more detail in the next two chapters; they are discussed here in relation to their role in curriculum design.

From the mid-1990s onwards, online resources have often been referred to as 'learning objects'. However, this concept is hotly contested, with definitions ranging from a restrictive view of learning objects as small digital resources through to whole units of learning with associated learning outcomes and assessment. Polsani (2003) suggests that there are now 'as many definitions of learning objects as there are users'. Wiley's definition is particularly popular: 'any digital resource that can be re-used to support learning' (2000), although he also defines a learning object as 'an independent and self-standing unit of learning content that is predisposed to reuse in multiple instructional contexts'. An alternative classification of resources (Littlejohn *et al.*, forthcoming) can be derived from Koper (2003), Rehak and Mason (2003) and Duncan (2003) and addresses the problem of describing the granularity of the resource *within the context of use*. It moves away from viewing granularity as an issue purely of aggregation of blocks of content, and is explicit about the degree to which information content is embedded within an activity or task-oriented learning context, describing four levels of resources:

*   Digital assets – normally a single file (e.g. an image, video or audio clip), sometimes called a 'raw media asset'.
*   Information objects – a structured aggregation of digital assets, designed purely to present information.
*   Learning activities – tasks involving interactions with information to attain a specific learning outcome.
*   Learning design – structured sequences of information and activities to promote learning.

The first two levels may be labelled 'information content' and, in isolation, have no learning or teaching effect. They acquire this by being placed within learning activities or designs.

Learning occurs within a context and is influenced by a set of inter-related factors. Biggs (1999) uses the phrase 'constructive alignment' and describes good pedagogical design as ensuring that there are no inconsistencies between curriculum, teaching methods, environment and assessment. In these terms effective learning activities are designed to meet a set of specified learning outcomes and assessment criteria through a series of tasks using a set of tools and resources. Creating the most effective conditions for learning therefore requires an understanding of these factors and their relationship to each other. The multitude of ICT tools now available provides new opportunities to enhance learning but also complicates the situation by providing another factor that practitioners need to take account of.

Therefore, there has been considerable criticism about focusing the design of learning solely at the resource level. As Mayes and Fowler (1999) point out, one problem in focusing on learning objects is that teachers tend to plan e-learning around 'instructivist' learning models, which focus on single learners accessing content. Thus, it does not help bridge the gap between current pedagogical theory and implementation. Recent developments in technology (which emphasise the dialogic and reflective dimensions of learning) allow us to go beyond simple re-purposing of content to support a wider range of pedagogical approaches, and in particular social-constructivist learning processes that emphasise the social dimensions of learning (Britain, 2004; Mayes and de Freitas, 2004). Interoperable, networked technologies have the potential to support students' collaborative activities, allowing them to source, create, adapt, integrate and store resources in a variety of formats. These new possibilities and the affordances of ICT tools mean that it is becoming easier to use technology to support social-constructivist methods of learning, such as collaborative learning through learning communities (Koper, 2004). These learning methods focus on the *process* of learning and on the learning activities students carry out in order to gain knowledge of concepts.

Beetham has described a learning activity as:

> an interaction between a learner or learners and an environment (optionally including content resources, tools and instruments, computer systems and services, 'real world' events and objects) that is carried out in response to a task with an intended learning outcome.
>
> (Beetham, 2004)

Conole *et al.* (2005) suggest that examples of learning activities can vary from simple tasks such as students reading texts, participation in asynchronous discussions, undertaking quizzes or tutorial exercises through to more complex examples such as situated learning, simulations, role-plays, concept-mapping or case-based scenarios.

To create learning activities practitioners have to make complex decisions about which tools and theories to use. One example of a resource that is designed to support practitioners in this process is the DialogPlus online toolkit, which guides practitioners through the process of developing pedagogically informed learning activities (Conole and Fill, 2005; Bailey *et al.*, 2006). The toolkit is underpinned by a taxonomy (Conole) that attempts to consider all aspects and factors involved in developing a learning activity, from the pedagogical context in which the activity occurs through to the nature and types of tasks undertaken by the learner.

Table 7.1 provides an overview of the learning activity taxonomy used in the toolkit. Learning activities are achieved through completion of a series of *tasks* in order to achieve intended *learning outcomes*. The components that constitute a learning activity can be defined as:

- The *context* within which the activity occurs; this includes the subject, level of difficulty, the intended learning outcomes and the environment within which the activity takes place. Learning outcomes are mapped to Bloom's (1956) taxonomy of learning outcomes and grouped into three types – cognitive, affective and psychomotor – and are what the learners should know, or be able to do, after completing a learning activity; for example they might be required to be able to understand, demonstrate, design, produce or appraise.
- The *pedagogy* (learning and teaching approaches) adopted. These approaches are grouped according to Mayes and de Frietas' (2004) three categories – associative, cognitive and situative, discussed in Chapter 6.
- The *tasks* undertaken, which specifies the type of task, the (teaching) techniques used to support the task, any associated tools and resources, the interaction and roles of those involved and the assessments associated with the learning activity.

However, one could argue that this is still very much a component-based approach, which is problematic because the relationships between the components are not well understood. Hence this still does not lead to providing a template for adopting a holistic approach to designing for learning where the 'sum of the components is greater than the parts'. The next section goes some way towards exemplifying this problem by describing other educational vocabularies that have been developed, highlighting their limitations and in particular the way in which the tacit aspects of practice, referred to in Chapter 2, are difficult to capture.

The development of educational vocabularies to describe practice

The outline of curriculum given at the beginning of this chapter as a nested set of processes from 'content' through to the inherently political and contextual holistic or 'lived' curriculum demonstrates the complexity of the process of curriculum design and in particular highlights just how difficult it is to articulate the design process. This is nicely illustrated by a historical review of the development of educational vocabularies, which has arisen in part because of the increasing impact of e-learning on educational processes and in part from the opportunity to create, store and share educational practice, afforded through the emergence of new technologies and in particular online portals and digital repositories. Such shareable databases require metadata in order to describe and access their content, which immediately gives rise to issues about how such practice can be adequately described. This goes to the heart of the tension outlined at the beginning of this chapter – namely that between adoption of an atomistic, content-driven description of content and a more holistic, contextual description. This section illustrates this by describing a number of key stages in the development of educational vocabularies in this area.

Conole *et al.* (2005) have undertaken a review of educational taxonomies that provides an historical perspective on these developments in relation to curriculum design. However, it should be noted that the development of taxonomies is a power-laden activity. Although it can be seen as a technical necessity, it can also be interpreted as technical experts and archivists seeking to control the way teachers are allowed to talk about their work and identities (Oliver, 2004).

At the heart of the issue is the fact that, if learning activities are to be re-usable, then they have to be described in commonly understood and standardised vocabularies that will allow users to source and share resources through searching or browsing. Recent and evolving taxonomies form the basis for standardised vocabularies. Also important is the parallel development of international standards for learning technologies that has grown in significance in recent years, in part in recognition of the importance of and need for interoperability. In line with this, current thinking in software development has shifted from the creation of 'monolithic all-in-one' IT systems to more of a 'pick and mix' approach, which is a consequence and recognition of the constantly changing and volatile nature of this area.

As discussed in more detail in Chapter 9, there is a range of organisations involved in the development of standards (see http://www.cetis.ac.uk/static/whos-involved.html for an overview); IMS IEEE Learning Technology Standards Committee (http://ieeeltsc.org/) and ISO/IEC JTC1 SC36 are among the leading standards/specifications bodies. The UK is represented in the international standards arena by CETIS (www.cetis.ac.uk). Of most relevance here is the work on the development of standards for learning objects and learning design. There is now a well-established standard for learning objects (http://ieeeltsc.org/wg12LOM/), although both the term itself and aspects of the standard are highly contested, in so far as the definition begins to try to consider the pedagogical aspects of the use of learning objects.

A number of projects have attempted to develop taxonomies that are broader in scope than focusing at the resource level. Of particular relevance here are those that tried to develop databases that in some way encapsulated practice

Table 7.1 Taxonomy of learning activities

Context			Task taxonomy					
Context	Learning outcomes	Pedagogical approaches	Type (What)	Technique (How)	Interaction (Who)	Roles (Which)	Tools and resources	Assessment
Aims	Cognitive	Associative	Assimilative	Arguing	Individual	Coach	Access grid tools	Not assessed
	Knowledge	Instructional system design	Reading	Artefact	One to one	Deliverer	Assessment software	Diagnostic
Pre-requisites	State	Intelligent tutoring systems	Viewing	Articulate reasoning	One to many	Facilitator	Bibliographic software	Formative
	Recall	Elaboration theory	Listening	Assignment	Group based	Group leader	Blogs	Summative
Subject	List	Didactic	Information handling	Book report	Class based	Group participant	Chat	
Environment	Recognise	Behaviourist	Gathering	Brainstorming		Individual learner	Data analysis software	
Computer-based	Select	Training needs analysis	Ordering	Buzz words		Mentor	Database	
Lab-based	Reproduce	Cognitive	Classifying	Case study		Moderator	Digital image manipulation software	
Field-based	Specify	Active learning	Selecting	Coaching		Pair person	Discussion boards	
Work-based	Draw	Enquiry-led	Analysing	Concept mapping		Peer assessor	Electronic whiteboards	
Audio-based	Finding out/discover	Problem-based	Manipulating	Crosswords		Presenter	Email	
Simulator	Pronounce	Goal-based scenarios	Adaptive	Debate		Rapporteur	Instant messaging	
Video	Recite	Reflective practitioner	Modelling	Defining		Supervisor	Voice over IP	
Lecture-based	Comprehension		Simulation	Discussion				
Seminar-based	Explain		Communicative	Dissertation/thesis				
Time	Describe reasons		Discussing	Drill and practice				
				Essay				

Difficulty					
Skills	Identify causes	Presenting	Cognitive apprenticeship	Exercise	Libraries
Creativity	Illustrate	Debating	Constructivist-based design	Experiment	Microsoft Exchange
Critical analysis	Question	Critiquing		Field trip	Personal digital assistants
Critical reading	Clarify		*Situative*	Fishbowl	Mind mapping software
Group/team work	Identify	*Productive*	E-moderating framework	Game	Modelling
IT	Understand	Creating	Dialogue/argumentation	Ice breaker	Models
Literacy	*Application*	Producing	Experiential learning	Interview	Project manager software
Numeracy	Use	Writing	Collaborative learning	Journaling	Search engines
Oral communication	Apply	Drawing	Activity theory	Literature review	Simulation
Practical	Construct	Composing	Apprenticeship	MCQ	Spreadsheet
Problem solving	Solve	Synthesising	Action research	Mindmaps	Text, image, audio or video viewer
Research	Select	Re-mixing	Reciprocal teaching	Modelling	Video conferencing
Written communication	Hypothesise		Project-based learning	Negotiation	Virtual worlds
Ability to learn	Infer	*Experiential*	Vicarious learning	On the spot questioning	VLEs
Commercial awareness	Calculate	Practising		Pair dialogues	Wikis
Computer literacy	Investigate	Applying		Panel discussion	Word processor
Criticism	Produce	Mimicking		Peer exchange	
Data modelling	Construct	Experiencing		Performance	
Decision making	Translate	Exploring		Portfolio	
	Assemble	Investigating		Presentation	
	Demonstrate	Performing		Product	
	Solve			Puzzles	
	Write			Question and answer	

Context	Task taxonomy							
Context	Learning outcomes	Pedagogical approaches	Type (What)	Technique (How)	Interaction (Who)	Roles (Which)	Tools and resources	Assessment
Foreign languages	Analysis			Report/paper				
Information handling	Break down			Role play				
	List component parts of			Rounds				
Information literacy	Compare and contrast			Scaffolding				
Interpersonal competence	Differentiate between			Scavenger hunt				
Management of change	Predict			Short answer				
Negotiating	Critique			Simulation				
Planning and organising	Analyse			Snowball				
	Compare			Socratic instruction				
Self management	Select			Structured debate				
Self reflection	Distinguish between			Test				
Synthesis	Synthesis			Voting				
Study skills	Summarise			Web search				
Critical analysis and logical argument	Generalise							
	Argue							
Writing style	Organise							
Library	Design							

E-literacy	Explain reasons
Listening and comprehension	*Evaluation*
Making notes	Judge
Oral presentation	Evaluate
Reading	Give arguments for and against
Referencing	Criticise
Research reading	Feedback
Inference and synthesis of information	Reflect
	Affective
	Listen
Selecting and prioritising information	Appreciate
	Awareness
Summary skill	Responsive
Time management and organisation	***Aesthetic***
	Appreciation
	Commitment
Moral awareness	
Ethical awareness	

Context								
			Task taxonomy					
Context	Learning outcomes	Pedagogical approaches	Type (What)	Technique (How)	Interaction (Who)	Roles (Which)	Tools and resources	Assessment
	Psychomotor							
	Draw							
	Play							
	Make							
	Perform							
	Exercise							
	Throw							
	Run							
	Jump							
	Swim							

through case studies or exemplars. For example, SeSDL (Scottish electronic Staff Development Library) is a library of educational resources in digital format (www.sesdl.scotcit.ac.uk). This example will be followed through to provide an illustration of how vocabularies are developed and adapted. SeSDL developed a taxonomy to help classify and retrieve resources, which covers the fields of educational development, educational technology, academic management, resources types and subjects. Therefore it went beyond a simple description at the learning object level to inclusion of wider contextual factors, trying in particular to focus on those relevant to practice. The educational development taxonomy consists of the following sub-categories: planning and preparation, instructional design, approaches to teaching, teaching and learning methods, educational environments, approaches to learning, outcomes of education, assessment and evaluation. The educational technology taxonomy was grouped into computer-mediated communication, virtual learning environments, groupware, courseware, computer-aided assessment, computer simulation, computer networks, internet, educational multimedia, human computer interaction, accessibility, embedding technology, legal and ethical issues, standards, and software packages. These groupings reflect the common terminology of the time, as well as the degree of maturity of the technologies available. Part of the challenge is the development of adaptive vocabularies that can cope with the rapidly evolving nature of the area.

Building on the experience of SeSDL, the SoURCE project (http://www.source.ac.uk) developed a Re-usable Electronic Software Library (RESL), a searchable database of case studies on re-using educational software. The database could be searched using keywords or browsed by subject, pedagogy, technology or strategy. Pedagogy was classified by the type of educational environment in which the event occurred (for example independent study, virtual environment or laboratory), the teaching and learning methods used (examples given included collaborations, demonstrations, discussions, small groups, peer teaching, presentation and seminars), the teaching and learning strategies adopted (for example active learning, constructivism, didacticism, experiential learning, resource-based learning, situated learning or student-centred learning), the educational outcomes (in terms of academic achievement and improvements), skills (analytical, communicative, computer literacy, numeracy, self-reflection, time management), and any associated assessment (including diagnostic tests, formative evaluation, peer evaluation, or summative evaluation).

Learning and Teaching Scotland developed a series of controlled vocabularies, partly based on SeSDL, which are used as part of the LT Scotland Metadata Information Model (LTS 2005). This included details on the target audience, the educational level, the context of the resource, the intended end user, the technical format, and the concept, nature and language of the resource. It also considered the principal use of the resource, listing for example classroom teaching, planning and management, support teaching, independent learning, and lesson development. In each case it is evident how each vocabulary has built on previous work, but also provides a more up-to-date reflection of the current practice and associated technologies.

A comprehensive review of educational vocabularies is provided by Currier *et al.* (2006), which includes an inventory of existing pedagogical vocabularies, including flat lists, taxonomies, thesauri, ontologies and classification schemes. The report highlights that vocabularies are being seen as increasingly important in terms of providing a bridge between practice and more abstract technical services and reference models (see Chapter 4 for more on the JISC e-learning framework and associated reference models). One of the most interesting parts of the report in terms of the argument presented in this chapter is the identification of the rise of 'folksonomies', which are defined as 'a new methodology for developing shared vocabularies'. Currier *et al.* (2006) go on to state that:

> Folksonomy systems allow community members, or users of a shared resource, archive, wiki, repository *etc.*, to assign their own indexing terms to resources ('tagging': a process previously known as natural language keyword indexing) and the system organises its interface by clustering the terms and/or the resources, although hierarchies of concepts are not always generated. Still in its infancy, this approach has both its proponents and its detractors.

Many of the taxonomies discussed so far are essentially atomistic in nature in that they provide a static representation of the components of learning; whereas learning design adopts a more holistic approach. There is a clear analogy here with the conceptions of curriculum design expressed earlier – starting with the content (syllabus) and then working through increasingly inclusive plans towards a holistic perspective.

The concept of learning design is generally discussed at two distinct yet interrelated levels. Designing for learning (or 'learning design' – lower case l and d) is the concept of designing activities that will support student learning. 'Learning Design' is the same idea implemented as an IMS specification. The important components in Learning Design are based around the concept of a 'unit of learning' (Britain, 2004). These components include learning objectives, roles, activities (*learning activities* or *support activities*), activity-structures, environment (including *learning objects and services such as chat rooms, quiz tools etc.*), resources and method.

The IMS Learning Design specification developed out of the educational modelling language originated in the Netherlands, which was developed in part to shift attention from a focus on content to process. Learning Design is defined as an application of a pedagogical model for a specific learning objective, target group and a specific context or knowledge domain. It specifies the teaching and learning process, along with the conditions under which it occurs and the activities performed by the teachers and learners in order to achieve the required learning objectives. LD is based on the metaphor of learning as a play instantiated through a series of acts with associated roles and resources. The core concept is that a person is assigned a *role* in the teaching–learning process and works towards certain *outcomes* by performing *learning activities* within a given *environment*. The environment consists of appropriate learning objects and services used during the performance of the activities. Koper and Olivier (2004) argue that e-learning specifications (such as the IEEE LOM) consider learning in terms of a process of consumption of content. They acknowledge that current educational practice is more complex and advanced than this and the learning design specification was developed to reflect this.

Modelling Learning Design requires further levels of representation, including the sequencing of activities into 'units of learning' or 'learning designs'. Activity templates can be sequenced in a linear or non-linear fashion to create 'learning designs', similar to lesson plans (Littlejohn and McGill, 2004). Moreover, individual students or groups of students might interact with activities in different ways, therefore the sequencing of learning activities can allow for personalised learning (Britain, 2004).

Interestingly, however, whilst these developments map on to the first three levels of the curriculum identified earlier, there is no obvious Learning Design equivalent yet for either the hidden curriculum or the emergent 'lived curriculum'.

Tools to support design

Practitioners use a range of tools and resources to support and guide decision-making in creating learning activities (Conole, 2005). Figure 7.1 shows the relationship between these and the three components (context, pedagogy and tasks) involved in designing a learning activity described earlier. Different tools and resources can provide support and guidance on: the context of a learning activity; the choice of pedagogy; the creation of associated learner tasks; or any combination of these. These tools and resources range from contextually rich illustrative examples of good practice (case studies, guidelines, narratives, etc.) to more abstract forms of representation that distil out the 'essences' of good practice (models or patterns).

Some common examples are as follows:

- Narrative
- Case study
- Peer dialogue
- Expert guidance
- Networked expertise
- Lesson plan
- Tips and tricks
- Demonstration
- Answer garden

Most work to date using Learning Design has seen instructional designers or teachers drawing on the pedagogical body of knowledge to prescribe learning processes. However, a new strand of research complementing this design tradition gives the specification a post-hoc, descriptive role. Drawing on theories of self-organisation and trail formation, and linked to work on constructivist curricula, paths through loose-ended networks of learning events are seen as emerging from the interaction between learners and learning events. These paths can be represented in IMS Learning Design and offered as navigational scaffolding for learners finding their way through constructivist curricula. Using the same representational language for both designed and emergent curricula opens the door to comparative research on the effectiveness of the two approaches.

Colin Tattersall

- Frequently asked questions
- Schema
- Wizard
- Template
- Toolkit
- Model and pattern

Within this range there is a hierarchy from contextually situated to more abstract and conceptual (see also Sharpe *et al.*, 2004). One of the benefits of articulating these is that it highlights their role in terms of providing a concrete mechanism for the re-use and re-purposing of learning activities.

Narratives and case studies tend to be rich and contextually located, which is valuable in that they describe the details of a particular pedagogical intervention. The drawback is that precisely because they are so contextually located they may be difficult to adapt or re-purpose. Practitioners also use a range of dialogic approaches to inform their practice, which enables flexibility as these provide an opportunity to clarify and discuss ideas with colleagues. Perhaps the most important of these are those based on peer dialogue – such as asking advice from a fellow teacher about how they have gone about setting up a teaching session. Conferences, workshops, staff development events, online networks and mailing lists provide more extended forms of peer dialogue and networked expertise.

Lesson plans provide a means of formalising learning activities and a framework for teachers to reflect in a deeper and more creative way about how they design and structure activities for different students and help achieve constructive alignment between theory and practice (Littlejohn, 2003; Conole and Fill, 2005; Fowler and Mayes, 2004). They are particularly useful in helping tutors to plan *blended learning* (i.e. the integration of technology-supported methods with face-to-face teaching), since they can be used to reflect explicitly upon different educational approaches. Examples of 'tips and tricks' include Salmon's suggested e-activities to promote effective online communication (Salmon, 2002).

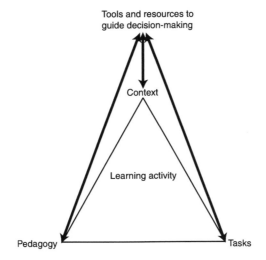

Figure 7.1 The relationship between tools and resources and a learning activity

Most commercial software now comes with some form of in-built help system. In addition many also provide templates or how-to wizards to guide the user through a particular set of activities. As a consequence, practice has shifted from a culture of reading the manual of instructions to a 'just-in-time' culture based on immediate need. Another type of guidance tool is exemplified by a tool for guiding practitioners through the process of learning design called LAMS (learning activity management system) (Dalziel, 2003). In LAMS, tools are organised so that users can pick and mix different types of learning activities.

Another category of support tool is toolkits that can provide a theoretical overview of an area and hence be used as a point of reference for decision-making (Conole and Oliver, 2002; Oliver *et al.*, 2002). A toolkit provides a structured resource that can be used to plan, scope and cost an activity (examples include the development of an evaluation plan, choosing and integrating different types of media into teaching, or managing information). By providing increasingly detailed layers of information, the user can follow up relevant issues when and if such detail is required. In addition, by providing a simple, logically organised structure, toolkits help to reduce the time required to plan work of this type. As described earlier, the DialogPlus is an example of a learning activity design toolkit that aims to guide practitioners through the process of developing pedagogically effective learning activities and appropriate use of relevant tools and resources (Conole and Fill, 2005).

Models and patterns provide more abstract forms of representation. Simplistically, a model is an abstract representation that helps us understand something we cannot see or experience directly. Kolb's learning cycle is probably the best-known experiential model (Kolb, 1984). Building on the work of Dewey,

Lewin and others, it presents an action-based or 'learning by doing' approach through a four-stage cycle (experience, reflection, abstraction and experimentation). Recently, Cowan has extended Kolb's learning cycle by considering explicitly how to plan interactive activities to support each of the four stages (Cowan, 2002).

A specific e-learning model that describes the stages of increasing competence in participating in an online community is Salmon's five-stage framework (Salmon, 2000) for supporting effective e-moderating in discussion forums, which emphasises the dialogic aspects of socially situated theoretical perspectives. Her stages are: access and motivation; online socialisation; information exchange; knowledge construction; development. As discussed in Chapter 2, this model has been incredibly popular and has been taken up and applied extensively. However, there has also been some criticism of the use of such models (Lisewski and Joyce, 2003). Because they are abstractions, practitioners may misunderstand how to apply the model effectively, by adopting a surface application of the model to their practice.

The tools and resources practitioners use to inform their practice have a number of benefits. First, they can be used as a means of sharing good practice between practitioners and enable re-use of learning activities, thereby creating economies of scale (Littlejohn, 2003). Second, examples of effective practice may be communicated to other teachers. This could aid practitioners in making informed decisions between comparable activities and approaches (Beetham, 2004). Third, they can be used as a framework for planning for accessibility, since resources can be replaced by other materials that closely match learners' needs. Fourth, they provide an effective means of communicating design requirements to developers, for example by providing outline lesson plans or schemas

---

For Bakhtin, understanding is a spark that occurs only when different perspectives are held together in tension, or, to put this another way, we learn by seeing things through our own eyes and the eyes of another *at the same time*. If learning is treated as an emergent property of dialogue between voices then it is always already affective as well as cognitive, since it depends on taking the perspective of another, social as well as individual, since even inner voices have personalities, and situated as well as unsituated, since every dialogue generates a 'third voice' or witness position beyond the actual interlocutors. Taking this dialogic perspective the educational design issues are firstly: how pedagogy can promote fruitful ways of responding to the other in a dialogue and secondly: how technology can best support learning dialogues by opening, maintaining and resourcing dialogic spaces in which different perspectives are held together in productive tension.

Rupert Wegerif

that illustrate to the developers the key stages involved in the process and the intended outcomes.

Despite a well-established practice of teachers adopting and adapting pre-designed resources such as case studies, lesson plans, etc., there is still little evidence of generic resources being developed and shared without specific subject content (Beetham, 2004). This is partly because it is difficult to abstract an activity that can be re-used across a range of subject disciplines (Britain, 2004).

Affordances of tools and resources

Different tools and resources have affordances that 'focus on the relationship between people and object, their creative and adaptive interaction with the environment rather than any compliant response to any designed features of that environment' (Conole and Dyke, 2004). Making the affordances (and in particular the benefits and limitations) of different tools and resources more explicit can help practitioners make more informed choices.

> The most striking claim of learning design remains the idea of a pedagogical meta-model, or put more controversially, that learning design is 'pedagogically neutral'. Systems that are able to instantiate many types of pedagogies from one flexible set of activity tools are a key goal for learning design software developers. While the first examples of learning design systems, such as LAMS, may fall short of this ultimate goal, they do provide indications of a new generation of e-learning software that go far beyond traditional courseware or Course Management Systems in their range of pedagogical possibilities.
>
> **James Dalziel**

The first affordance, *accessibility*, can be considered in terms of the degree to which a tool or resource is easily accessible to practitioners – both in terms of ease of retrieval and simplicity. *Speed of change* refers to how adaptable a tool or resource is and the degree to which it can be personalised. *Diversity* focuses on which tools or resources offer diverse and different experiences tailored to individual needs. *Communication and collaboration* centres on the degree to which they offer opportunities for communication and collaboration (for example a 'peer dialogue' offers better communicative interaction than a 'lesson plan'). *Reflection* refers to the degree to which the user can reflect on and adapt their thinking – toolkits, for example, are designed to encourage the user to revisit and adapt concepts. *Multimodality* is the degree to which a tool or resource offers different navigational routes and forms of interaction, as well as the degree to which it can be tailored to different user needs – toolkits, therefore, because they are designed to be adaptable and offer different navigation routes, are more *multimodal* than fixed lesson plans. *Immediacy* refers to the degree to which the tool or resource is relevant to the end user, and is related to the degree of contextualisation possible. *Monopolisation* centres on the issue of 'one-size-fits-all' type tools or resources with more bespoke, contextually located examples. A bespoke tool or resource will meet particular needs but may be more difficult to re-purpose and adapt, whereas a generic one has more applications but may have less of an impact. Finally, *surveillance* refers to the degree to which the tool or resource has in-built tracking and recording mechanisms and the issues this might raise for the end user.

Conclusion

This chapter has focused on curriculum design and has described the range of tools and resources used by practitioners to make more pedagogically informed choices about designing learning activities. Curriculum is seen as far more complex than simple course content or syllabus; rather it is composed of multiple layers of contextually located and specific factors that need to be taken into account. However, these broader aspects of the nature of curriculum are also by their nature more difficult to quantify, to define, to pin down. There are echoes here of the arguments presented in Chapter 6, where a similar situation is seen on moving from content-focused, individualised delivery of knowledge through associative ('transmissive') theories to those that embrace a broader contextual interpretation (such as socially situated theories). Encapsulation of these 'fuzzier', non-defined aspects of learning in technological terms is still problematic – this is illustrated in this chapter by consideration of the developments of educational vocabularies to capture and share educational good practice that have arisen in the last decade. The chapter tries to demonstrate the complexity of learning design, pinpointing the range of factors that practitioners need to consider when creating learning activities and suggests the range of tools and resources that are increasingly being developed and used to achieve this.

Chapter 8

Designing digital resources for learning

Jane Seale, Tom Boyle, Bruce Ingraham, George Roberts and Claire McAvinia

Introduction

In this chapter, the design of specific educational resources is examined. Resources can be variously defined, but in this context they are perhaps best understood in comparison to books and other print-based artefacts that are used conventionally as educational resources. Thus at one level we may understand these resources as physical or digital objects that need to be stored, classified, accessed and used, while at another we may wish to understand how best to structure and create individual resources to ensure that they successfully underpin the learning process.

In the case of print-based technology, there are established conventions about how to write learning materials, print them in usable formats, and store and retrieve them for use on demand. For the resources emerging from contemporary learning technologies designers do not always have such an understanding, but they need to develop this if they are to improve the educational experience of learners. In order to develop such an understanding, we address in this chapter three key design issues, and illustrate each by focusing on different partners within the designer, learner and resource relationship:

- Designing for learning: a focus on the designer
- Designing for accessibility: a focus on the learner
- Designing for re-usability: a focus on the resource.

Each of these relationships will be explored in turn.

Designing for learning: a focus on the designer

The primary concern of this section is with design as practice. Therefore, we start with the designer not the learner, address the 'channel' for communication before the learning objective, and argue that the learner is not the only audience for whom the design will be intended. This results in a designer-centred approach rather than a conventional student-centred approach. Wenger (1998: 229) asserts unambiguously that: 'learning [itself] cannot be designed: it can only be designed for – that is, facilitated or frustrated'. Designing for learning therefore involves the designer taking an orientation, assuming a stance and acquiring a posture. Each of these ideas will be explored below.

Orientation

Orientation is the position that a designer takes in relation to pedagogy and how knowledge is constructed. When addressing issues of orientation a number of questions automatically spring to mind, such as why start with orientation and what does this mean?

One feature noted by many learning technologists is that when making the design of resources for learning explicit, rather than reproducing the familiar forms of teaching, the whole process of learning and teaching is articulated as if new (Mason, 2001). The introduction of technology into education remediates teaching and learning. Such remediation can be uncomfortable, leading to reflection on the practice of teaching and learning. Such reflection is not always an explicit feature of the practice. Orientation is therefore important in order to communicate a sense of one's personal values, context and style.

Laurillard (1994: 181–2) introduces her design approach with a characteristically direct statement: 'The design of learning materials for any medium should always begin with the definition of objectives and analysis of student learning needs ... The student is considered primarily as a future expert at this stage.'

Laurillard goes on to say that learning objectives 'have to be' precise, necessary and complete (1994: 186). She then leads her learners through a process, which, if followed, would produce such learning objectives.

This approach is entirely well intentioned. Pragmatically, the approach could work. But it is problematic for two reasons: the presumption of a deficit model of learning where the student is not yet considered to be an expert; and the presumption that completeness will be possible in the expression of a learning objective.

High-quality learning and teaching sets ground rules and provides alternative modes of participation, exemplifies models of engagement, and gives access to the experience of the instructor in order to develop understanding. Good learning relationships are based on reciprocity, authenticity and credibility, where co-elaboration of knowledge is shared (Brookfield, 2001; Jones, 1999a). However, if a designer lacks the self-awareness to recognise their own values, context and style, the resources they design will reflect this uncertainty; authenticity and credibility will be compromised, reciprocity will be manifested in conflict and, while knowledge may be transmitted, the outcomes will be uncertain. To illustrate the influence of orientation on design, we offer four examples, which focus on positivism, social perspectives, pedagogical pragmatism, and tacit communitarianism.

Positivists, as outlined in Chapter 2, take a 'traditional' empirical-idealist view of reality as being objectively 'out there' (Feigl and Brodbeck, 1953). Human beings are postulated as rational individuals whose behaviour can be predicted. A designer with a positivist orientation may therefore aim to transmit a body of rules, principles and procedures and view learning as about moving from a state of containing less knowledge to a state of containing more knowledge.

Social learning theorists view knowledge as emergent rather than given or discoverable (Vygotsky and Cole, 1978). Knowledge arises from social practice, there is variation in what is known and how it is known and this variation is context-dependent (Goodman *et al.*, 2003; Scollon, 2001). A designer with a social learning orientation may therefore aim to facilitate learning that is constructed from the personal meanings derived from social interactions and conflicts.

Pedagogical pragmatism explicitly acknowledges the cognitive disconnect in much learning and teaching practice (Roberts and Huggins, 2004). For example, people assert their constructivist credentials yet use behaviourist methods as extrinsic motivators or where learners assert their desire for student-centred programmes yet ask 'is it in the exam?'. Therefore, a designer who takes on an orientation of pedagogical pragmatism aims to acknowledge conflict but does not require resolution of that conflict.

Tacit communitarianism is the pedagogy of normalisation, which asserts that teaching is about reproducing a community of practice through its many tacit codes (Bauman, 2002). The aim of designing for learning in this case might well be to create 'people like us'.

Each of these positions has obvious implications for the kind of design that someone might wish to create; however, the situation is further complicated by the remaining two properties.

Stance

Stance refers to the position that designers take when considering the factors that frame their approach and thinking. In assuming a stance, a designer attends to the channel (e.g. environment, technical specifications); the relationship that learners (and designers) will have with the resource (e.g. what are the teaching and learning styles that the resource might be called upon to support?); and finally the topic (what is the subject, discipline or field in which the resource will be placed and used?). This may appear to contradict the conventional student-centred approach, but this is only an honest admission of what actually has to go on when communication is established through resources. This raises the question 'to what extent can we presume that the design of resources for learning is an act of communication?' Designers are communicating through resources for learning, but those who appropriate the resources are not necessarily interested in this. This is illustrated in Scollon's ethnography of media communication (Scollon, 2001), where media events (like learning) are not the channels for communication as they may purport, but contexts for communication where the actor network is extraordinarily complex.

Posture

Posture refers to the designer's awareness of the relevant users, audiences or stakeholders of the resource. Designing resources for learning is a discursive act, which impinges upon the posture of the actor – in this case the designer. Posture takes into account the stakeholders in the discourses into which the resource is launched. Key stakeholders are the recipients (learners) and referees (third party agents such as a project funding body) of learning resources. Designing for learning may therefore involve a trilateral relationship between designers, referees and recipients in which the posture of the designer is influenced along with the practices that they adopt (Roberts and Huggins, 2004).

Recipient design is a body of practice that presumes an audience and designs for an idealised representative of that audience. Manuals for the design of resources for learning often exhort the designer to enact the role of the idealised learner, to advocate for the learner or to interpret for the learner. Referee design as a practice looks over the shoulder at a third party: a validating authority, a project funding body, policy-makers or, more often, a notional embodiment of society at large, with its conventional sense of what is permissible (Roberts and Huggins, 2004). Designers can resolve questions of posture by assuring that the referee is the recipient and the recipient is the referee.

Learning design and relationships between designer, learner and resource

The challenge of designing for learning is to make explicit that resources are appropriated for learning by learners. That act of appropriation is an act of design. The learner takes something that may have been made for learning – a 'learning object' – and learns from it. Whether they learn what was intended is not entirely in the control of the originator of the object. The learner will fit that object into their world-view, in part subversively. Design for learning makes explicit the false dichotomy between teachers and learning designers on the one hand and learners on the other. In learning to learn the learner must become a designer for learning: and in designing for learning the designer must, equally, be a learner.

Standards and tools for representing design for learning (for example IMS Learning Design) are now emerging. These offer potential to separate out structure from implementation in a way that can be handled by computer systems. Having firm ways to represent the designs does not ensure learners will acts as designers intended and it could well be that this approach to design emphasises the importance of the subversion of the learner and their opportunity to take part in the design.

Patrick McAndrew

Designing for accessibility: a focus on the learner

Over the past five to seven years a wide range of accessibility tools and guidelines have been developed, with the intention of guiding designers through the issues they need to address in order to ensure that the electronic resources they design can be accessed by people with disabilities. The most influential of these guidelines is the WAI Web Content Accessibility Guidelines (Chisholm *et al.*, 1999; Caldwell *et al.*, 2004), which are heavily influenced by the 'design for all' principles. These guidelines are therefore quite generic in nature and do not distinguish between different kinds of learners. There are, however, a growing number of alternative accessibility guidelines that are being developed to address the needs of specific groups of disabled learners.

The most common disability-specific guidelines to be developed are those for dyslexia (e.g. Rainger, 2003; Powell *et al.*, 2004). The existence of what could be perceived as competing guidelines (although many of the alternatives to the WAI guidelines incorporate some of the recommendations contained within them) highlights a design tension and offers a real challenge for designers: should they design for all learners or should they design for the specific needs of some learners?

Designing for all learners

Approaches to designing for accessibility have been heavily influenced by the Universal Design approach to design, which is also known as Design for All, Barrier Free Design or Inclusive Design (Burgstahler, 2002). The underpinning principle of Design for All is that in designing with disability in mind a better product will be developed that also better serves the needs of all users, including those who are not disabled (Vanderheiden, 1996).

Thompson (2005) offers a number of examples that illustrate how universal web design can benefit a range of users. For example, text alternatives for visual content (e.g. providing ALT tags for images) benefit anyone who doesn't have immediate access to graphics. While this group includes people with visual impairment, it also includes those sighted computer users who surf the web using text-based browsers, users with slow internet connections who may have disabled the display of graphics, users of handheld computing devices, and users of voice web and web portal systems including car-based systems.

The following case study provides another example of how 'designing for all' can produce multiple benefits: in this case, readability *and* accessibility.

Central to the Universal Design approach is a commitment that products should not have to be modified or adapted. They should be accessible through easily imposed modifications that are 'out of the box' (Jacko and Hanson, 2002: 1). Products should also be compatible with users' assistive technologies, such as screen readers and voice recognition systems (Thompson, 2005). Design approaches to accessibility, such as 'Design for All', challenge designers to become familiar with specialist assistive technologies. By engaging with the technology

---

Case study: Implementing iPALIO

In 2001 the University of Teesside decided to adopt 'Multi-PALIO', the Open Learning Foundation's (OLF) course in Open and Distance Learning to support staff development in this area. The existing course was paper-based and consisted of some 1,500 pages of text divided into 57 units. Each unit is self-contained and may be used either in isolation or in any combination to meet the particular needs of particular learners. In effect, it is a paper hypertext and as such eminently suitable for use online and the decision was taken to convert the entire text into an electronic format suitable for actually reading online.

The process of creating the new version of the course now known as 'iPALIO' (OLF, 2003) is reported in Ingraham and Bradburn (2003a), but the important issue here is that making a text usable online is not merely a matter of the suitability of its structure. Much more importantly, the text must be so designed as to be comfortably readable from computer screens. Since much conventional wisdom about reading from computers is very negative, this posed a challenge for the project – how to understand and overcome the issues involved in making large bodies of continuous text comfortably readable online. Significantly, it rapidly became apparent that 'readable' text met most of the requirements of 'accessible' text; and that, as such, if one approached the problem from a Design for All perspective it would be possible to develop strategies that would make large bodies of text accessible onscreen to the widest range of readers.

In order to actually undertake the conversion of the materials it was necessary to create cascading style sheets (CSS) that could be applied to the existing text in order to convert it into a format that met both the best available guidance for producing readable onscreen text (e.g. Davidov, 2002; List, 2001) and the best available guidance for creating accessible text (e.g. Web Content Accessibility Guidelines). Like others, the team found that existing guidelines were by no means unproblematic and that it was necessary to create a coherent subset of these to address the specific issue of making large bodies of text readable and accessible onscreen. These guidelines, the style sheets and a range of other related information are freely available online (Ingraham and Bradburn, 2003b).

This may all seem to be something of a large hammer to crack a small nut, but, despite the important affordances of multimedia computing, the bulk of academic discourse is still largely conducted through large bodies of continuous text. As such, adopting a Design for All approach to the dissemination of this text may not only afford new access to those for whom printed paper is problematic, but also access by all to other affordances that contemporary technology permits to the conduct of scholarly activity.

(Landow, 1997; Ingraham, 2000).

---

produced for learners with disabilities, we may find tools that could be brought to other users as learning technology tools. This in turn links to the issues of how we may wish to develop areas of specialisms within learning technology practice.

Will we eventually have a community of learning technologists specialising in access and assistive technology? If so, how will these specialists make links to the generic support services for learners and teachers as a whole?

Whilst some purists argue that Universal Design is about designing for everyone, the majority of proponents agree that designing for the majority of people is a more realistic approach (Vanderheiden, 1996; Bohman, 2003a; Witt and McDermott, 2002).

Designing for individual learners

There are some who feel uncomfortable with the principles of universal design because they appear to relieve educators of the responsibility of addressing individual learners' needs. For example Kelly *et al.* (2004) argue that, since accessibility is primarily about people and not about technologies, it is inappropriate to seek a universal solution. They argue that, rather than aiming to provide an e-learning resource that is accessible to everyone, there can be advantages in providing resources that are tailored for the student's particular needs.

There are also some who warn that no single design is likely to satisfy all different learner needs. The classic example given to support this argument is the perceived conflict between the needs of those who are visually impaired and those who have cognitive disabilities. For example, a dyslexic person's desire for effective imagery and short text would appear to contradict the visually impaired user's desire for strong textual narrative with little imagery. However, Bohman (2003b) provides a counterbalance to this argument stating that, while the visual elements may be unnecessary for those who are blind, they are not harmful to them. As long as alternative text is provided for these visual elements, there is no conflict. Those with cognitive disabilities will be able to view the visual elements, and those who are blind will be able to access the alternative text.

User-centred design

Whether designing for all students or individual students, accessible design approaches share many similarities to user-centred design approaches in that the learner is the central focus of the design approach. Alexander (2003) defines user-centred design (UCD) as a development process, with three core principles:

- Focus on users and their tasks: a structured approach to the collection of data from and about users and their tasks. The involvement of users begins early in the development life cycle and continues throughout it (user profiling).
- Empirical measurement of usage of the system: the typical approach is to measure aspects of ease of use on even the earliest system concepts and prototypes, and to continue this measurement throughout development (user testing).
- Iterative design: the development process involves repeated cycles of design, test, redesign and retest until the system meets its usability goals and is ready for release.

An alternative approach is to allow the learner to choose to interact with a resource in the way that suits them. Not universal design, not designed for the individual but adaptive design that enables learning by accommodating accessibility, pedagogical or environmental needs. This point highlights the need to support the designer in developing an empathy with the disabled learner. The designer cannot understand the outcomes of an automatic checker nor the relevance of guidelines if they don't appreciate the effect of the design decisions they take. This can be achieved through appropriate accessibility training with the introduction of videos and simulations of the disabled learner's experience when interacting with online resources (Pearson and Koppi, 2006 in press).

Elaine Pearson

UCD in the field of disability and accessibility is attractive because it places people with disabilities at the centre of the design process, a place they have not traditionally been. As Luke (2002) notes: 'When developers consider technical and pedagogical accessibility, people with physical and/or learning disabilities are encouraged to become producers of information, not just passive consumers.'

Accessibility and relationships between designer, learner and resource

When designers attempt for the first time to address accessibility issues, the first thing that their peers and colleagues do is to point them to accessibility tools (e.g. Bobby, LIFT, A-Prompt), standards (e.g. Section 508 standards) and guidelines (e.g. WAI Web Content Accessibility guidelines). This has meant, however, that the relationship between designer and learner has become heavily mediated by accessibility tools, standards and guidelines. Designers' attention can therefore be taken away from learners, which may adversely affect their practice and therefore the quality of the resources they produce (Seale, 2006).

Designing for re-usability: a focus on the resource

Having focused on the designer and the learner, this final section considers the resources themselves. Designing resources that can be re-used is closely associated with the concept of 'learning objects' (which is discussed in more detail in Chapters 7 and 9). The approach to learning objects in this section is summarised well in the definition given by Polsani (2003): 'A learning object is an independent and self-standing unit of learning content that is predisposed to reuse in multiple instructional contexts.'

A Learning Object: A concept more than an entity

The term learning object comes with a high degree of baggage these days. Different people assume totally different meanings for the term. It is impossible to find agreement between experts on what is and what isn't a learning object. It is impossible to find agreement on how big (or small) a learning object should be, on the instructional elements that should or should not be contained. Perhaps the solution is not to think of learning objects as entities, but as a concept with multiple representations. The concept of learning objects describes digital resources for learning that are interoperable, discoverable and sharable. With this approach we can save a lot of arguing over describing discrete attributes for objects and decisions as to when an object is or isn't a learning object. And we can concentrate on finding meaningful and successful ways to implement them.

Ron Oliver

Laurillard (2002) points to a distinction between what she terms calls 'the knowledge engineering' of e-learning and pedagogical design. Knowledge engineering work has been concerned with the development of specifications and standards that underpin the exchange and re-use of learning objects. This standardisation work, however, does not address the issue of how to design high-quality learning objects. The function of these specifications is to support transfer and interoperability across different learning management systems. The standards are argued to be pedagogically neutral (although the assertion of neutrality is contested by some researchers and practitioners). They can be used to package and describe any learning object, irrespective of its pedagogical value. The focus of this section is on the design of pedagogically effective learning objects.

The design of re-usable learning objects (RLOs) must tackle two major issues: the structural and the pedagogical design of learning objects. We need structuring principles to develop resources that have maximum potential for re-use, and pedagogical principles to ensure that they produce effective learning experiences.

Structural design of re-usable learning objects

Learning objects must possess certain structural properties if they are to act as standalone units. There are two important structuring principles that help achieve this goal. The first principle is that of cohesion: each unit should do one thing and only one thing (Boyle, 2003; Bradley and Boyle, 2004). Learning material should be included in the RLO only if it contributes to attaining the learning goal. No extraneous material should be included. This principle tends to go against the tendency for elaboration, which many tutors engage in naturally. However, if material referring to other goals or concepts is introduced this will make it more difficult to re-use the RLO in a different context.

The second structuring principle is 'de-coupling', or more accurately, minimised coupling. This principle states that the unit should have minimal bindings to other units. Thus the content of one learning object should not refer to and use material in another learning object in such a way as to create necessary dependencies, since one object then cannot be used independently of the other. The two principles combined state that the RLO should include only instructional material directly related to the learning goal, and exclude or strictly control all navigation or content references to external sources. The typical hypertext document with several embedded hyperlinks is thus a very poor candidate for a learning object.

> There is a dichotomy between the poor re-usability of hypertexts (which are commonly used in e-learning and feature large chunks of linked text) and re-usable learning objects which can be designed to be adaptable to learners' needs and preferences. As long as hypertexts are a dominant resource in e-learning, the opportunities for resources that are adaptable to the learners' requirements will be limited. Designers should be encouraged to reconsider the way that they wish to present their resources and re-think their approach to the learning and teaching process in the digital environment.
>
> **Elaine Pearson**

In working with tutors in developing RLOs it is clear that many tutors have to work at developing this discipline. They tend to initially develop 'objects' that have three or four learning goals instead of one. They may struggle to focus on dealing only with the material required for this learning goal (cohesion) and to exclude references that may tie the object too tightly to the original context of use (decoupling). There is clearly a debate over the pedagogical value of authoring in this way. However, there is considerable value in the demand for clear, lucid, uncluttered communication. It forces tutors towards a learner-centred 'simplicity' in communication that many tutors have to struggle to achieve. This is particularly valuable in 'extreme learning' domains where there are high failure rates, such as mathematics and programming. The requirement to break complex, instructional material into learning objects places a demand on tutors that can have considerable benefits for students.

It may be, however, that this approach is resisted as inappropriate in certain topic areas or disciplinary contexts. Highly analytic subjects such as programming would appear to lend themselves well to the creation and use of self-contained, decontextualised resources for learning. On the other hand, highly synthetic subjects such as the social sciences may be less hospitable domains for the deployment of such resources.

What is the useful size of a learning object? Boyle suggests micro contexts or self-contained objects. However, successful cases for re-use in the SoURCE project (see e.g. Laurillard and McAndrew, 2003) described mid-scale implementations that needed understanding of context and intentions before re-use to get the same results. Without that the re-use could still be successful, so offering a more interpreted view of re-use as inspiration.

Patrick McAndrew

The pedagogical design of re-usable learning objects

Wiley criticises the widespread approach to learning objects as carriers of traditional didactic pedagogy: 'Disappointingly, while they harmonize well with 1980s learning research, the assumptions of current learning objects approaches frequently contradict recent research on learning' (Wiley, 2003: 1).

The approach is to use learning objects as containers for the transmission of information. This approach embodies a passive, didactic transmission model of learning. Wiley argues that this approach may be useful for low-level training but it is unsuitable when deeper learning is required. Implicit in this approach is the tendency to view learning objects as encapsulated content. Boyle argues, however, that RLOs should be treated as 'micro contexts' for learning (Boyle and Cook, 2001). Each micro-context consists of content with appropriate interactivity organised around the achievement of an educational goal. The concept of learning objects as micro-contexts for learning opens up rich possibilities for pedagogical design. These possibilities will be illustrated by an examination of the learning object introduced in Figure 8.1.

The object in Figure 8.1 is built around one learning goal, understanding the 'while' loop in the Java language (there are three looping constructs in Java; each looping construct has its own RLO). This RLO is taken from a project that led to substantial improvements in a first-year introductory programming course taken by over 600 students (Boyle *et al.*, 2003).

The aim of the RLO in Figure 8.1 is both to engage the learners and to ease the transition into the (more abstract) use of the loop construct in programming. This is followed by screens providing user-controlled visualisation of the execution of a loop in Java. The first example involves moving a car across a screen. The second example involves moving a submarine (it has to be a submarine as the zero origin for counting in the vertical dimension in programming is taken as the top right of the screen). These provide highly visual examples of the execution of the 'while' loop. The learners can step through the animated code at their own pace. Alternatively an experienced student may navigate past the animation entirely by using the buttons on the bottom of the screen. At the end of the object, scaffolding is used to help the student make the transition to using the code in a full editor/compiler environment. The concept of scaffolding is a rich constructivist

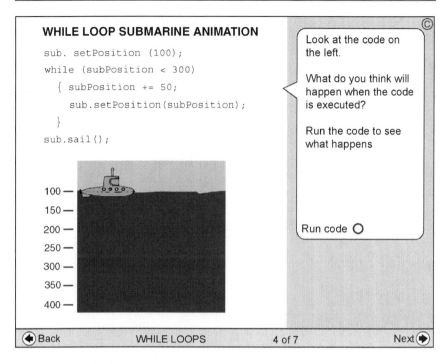

Figure 8.1 An example of a learning object developed for the teaching of introductory programming

technique (Linn, 1996; Hammond, 1995; Rosson *et al.*, 1990) that has a deep basis in the psychology of learning (Bruner, 1975; Vygotsky, 1962). The technique was implemented here by allowing students to construct the appropriate Java code by selecting from the options provided. The students get feedback after each line selected. The students can thus test their code construction skill in a supportive environment before moving to the more demanding editor/compiler development environment.

A learning object can thus be cohesively focused on one learning goal and be pedagogically quite rich. The combination of cohesive, pedagogically rich learning objects may be particularly beneficial in demanding domains where there are normally high failure and dropout rates.

Conclusions

In this chapter we have addressed three design issues – designing for learning, designing for accessibility and designing for re-usability – and used these issues to explore the relationship between the designer, the learner and the resource. Having explored these issues, several implications can be identified.

Designing for usability is not simply a matter of conforming to established guidelines; instead it involves designing in a way that recognises – and encourages – the learners' ability to use resources for their own ends. It is thus an act of expression, and of communication. Repositioning design in this way makes it clear that the creation of digital learning resources is not a 'neutral' or techno-rational act. As well as requiring a degree of pedagogical and technical competence, this also demands a spark of creativity.

Designers invest 'something of themselves' in the resources that they produce, including their beliefs about what constitutes effective learning. Many of the tensions around the use and re-use of digital learning resources may be a consequence of the extent to which the designers' investment is denied or ignored. Balancing such complex issues may involve the acquisition of new design skills. This has implications for professional development.

One of the aspirations of this book is to highlight the different voices and tensions in the learning technology arena. By exploring the relationship between the designer, the learner and the resource this chapter highlights the potential for tension in this relationship and offers an insight into how the design of resources may be influenced by one or many voices.

Chapter 9

Managing educational resources

Allison Littlejohn, John Cook, Lorna Campbell,
Niall Sclater, Sarah Currier and Hugh Davis

Introduction

This chapter explores issues around the organisation and management of educational resources. It discusses some of the current tools available to help academics and support staff to manage these, in particular highlighting the importance of learning technology interoperability standards in supporting more effective use and re-purposing of such resources. Finally it investigates some of the associated issues (pedagogical, technical, cultural) that may inhibit effective content management and provides insight into ways in which these challenges might be addressed.

In the previous chapter the authors outlined a vision of how learning resources might be developed, shared and re-used by teachers and learners in order to realise economies of scale. As part of this vision, re-usable resources (or 'learning objects') act as a new currency of exchange within a 'learning object economy' (Campbell, 2003). However, effective re-use of resources requires careful management of materials. Resource management is supported by a range of tools that allow learning materials to be easily stored, accessed, re-used and re-purposed.

Chapter 6 illustrates that learning is more complex than the simple acquisition of information. The development of effective learning is about more than making content resources available to students; it is about how resources are used within particular learning activities in specific contexts. With this in mind, we argue that most current content management tools do not allow academics enough freedom and flexibility in course design and development to utilise educational resources effectively, nor do they allow easy resource re-use and sharing. Given that a central theme running throughout this book is the complex and multi-faceted nature of e-learning, this is a key issue that needs to be addressed if educational resources are to be used extensively, effectively and flexibly in the future.

Organisation and management of educational resources

Information management skills are now an integral aspect of education (Longo, 2001). This is because managing learning resources is a complex process, involving a number of key elements associated with storing, retrieving and re-using resources

(Littlejohn, 2005). Realising these elements requires library and information professionals to work closely alongside teaching professionals. The expertise required to manage electronic resources is being combined with the expertise of learning technologies, leading to a convergence of work on digital libraries, educational resources and e-learning interoperability standards.

In support of sharing and re-use of e-learning resources within and across institutions, disciplines and other communities of practice, a number of standards-based measures are now being implemented. Real-life implementations feed back into standards development, allowing continuous, iterative improvement of both standards and tools and these real-life implementations lead to iterative improvements of the standards.

There are a number of different ways in which learning resources are organised and managed. This section describes three common examples and discusses their advantages and disadvantages, beginning with virtual learning environments (VLEs), which have been widely implemented in recent years. This is followed by a look at digital repositories, which are a more recent development designed to facilitate management and sharing of the kinds of resources delivered via VLEs in a sustainable and efficient way. We then examine one specialised application of repositories: the storing of assessment items in an item bank. Finally, we highlight a range of issues associated with managing educational resources.

Virtual learning environments

A virtual learning environment (VLE) is a collection of tools that support learning processes. These tools include online discussion forums (through bulletin boards or chat facilities); tools for submission of group work; assessment tools (such as computer-marked tests, computer-managed submission of essays, and e-portfolios); access to teaching resources (for instance course notes, handouts or simulations); and administrative course information. The first generation of VLEs were popular because they allowed ordinary practitioners to set up online courses without the need for intensive IT training. Most VLEs have simple interfaces that support tutors' design and development of online or 'blended' courses. This enables tutors to concentrate on course design issues rather than worrying about technical issues – a factor that dominated earlier online course developments (Littlejohn and Peacock, 2003).

As discussed in Chapter 4, there are many terms to describe such online course creation environments; including electronic learning environment, course management system (CMS), learning management system (LMS) and managed learning environment (MLE), each emphasising different aspects of the software and reflecting regional differences. For example, the term VLE has been used extensively in the UK. This term contrasts with the more encompassing term, MLE, which generally refers to a VLE linked to other institutional systems such as student records, finance or the library system. The meanings of these terms are somewhat fluid and contentious, as outlined in Chapter 5. However, the common feature of these systems is that they integrate e-tools that can be used to support a range of teaching and learning activities.

There are two main types of VLE: commercial off-the-shelf systems and open source software. The most popular commercial system in the UK is Blackboard (http://www.blackboard.com). Other systems that were developed by individual universities and adopted within other institutions include COSE (http://www.staffs.ac.uk/COSE/), COLLOQUIA (http://www.colloquia.net/) and Bodington (http://bodington.org/index.php). Open source software includes Moodle (http://moodle.org/), which is becoming increasingly widely adopted. Most institutions implement a single, centralised VLE linked to the student record database.

At the time of writing, most universities and colleges within the UK have implemented a VLE system. Evaluation studies have revealed that VLEs are mainly used to 'deliver' lecture materials and slides to students (Britain and Liber, 2004). Few practitioners use VLEs to support active forms of learning, for three main reasons. First, some learning environments have been designed around limited educational models (for example the lecture-tutorial model). Resulting from this, many current VLEs offer limited opportunity for the development of courses based on more diverse pedagogical models or which enable multiple course models. Since most systems adopt specific pedagogical approaches that tend to be fixed, this allows any one VLE to be used within only a limited range of contexts. Consequently, using VLEs to support 'active' forms of learning, such as problem-based learning, may require imagination and skill on the part of the academic. VLEs can be equally uncompromising in allowing students to actively negotiate assessments, set up online discussions, or develop and upload their own learning resources.

Second, once a system has been adopted, it is difficult to transfer courses to other systems; therefore tutors are 'locked in' to a single system.

Third, an additional problem with VLEs is in re-using resources. Re-use of resources can be employed at three levels: content, activities and course design. Materials purchased from publishing houses or bespoke resources created by audio-visual units can, in theory, be redeployed across several different modules. Student *activities*, such as online discussion tasks, group project assignments, computer-marked and computer-managed assessments and simulations, can also be re-used. However, VLE systems, such as Blackboard, do not allow for easy resource sharing, resulting in duplication of materials. This shortcoming can frequently lead to further problems, since multiple copies of single resources may have to be updated individually. More recently, storage and management of VLE resources is being carried out within digital repositories, as discussed in the next section. This allows resources to be stored, shared and re-used more easily, often in the form of granular 'learning objects'; it also utilises the application of open learning technology interoperability standards to allow the development of more flexible, sustainable systems.

Digital repositories

As discussed above, learning resources, or 'learning objects' may be developed and delivered via a VLE; however, VLEs are not designed for the sustainable management of such resources. A digital repository is a tool that can support the storage, sharing and re-use of learning resources or learning objects; repositories also have wider applications for other kinds of resources: 'In simplest terms, a digital repository is where digital content, assets, are stored and can be searched and retrieved for later use. A repository supports mechanisms to import, export, identify, store and retrieve digital assets' (Hayes, 2005).

A repository of learning objects may be based in an institution (e.g. Edinburgh University's LORE: http://www.lore.ed.ac.uk/index.html), within a cross-institutional subject- or discipline-based community (e.g. SIESWE Learning Exchange: http://www.sieswe.org/learnx/about.html), or regionally or nationally funded and managed (e.g. YHLearning: http://www.yhlearning. org.uk/ and Jorum: http://www.jorum.ac.uk/). Any number of these repositories may be linked in a network via cross-searching services or collections of meta-data harvested via the OAI-PMH protocol. They may also be included in wider networks of digital resources including ePrint archives, institutional portals, digital libraries, and internet gateways or hubs. A more recent development is the concept of peer-to-peer repository networks allowing individuals to share resources held on their own hard drive, in much the same style as Napster, for example the LionShare project at Pennsylvania State University in the US (http://lionshare.its.psu.edu/main/).

> Good quality metadata is critical to successful searching of digital reposi-tories. Many librarians have real concerns about the quality of meta-data that has been added by authors or creators of digital objects. These people often cannot see the real ben-efit of adding metadata nor understand the complexity of subject indexing. This factor will greatly reduce the value of the digital reposi-tory.
>
> **Jane Secker**

One major difference between repositories and traditional digital libraries is the idea that creators and users of resources may deposit mate-rials directly into repositories. Most of the early digital repositories did not envisage employing a librarian or other information professional to oversee the management of repositories; the idea of inexpensive, highly dynamic, user-based services has underpinned the thinking and development of these initiatives. However, as repositories have become more widely implemented and problems with this approach have emerged, this has begun to change, although the emphasis on the needs and expertise of teachers and learners has remained central (Currier *et al.*, 2004). There are some specialised applications of repositories, one of which – assessment itembanks – is discussed in more detail in the next section.

Assessment tools

Given the unique importance of assessment in the learning and teaching life cycle, assessment resources deserve particular consideration and raise a number of unique issues. Chapter 10 highlights a number of benefits in using technology to assist with the assessment process. A growing number of assessment engines are available as stand-alone systems or embedded within VLEs. A major problem is that building up banks of assessment items is a time-consuming process. As with other forms of educational content, it is advisable to maintain these items in a platform-independent, interoperable, shareable format. This allows for three major benefits. First, authors can have confidence that the items they create have been future-proofed. Second, institutions can transfer assessment items to an upgraded system. Third, questions may be uploaded into different assessment systems for different purposes, for example they may be accessed via a VLE system for formative assessment purposes and later via a high specification secure assessment system for summative examinations. This level of interoperability enables the exchange of content between individuals and institutions using different systems. A market in which institutions can buy and sell questions and tests from the commercial sector is more likely to emerge once such a standard is widely adopted.

There is currently only one set of standards that has a degree of acceptance among some of the leading vendors of VLE and assessment systems – IMS Question and Test Interoperability (QTI). QTI focuses on four main areas:

- Assessment, section and item – the content of the assessment.
- Results reporting – the results after the test has been taken.
- Selection and ordering of sections and items.
- Outcomes processing – compiling question scores into test scores.

Although in theory QTI enables systems to interoperate, in practice there is little evidence that assessment content can be exchanged satisfactorily between systems, even though vendors of assessment software systems may claim 'IMS compatibility'. To overcome this issue, the UK-based CETIS Assessment Special Interest Group aims to develop common practice among systems developers (http://assessment.cetis.ac.uk/). The group has produced a rendering engine that is designed to accommodate many interpretations of the QTI specifications. A reference set of examples that embody the common practice agreed between developers is being produced. Details of ambiguities are being collated and made available via a searchable information resource.

Agreement of common practice between assessment system vendors will promote further interoperability and will bring support for further development of item banks by various organisations. One such initiative that has already built up a large bank of peer-reviewed items is the Electronics and Electrical Engineering Assessment Network (e3an: www.e3an.ac.uk). A key issue that has been addressed by the project is that of assessment item metadata. Item authors are required by E3an to complete all metadata fields in the Microsoft Word templates it provides for the entering of assessment items but restricts these to a relatively small number.

A second project of interest, COLA (www.coleg.org.uk/cola), has developed a bank of items and assessments for the Scottish Further Education sector. COLA uses an adapted version of the e3an templates to gather assessments from authors. These are then processed by a program that generates the QTI and the associated metadata. The IEEE Learning Object Metadata standard has been applied directly to assessments and items in the COLA project, using a new application profile developed for the project (Sclater, 2003).

It is likely that assessment items, like learning objects, will in the future have 'secondary' metadata that describes when and where an item has been used. This will enable assessment items to be used by learners and practitioners in more imaginative and dynamic ways than is currently possible.

Issues in managing educational resources

In the previous section we examined three major systems used in the management of educational resources. However, the development and implementation of such systems has not solved all of the arising problems and issues. In this section we examine issues that inhibit the sustainable management and use of learning resources, and discuss possible solutions.

Interoperability

As the concept of sharing educational resources has gained currency, there has been a parallel awareness of the importance of learning technology interoperability standards and specifications. These are open standards and specifications that are designed to facilitate the description, packaging, sequencing and delivery not only of educational content but also of learning activities and learner information. Learning technology interoperability standards help to

> Technological developments such as digital repositories and adherance to standards are important; however, the key challenge is actually one of ensuring that academic staff are equipped with the wide range of information literacy skills to discover, access, use, and re-use learning objects in an appropriate and ethical manner, without infringing the rights of others. The use of creative commons licences, for example, presents a real problem in educating staff about what they can and cannot do with a resource when they re-use it.
>
> **Jane Secker**

ensure that resources are *portable* – allowing users to move resources between proprietary systems, preventing 'lock-in' to single software packages; *durable* – ensuring that resources will remain accessible as systems and platforms change; and *re-usable* – enabling practitioners to re-use resources in different contexts and to tailor resources to meet their own requirements and those of their learners.

A wide variety of international bodies and consortia are currently involved in the development of learning technology interoperability standards and specifications. These include the IMS Global Learning Consortium, the American Department of Defence, the Institute of Electrical and Electronic Engineers, the Comité Européen de Normalization/Information Society Standardisation System Workshop – Learning Technologies, and the International Standards Organisation. These organisations have made rapid progress in producing standards and specifications that facilitate interoperability in many areas of online education and training. Examples include:

- The IEEE Learning Object Metadata and Dublin Core Metadata standards, which support description and discovery of resources.
- The IMS Digital Repositories Interoperability, which supports development of interoperable repositories.
- The Open Digital Rights Language, which allows intellectual property rights data to be recorded in a standard way, and shared and enforced.
- The IMS Content Packaging specification, which allows learning objects to be packaged and transported between systems with their internal structure intact.
- The IMS Learning Design and IMS Simple Sequencing specifications, and the ADL Shareable Content Object Reference Model (SCORM), which allow the planning, structuring, delivery and sharing of learning activities.
- The IMS Question and Test Interoperability specification, which allows for the creation, delivery and sharing of computer-aided assessments.
- The IMS Learner Information Package and IMS ePortfolio specifications, which enable creation, maintenance and sharing of records for lifelong learning.
- The IMS Definition of Competencies and IMS Enterprise specifications, which record and share learner information across enterprise systems and educational systems.
- The IMS Accessibility specification and the W3C Web Accessibility Initiative, which aim to ensure that educational content is accessible to all users.

In the UK, the Centre for Educational Technology Interoperability Standards (CETIS: http://www.cetis.ac.uk) is a national service that assists educational institutions and other stakeholders with uptake, implementation and use of these standards; their website and other resources are helpful tools for further investigation. However, technical interoperability standards for learning resources do not automatically solve all of the problems in resource management. The next sections

Although this describes a typical life cycle it is certainly not the only life cycle. Learning objects may be used in many ways – in wikis, blogs, emails, reading lists, and other ways which haven't even emerged yet. Not all of these tools will ever support the important standards described here. It is therefore very important for a learning object in a repository to be usable without having to download it. This is achieved by creating a reference for the learning object so that the object remains in the repository but the reference (usually a URL) can be used anywhere. The learning object can then be inserted into any educational tool whether or not it supports the interoperability standards. This approach is also useful when learning objects are shared between institutions using different VLEs. The same learning object can be used in different VLEs simultaneously by referring to a single object in the repository rather than downloading multiple copies.

Charles Duncan, Intrallect Ltd

go into more detail on packaging and metadata for learning resources, followed by discussion on the wider pedagogical and cultural issues.

Interoperability, the learning object life cycle and content packaging

The life cycle of a learning object that may be used in a VLE or other online learning scenario or tool involves the following processes (although not necessarily strictly in this order): creation of the object; standardised packaging for interoperability and portability; metadata creation (or cataloguing); upload to a repository; discovery by subsequent users of the repository via searching or browsing; downloading of the object for use in another VLE or other learning scenario; changing the object to suit the needs of the new user; and possibly uploading the new object to the repository, going through the same procedure of packaging and metadata creation (Dalziel, 2005). The IMS Content Packaging specification ensures that learning resources may be transported between e-learning systems such as authoring tools, repositories and VLEs. Tools such as Microsoft LRN and the RELOAD Editor (http://www.reload.ac.uk/) are available to ensure teachers and other users may package resources using this specification. However, although these tools, alongside repositories, support creation and management of metadata, they do not in and of themselves solve the metadata management problem.

Metadata: more than a technical interoperability issue

The tools described above generally allow for metadata to be created for the object at the point of packaging, while some repositories allow for metadata to be imported or created at the time of upload. Metadata for learning objects will usually be created in conformance to a learning resource metadata standard such as the IEEE Learning Object Metadata (IEEE LOM), which allows for standard library-style attributes to be described such as author, title and subject classification. Additionally, these standards also allow for educational attributes to be described, such as the intended audience, difficulty, educational level, or the length of time it takes to work through the resource. Many of these metadata elements may be utilised in searching or browsing for an object by subsequent users, hence quality control of metadata is important in order that resources are not lost within a repository. Metadata elements may also be examined by the user once an object has been found, in order to decide whether the object will meet their needs.

The issue of metadata quality is of vital importance to the management of these processes. The development of appropriately specified metadata standards has been the first step; development of application profiles that describe how individual initiatives will use a metadata standard has been an important next step for ensuring that different repositories may be searched across with some consistency of results. The vocabularies necessary to populate the metadata must also be agreed upon and specified, including educational attributes and concepts, as well as subject discipline, keyword and curriculum-based vocabularies. This process is complex and ongoing, particularly within the vastly heterogeneous international field of education. Finally, the high-level management of quality assurance for all of the metadata is now being looked at, with researchers investigating who should create which metadata elements, how metadata creation tools may be developed to best support the process, and what are the important attributes that teachers and other users may wish to search or browse by or look for in a metadata description of an object (Currier *et al.*, 2004).

Another type of metadata that may increasingly become central to the sharing and re-use of educational resources is sometimes referred to as secondary metadata. This is metadata created by users of resources, describing how the resource was used, what they thought of it, or what success or otherwise they had with it. It is often likened to informal peer review, or to Amazon.com book reviews, and has been developed for some time in the Merlot web catalogue (http://www.merlot.org/) for user sharing of educationally useful resources. While it is still unclear to what extent users will want or use such metadata, it has been flagged in numerous e-learning arenas as something that may need to be developed in order to fully support the usability, uptake and effectiveness of e-learning.

However, even with adequate systems and procedures to support the packaging, storage, description and discovery of learning objects and other educational resources, there are wider pedagogical and cultural issues that warrant attention. These are summarised in the following sections.

Wider issues with learning objects

As discussed earlier, in recent years electronic learning resources of the type delivered in a VLE have been referred to as 'learning objects' (Littlejohn, 2003). If we want to use these resources effectively to support learning, it is important to develop a model for understanding learning objects and their potential use (Boyle and Cook, 2003). However, there is a significant problem with current approaches to standardisation, which have taken a strongly technological approach to solving the problems of re-use and recombination; for instance, metadata information associated with learning objects does not have a strong pedagogical base. Metadata, which is essentially 'data about data', and comprises the catalogue information about a resource, provides ways of describing and locating objects. This metadata may be extended to include information about the instructional role of the learning object. However, there are limitations to the use of adding descriptive data without a clear theoretical base (Boyle and Cook, 2001).

An alternative basis for demarcating basic learning objects is the identification of minimal meaningful educational objectives that provide the basis for learning objects (Boyle and Cook, 2003). As discussed in Chapter 8, learning objects can be viewed as 'learning microcontexts' structured to achieve these educational objectives. In other words, they explicitly consist of the content and the pedagogical processes required in order to achieve specific educational objectives. Learning objects can be based on minimum basic learning units that it does not seem pedagogically sensible to subdivide. Thus if there are three types of loops in a programming language then one learning object is produced for each loop type.

Mayes (2003) contends that 'to be useful, learning objects will require the mediation of human (teacher) judgement, even though these judgements can operate in a very distributed way'. Clarifying the pedagogical models that might be used to underpin the development of the learning object economy becomes especially important when we consider that the prime reason for the dramatic uptake and interest in VLEs is the versatility of the tools they offer to practitioners. From another perspective, we could observe that all of the pedagogical intelligence and adaptivity within VLEs comes from the community of practice – the human teachers, peer tutoring, learning support, etc. A major issue, then, is that the 'one size fits all' approach offered by VLEs does not provide adequately for learning dissimilarities present even in a small group of learners. How, then, do we address this issue and realise the potential of the learning object economy? What is needed is a partnership between researchers and practitioners in order to formulate pedagogically enriched models for the re-use of learning objects. Such a model-building partnership is needed if we are to build the stronger versions of how people conceive of re-usability.

Learning design

Despite the achievements outlined above, there has been some concern that learning technology standards and specifications are failing to deal with the actual process of learning in all its complexity. So, while it has been possible to deliver simple linearly sequenced resources to individual learners, there have been few specifications that allowed teachers to plan and share complex learning scenarios involving multiple cohorts of students working individually and collaboratively and undertaking a wide range of tasks and activities.

This fundamental gap is being addressed in the current interest in Learning Design (and more broadly in the wider work on designing for learning). The IMS Learning Design specification, which is based on the Educational Modelling Language developed by the Open University of the Netherlands, enables teachers to create and share complex pedagogical frameworks and learning scenarios that are described in terms of roles, activities and resources (Liber and Olivier, 2003). The development of these pedagogically informed specifications brings us a step closer to achieving the goal of being able to create and share complex and engaging learning activities that are capable of meeting the needs of all learners regardless of their individual learning styles of requirements.

Systems based on IMS Learning Design allow tutors to design courses in a much more flexible and intuitive way. An example is the Learning Activity Management System (LAMS), which allows tutors to plan (or storyboard) their learning activities using a graphical drag and drop interface (Dalziel, 2005). Issues associated with designing for learning are discussed in more detail in Chapter 7.

Pedagogical issues

So far the discussion has focused on the technical aspects of educational resource management and associated issues of metadata, interoperability and standardisation. However, there are also fundamental issues at a pedagogical level, as tutors and learning facilitators often find it difficult to discover appropriate resources. Indeed, important issues exist relating to support for staff who are re-using learning objects. Beetham *et al.* argue that the main barriers to re-use appear to be cultural at both individual and institutional levels (Beetham *et al.*, 2001). Practitioners require support in moving from individual development of learning resources and courses towards team-based collaborative development and re-use within learning communities.

From the course creator's perspective, interoperability would free the course construction activity from time-consuming search and crop-to-fit exercises (i.e. customising located material to fit a particular educational objective). The assumption is that each object within the resource could be described in its own right as well as be a part of a bigger object, which in turn could be contained by a bigger object, and so on. This flexibility would allow the possibility of construction of entire courses by the integration of various sets of metadata referenced materials. One author's resources could be integrated in numerous learning systems. However, the question as to whether this would improve the overall quality of learning materials has not yet been resolved.

Cultural and organisational issues

By sharing resources tutors have access to a much wider pool of educational materials and expertise. However, this is not yet part of the established culture and organisation of most institutions. Tutors require incentives to change their working practice towards the sharing and re-use of resources. However, they may have concerns over a number of issues, including quality assurance of resources; peer review of resources (secondary metadata); digital rights management; the management of digital repositories and re-usable content; and resource description and semantic interoperability, not to mention drivers such as professional development and recognition for teachers. There are numerous current studies investigating these issues in progress at the time of writing, e.g. the JISC Digital Repositories Programme project 'Community Dimensions of Learning Object Repositories' (CD-LOR: http://www.jisc.ac.uk/index.cfm?name=project_cdlor). The changing web landscape, however, heralds even more fundamental changes in how individuals interact with technology; these changes will have an impact on learning.

Personalised learning

Individuals are becoming more and more accustomed to personalisation in the use of web services. For example, personal profiles help to elicit individual suggestions when shopping on Amazon. Increasingly learners are likely to enter educational institutions expecting similar forms of personalisation to support their learning. Personalised learning has the potential to challenge, support and motivate the learner at the appropriate level, and it may enhance the acquisition of knowledge. This area is still in the early stages of investigation; in the UK, the JISC has funded a number of studies related to personalised learning, which are underway at the time of writing, for example the PLE Reference Model project (http://www.elearning.ac.uk/news_folder/ple/view).

Future challenges

The vision of a learning object economy implies the existence of distributed, digital repositories serving communities of users across multiple institutions, educational sectors and nations. Harnessing this potential requires major strategic reorganisation not just within and across institutions but also across different educational sectors for a number of reasons. First, at a cross-institutional level, obvious conflicts exist between institutional competition for students and the collaboration implied by a learning object economy. Second, to get maximum value out of the development of re-usable resources they should be shared across disciplinary communities, but this kind of cross-disciplinary sharing is not a strong feature in education. Disciplines differ in their languages, in their methods of enquiry and in their social and cultural organisation (Becher and Trowler, 2001). Third, at a transnational level, cultural and language differences add a further complexity to the idea of resource sharing. However, on a more positive note, globalisation coupled with the increased availability of new content management tools and, indeed, broader web-based tools, such as peer-to-peer sharing, are resulting in the emergence of real and virtual communities in which previous barriers to collaboration are being broken down. The resulting new and emerging teaching and learning processes are discussed in Chapters 6 and 7.

Chapter 10

E-assessment

Niall Sclater, Gráinne Conole, Bill Warburton
and Jen Harvey

Introduction

Assessment is *the* key driver for learning. It enables the certification of learning and can facilitate learning in its own right (Boud, 2000). While students have always learned strategically based on what they perceive as the assessment requirements of their course, increasing demands on their time mean that obtaining a qualification is the fundamental driver for growing numbers of learners. The introduction of student fees, reductions of grant assistance and greater costs of living mean that most undergraduates now juggle paid employment with their studies. Fewer turn up for lectures, particularly when their lecture notes are posted online, and there is less time to read books peripheral to the core subject matter that will be assessed. At the same time, the explosion in resources available on the internet and the resulting information overload forces many students to base their learning activities solely around the assessment requirements of their course.

A distinction is drawn between summative assessment (administered for grading purposes) and formative assessment (providing feedback to assist the learning process). Diagnostic assessment is used by tutors to determine students' prior knowledge (Bull and McKenna, 2004; O'Reilly and Morgan, 1999). Other categorisations include formal/informal (invigilated or not) and final/continuous (at the end of a course or throughout). Sclater and Howie (2003) distinguish the following applications of e-assessment: 'credit bearing' or high-stakes summative tests, continuous assessment, authenticated or anonymous self-assessment, and diagnostic tests that evaluate the student's knowledge before the course to assess the effectiveness of the teaching.

The fundamental difference in the way formative and summative assessment is perceived in face-to-face activities is carried over to the online learning world. Where the online activities are themselves entirely optional, summative assessment-focused students are less likely to engage with them than if they directly contribute to the final course mark. It thus becomes important if assessments are purely formative that they are regarded as providing practice or helping to learn content and skills relevant for a later summative assessment.

Suppose formative assessment is about evoking feedback. It might be represented as follows:

Feedback on ... Feedback from	Formal interactions, e.g.	Non-formal interactions, e.g.
Teachers	Electronic assignments	Conversations in labs, design studios, etc.
Technologies	On-line quizzes	Simulations, CAD, such as SolidWorks
Peers	Peer marking	Coffee conversations
Others (workplace colleagues)	Mentor reports	Daily interaction
Self	Self-evaluation	Self-regulation (a continuous business)

Notice that this model is about designing learning environments that maximise interactivity. The emphasis is on the design of learning, with assessment as an inevitable product of interaction. This view plays to some of the strengths of online devices for stimulating and supporting trust, play, disclosure, exchange, risk-taking, feigning and learning. It implies a more extended account of the role of new technologies in supporting e-learning – this chapter is good on assessment methods and tools that support activities mainly in the white cells.

Peter Knight

In the same way that assessment is key to learning in traditional forms of higher education, e-assessment is a critical part of the e-learning domain. Many attempts to convert traditional courses to web-based courses have failed to inspire students because they are essentially page-turning activities that do not use the technology to provide interactivity and automated feedback. The ability to interact with the computer by answering questions to ascertain the level of knowledge and understanding gained helps to ensure a more engaging online experience. Where detailed feedback is provided automatically based on the input of the learner, the knowledge of their level is supplemented by new learning content, which can confirm or enhance their understanding of the subject.

The evolution of e-assessment

The use of technology in assessment is not new. Systems to provide multiple-choice questions and have students select the right answer are technically trivial to implement and there are therefore myriad examples of basic automated testing programs. These have recently moved out of formal education into mainstream society so that automated testing is now an essential element of the UK driving test and is even required for citizenship applications.

Various terms to describe the use of technology in the assessment process have emerged. Among the most commonly used is *computer-assisted assessment* (CAA), defined by Bull and McKenna (2004) as 'the use of computers for assessing student learning'. This incorporates optical markup reading (OMR) technologies that are still commonly used by institutions to digitise and mark the paper-based responses to multiple-choice questions. This can be thought of as an intermediate technology similar to the fax machine, which temporarily bridges the divide between the paper-based and digital worlds before the digital technologies are ubiquitous. It incurs a considerable administrative overhead but avoids the need for every candidate to be placed in front of a computer.

Computer-based assessment is a development of CAA where the assessment is carried out entirely on the computer. Where this takes places via a web browser it is referred to as *web-based assessment, online assessment* or, increasingly, *e-assessment*. The e-assessment process includes, of course, much more than the sitting of the test; it incorporates (i) the creation, storage and delivery of assessments, (ii) the capture, marking, storage and analysis of candidates' responses and (iii) the collation, return and analysis of their results (SQA, 2003).

The advent of the web and associated technologies in the early 1990s had a number of significant impacts on CAA. First of all it meant that testing software was entirely independent of the learners' machines; all they now needed was a web browser while the testing software sat on the web server. As browsers became ubiquitous, most students could access tests from computers at home or at least in a university-provided lab. A second impact of the web has been the increased ability to integrate tests with learning content. It therefore became easier to provide an integrated online learning and assessment experience. The implementation of virtual learning environments at almost all universities made it relatively straightforward for staff to author online assessments for their students. In fact the online assessments often provided the 'fun' element – the active part that brought alive otherwise uninspiring text-based materials. A third impact of the web was that it became possible for staff to manage the assessment processes much more closely. Assessments could be released automatically at certain points in the course that related to the subject matter covered. Staff could monitor student participation and areas that were giving them problems so as to provide remedial assistance and improve their teaching materials.

Addressing criticisms of e-assessment

While the web has undoubtedly made automated assessment easier to deliver and administer, it has done little to address two fundamental criticisms: 'How can computer-marked tests assess higher levels of understanding?' and 'How do you know the person submitting the assessment is who they say they are?'

Assessing at different cognitive levels

The most common question type used in e-assessment is multiple choice, where the student is asked to select one from, say, five options. A more demanding variant is the multiple-response question where more than one option can or must be selected from the list. Other objective question types include putting words or phrases into the correct order (sequencing) and matching pairs of words. Images can enable other forms of objective questions where learners are required to click on a particular part of an image (hotspot) or drag objects on to a diagram (drag and drop). Such question types have proved useful for subjects such as geology where it is necessary to be able to identify rock formations visually.

Objective question types are ignored outright by many university lecturers who, while they may acknowledge their role in assessing the recall of basic knowledge and comprehension, consider them inappropriate for assessing the 'higher order' learning outcomes identified by Bloom *et al.* (1956), such as application, analysis, synthesis and evaluation. Outcomes at the lower end of Bloom's taxonomy are traditionally assessed on a convergent basis (i.e. only one 'correct' answer), whilst higher-order outcomes are most readily assessed divergently (a range of informed responses and analyses is permissible) (McAlpine, 2002a). Convergent assessments can be readily constructed using objective items, but divergent assessment has traditionally relied on longer written answers or essays.

The fact that correct answers can be guessed becomes less critical the more questions there are in a test and the more possible responses to each question that are present (though four responses can be perfectly adequate for discriminating between different competences over a whole test). Guessing can be countered by negative marking, which aims to penalise those who make an attempt at a question they do not know the answer to rather than leaving it blank. Another strategy is the use of confidence measures where students are asked to specify how confident they are that their answer is correct (Davies, 2002). The mark for a correct response is therefore augmented by strong confidence or reduced by weak confidence. A confidently answered but incorrect response, if combined with negative marking, would incur a penalty.

More credible to some teachers than multiple-choice questions are those where the learner is required to type an answer rather than select one from a list. The most basic form of this is a question where the student enters a single word or short phrase as the answer. If there are a very few possible responses it becomes possible to anticipate all possible correct answers and assess the response automatically. This can be complicated by typos and poor spelling, although there are algorithms now available that compensate for these. Longer sentences can also be assessed automatically and fairly accurately using natural language processing techniques.

The 'killer application' for online assessment may be the automatic assessment of essays. The US-based Educational Testing Service has developed software to analyse longer pieces of writing and identify errors in grammar, usage, mechanic and style. It is claimed to do so as accurately as human markers. However, we are still a long way from being able to assess creativity and originality automatically.

Authentication and plagiarism

Knowing if a candidate is who they say they are and whether their work is their own remain two of the biggest barriers to the use of summative online assessment at a distance. Students can be authenticated by *knowledge* (of a username, password, pin number), *ownership* (an object the student owns such as an ID card) or *characteristic* (e.g. iris or fingerprint recognition) (SQA, 2003). These techniques are either impractical or open to abuse at a distance, so, for summative tests, face-to-face examinations (whether paper-based or computer-based) are still considered essential by most higher education institutions.

The internet provides many opportunities for students to plagiarise, ranging from the copying and pasting of text from web pages to buying entire essays from essay banks (Marais *et al.*, 2005; Caroll, 2002). However, requiring students to submit essays in digital format means they can be checked for plagiarism more easily than if they are supplied on paper. Techniques for plagiarism detection include tools that match essays to those submitted by other students in the cohort (and previous cohorts). Other tools search the web for text that bears similarities to that submitted by the students. They can highlight text that is identical and allocate a percentage to the amount of an essay that has been plagiarised. Further algorithms detect changes in style within an essay. If American spellings suddenly appear in an otherwise UK-style essay, for example, this can suggest plagiarism.

In an age where it is important to be able to synthesise materials from many sources some lecturers are taking the decision to allow a small percentage of students' work to be plagiarised, though this clearly breaks with traditions of academic integrity (Price, unpublished work).

Paper versus machine

CAA allows for more complex item types than paper-based assessments, and also enables the use of audiovisual materials and iterative interactions between learner and computer. One continual finding is that direct translation of paper-based assessments into online assessments is inappropriate; there is a need to revisit question formulation, reflecting on what it is intended to test. The process of creating questions for online delivery can therefore challenge the validity of paper-based questions as well. The use of steps for some kinds of questions (for example in maths) has also proved valuable in terms of enabling teachers and researchers to get a better understanding of the student learning experience and how they tackle questions (Ashton *et al.*, 2003). This raises important issues about how CAA software systems record and report on student interactions. The reporting mechanisms available within CAA systems provide much richer data about the students than were available from paper-based assessments.

The format of an assessment affects validity, reliability and student performance. Paper and online assessments may differ in several respects. Various studies have compared paper-based to computer-based assessments to explore this (e.g. Outtz, 1998; Ward et al., 1980; Fiddes et al., 2002). In particular the Pass-IT project has conducted a large-scale study of schools and colleges in Scotland, across a range of subject areas and levels (Ashton et al., 2003; Ashton et al., 2004). Findings vary according to the item type, subject area and level. Potential factors include the attributes of the examinees, the nature of the items, item ordering, local item dependency and the test-taking experience of the student. Additionally there may be cognitive differences and different test-taking strategies adopted for each mode.

Policies and initiatives

While assessment technologies are now at a reasonable stage of maturity and available at a basic level through most universities' virtual learning environments (VLEs), take up has been minimal in all but a handful of UK institutions. Certain pioneering institutions and individuals have, however, invested heavily in the technologies, and various initiatives from the national funding councils and JISC have helped to develop the area.

One initiative regarded as having a significant impact was the HEFCE-funded Computer Assisted Assessment Centre project (Bull and Hesketh, 2001), led by Luton University. The Centre organised dissemination activities and produced a number of useful publications (e.g. Bull and McKenna, 2004). Recent national funding has been aimed at more practical and specific developments of tools, interoperability specifications and assessment content.

The Scottish Computer Assisted Assessment Network linked several Scottish universities from 1991 to 2001 and produced an interoperable format for assessment content. However, the community's focus then moved to the IMS Question and Test Interoperability (QTI) specification (IMS, 2005), which developed a common format to allow questions, tests and results to be exchanged between online assessment systems. Interoperability is important for transferring questions between systems and for practitioners who design questions within one tool and deliver tests in another.

Lay and Sclater (2001) identify two more reasons for e-assessment interoperability: first, to ensure that the item banks are accessible when current systems are no longer in use; and second, to permit student assessment data to be transferred to institutional student records systems. Another important driver for interoperability is to preserve users' investments in existing questions and tests when moving between institutions or to different e-assessment systems. The IMS Consortium's QTI specification is a valuable starting point, but clearly there is a need for further work. There is also little evidence that most e-assessment system vendors take interoperability seriously (Sclater et al., 2002).

In order to establish and embed the QTI specification, the Technologies for Online Interoperable Assessment (TOIA) project was funded by JISC to produce an assessment system based on QTI (Conole and Sclater, 2005). The system was made available freely to all UK higher and further education institutions. Meanwhile JISC's ambitious e-Framework for Education and Research funded a range of projects to develop various web services in the assessment domain. One project developed the web services to package and attach metadata to questions (SPAID, 2005); another developed marking services (APIS-MS, 2005); while a further one concentrated on delivering mathematical questions via web services (Serving Maths, 2005).

These are all part of the developing e-assessment domain mapped out by the Framework Reference Model for Assessment (FREMA) project (Millard *et al.*, 2005), also funded by JISC. FREMA developed two concept maps, one to do with the processes involved in e-assessment such as authoring items, quality assuring them, exchanging them with others, scheduling assessments, managing users, delivering asssessments to students, marking them and providing feedback. The other concept map concentrated on entities in the e-assessment domain. These were categorised as:

- *stakeholders* – all people and organisations involved in the e-assessment process
- *delivery context* – the environment in which candidates are assessed
- *infrastructure* – the associated institutional information systems relevant to assessment
- *pedagogical context* – the educational motivation for assessment
- *interaction type* – the question types available to learners
- the *roles* users have in the assessment process
- *specification* – the legislation, standards, specifications and guidelines relating to e-assessment
- *activity* – the techniques used to assess candidates
- the *data* relating to the assessment process
- the various *reports* available after an assessment or group of assessments.

Each one of these categories maps on to the relevant organisations and individuals involved, descriptions of the web services available, the software packages that implement them and the relevant standards and frameworks.

Item banks

Item banks are collections of questions, often produced collaboratively across a subject domain, that can be grouped according to difficulty, the type of skill or the topic. Security issues are particularly important with high-stakes assessments; use of larger pools is one strategy that can help deter cheating. Controlling item exposure and maintaining the security of item banks is likely to continue to be an active area of research and development.

While higher education continues to develop frameworks, software and services to facilitate e-assessment, a number of initiatives emerged in parallel to develop assessment content. Notable among these was the Electronics and Electrical Engineering Assessment Network (e3an, 2005) led by Southampton University and the COLEG OnLine Assessment project (Sclater and MacDonald, 2004), producing questions across the Scottish further education curriculum. Both of these projects put considerable effort into thinking about the types of questions that could be offered, the way in which they would be captured by question authors, the format in which they should be stored, and the metadata that needed to be captured along with the items to facilitate browsing, searching and retrieval.

While both projects made their questions available via the internet, they considered that questions would best be gathered using templates in Microsoft Word, then they used a separate software application to convert these to the IMS QTI format. The COLA project had a rare success with interoperability by enabling its items to be run in four separate VLEs and two assessment management systems. COLA also produced an application profile (Sclater, 2003) of IEEE's standard for Learning Object Metadata, which detailed the various metadata fields required for all the project's items and assessments. This document was in turn an input to the assessment-specific metadata defined in v2.0 of the QTI specification.

What both the e3an and the COLA projects produced was an embryonic item bank. There was, however, no appropriate type of repository in which to store these items and allow people to search for the items based on their metadata, try them out and then transfer them seamlessly to their local assessment systems. JISC therefore funded a further project, the Item Banks Infrastructure Study (Sclater, 2004), to examine a possible system of distributed item banks where organisations could purchase or exchange collections or *pools* of items from other institutions. The resulting report presents a comprehensive vision of a distributed item bank system for UK education. It examines the legal, service delivery, security, metadata, access and authentication issues surrounding such a system and presents a system requirements specification for a distributed item bank system. No such system yet exists and, despite the fact that many people feel it is pointless to replicate the development of assessment items in every university in the land, there is no evidence as yet of an emerging assessment item economy, let alone the long-predicted 'learning object economy'.

The ability of objective items to explore the limits of a participant's ability is developed by computer-adaptive testing (CAT). CAT involves issuing questions of a difficulty level that depends on the test-taker's previous responses. If a question is answered correctly, the estimate of their ability is raised and a more difficult question is presented and vice versa, giving the potential to test a wide range of student ability concisely. For instance, Lilley and Barker (2003) constructed an item bank of 119 peer-reviewed items and gave both 'traditional' (non-adaptive) and CAT tests to 133 students drawing on item response theory as a model. Students' results from the CAT test correlated well with their results from the traditional version and they did not consider the CAT test unfair. Because CAT items are written to test particular levels of ability they have the potential to deliver more accurate and reliable results than traditional tests.

Analysing e-assessment

One of the benefits of e-assessment is the opportunity to record student interactions and analyse these to provide a richer understanding of learning. A variety of analyses can be run to assess how well individual questions or students perform. Weak items can then be eliminated or teaching strategies adapted. Automatically recorded data can be used in a variety of ways, for example to look at the relationship between answering speed and accuracy. Care is needed, however, in interpreting results, for incorrect responses may indicate a more sophisticated understanding by the student than might at first appear; for example, unusual use of grammar in a foreign language test might be a result of higher cognitive understanding by the student.

Assessments need to be both valid and reliable. An advantage of e-assessment is that it offers consistency in marking. A range of methods is possible for scoring, from simple allocation of a mark to the correct response through to varied, compound and negative scoring. Two main methods are used for item statistics: Classical Test Theory (CTT) and Latent Trait Analysis (LTA) (Rasch analysis and Item Response Theory: IRT). The former is simpler and evaluates at the level of a test, whereas the latter looks at individual questions (McAlpine, 2002b). Boyle *et al.* (2002) explore the use of CTT, IRT and Rasch analysis with a set of 25 questions used by 350 test-takers. They conclude that the present approach by many practitioners of neglecting the rigorous quality assurance of items is untenable, and that this is particularly problematic for high-stakes assessment. Boyle and

There is a danger when we concentrate on the development of reliable methods and tools for summative assessment that we may miss two bedrock questions: Why should anyone *trust* our cumulative assessment that a new graduate is skilled, say, in 'communication'? How are people outside our departments to know what an upper second class degree *means* – what sort of performances and judgements does a judgement signify? The danger is that e-assessment experts may concentrate on the refinement of methods and tools. But what value is there in more exquisite tools if there is uncertainty about the final award or warrant to achievement – about its meaning and trustworthiness? Interestingly, these are issues that the on-line community has had to address in general terms. It would be timely to think about them in terms of the ways we warrant student achievement.

Peter Knight

O'Hare (2003) recommend that training in item construction and analysis should be obligatory for staff who are involved in developing CAA tests and that items should be peer-reviewed and trialled before use.

Cheating, however, can be reduced by proper invigilation, by interleaving participants taking different tests and by randomising item and response order (BSI, 2002). Other tactics include the use of item banks to present different but equivalent items to each candidate.

A code of practice for e-assessment (BSI, 2002) acknowledges that increased use of CAA 'has raised issues about the security and fairness of IT-delivered assessments, as well as resulting in a wide range of different practices'. The code aims to enhance the status of e-assessment and encourage use by demonstrating its fairness, security, authenticity and validity. However, the document's focus on the delivery of CAA tests could lead to the relative neglect of earlier stages in the preparation and quality assurance of assessments. As Boyle and O'Hare (2003) contend: 'A poor assessment, delivered appropriately, would [still] conform to [the standard].'

Scaling up e-assessment

A Roadmap for e-assessment

This chapter elucidates the benefits of e-assessment and clearly points to further research into text-based analysis of student responses. However, how do other experts working in this domain view the future? JISC commissioned a study to explore UK e-assessment activity and to produce a roadmap. Findings to date suggest that most experts expect e-assessment to make a significant contribution in providing quality and usage of assessment by 2010. They also believe, as champions in the field have shown, that the introduction of technological change can facilitate reflection upon old practice and encourage a significant revision of assessment tasks. It is policy pressure which is perceived as the main driver in the post-16 sector. The main driver at a super-institutional level is a move towards a new generation of self-reflective learners who will be able to identify their own learning needs. Both the post-16 and higher education sectors suggest the adoption of formative e-assessment can affect student retention, and changes in pedagogical practice have been noted when such systems are in place. However, there is a plea that current innovative practice should not be stifled by the introduction of VLEs. One way forward is to build more open source products that can be shared, improved and tested by large communities. Who knows where we will go from there?

Denise Whitelock

An obstacle to the uptake of CAA is that it is often implemented by individuals on an *ad hoc* basis with no overarching strategy or institutional IT infrastructure. This may delay or prevent embedding (Boyle and O'Hare, 2003; Bull, 2001). Bull (2001) asserts that: 'Retooling is a challenge which impacts on research and development, requiring a high level of resourcing for academic and support staff in order to maintain pace with technological and software developments.' The risks of small-scale development include practitioner isolation and underfunding, although one possible benefit is that practitioners are more in control of the process (Kennedy, 1998). Higher education institutions that are implementing e-assessment centrally encounter risks and benefits on a different scale. Scaling up for full-scale institutional deployment seems likely to depend more upon the resolution of cultural than technical issues. Bull (2001) points out that 'the organisational and pedagogical issues and challenges surrounding the take-up of CAA often outweigh the technical limitations of software and hardware'. This finding is mirrored in the issues associated with the uptake of other learning technologies (e.g. Seale, 2003).

Traditional assessment practices are now reasonably well understood. Even so, not all traditional assessments run smoothly. Many barriers and enablers for traditional assessment are also relevant to e-assessment. The emergence of e-assessment has forced the re-examination of these dormant issues in traditional practice. An argument for establishing good e-assessment practice at an institutional level is that it triggers the re-examination of assessment practice generally (Bull and McKenna, 2004).

Several approaches have been taken to identifying factors governing uptake. Stephens and Mascia (1997) conducted the first UK survey of CAA use in 1995, using a 10-item questionnaire that attracted 445 responses. They identified the need for institutional support (training and resourcing) allowing time to develop CAA tests, making CAA a fully integrated part of existing assessment procedures (rather than an afterthought) and subject-related dependencies. Important operational factors were familiarisation with the tools, well-planned procedures that addressed security and reliability issues, and involvement of support staff.

Warburton and Conole (2003) undertook a detailed survey of the barriers and enablers to the uptake of CAA. The greatest institutional barrier was seen to be cost, in terms of both personal time and the expense of commercial software. Unrealistic expectations coupled with inherent conservatism and lack of technical and pedagogic support were also cited. Respondents were less concerned with system integration, security or copyright issues. Another obstacle was the perceived steep learning curve associated with the technology and constructing specialised e-assessment question types. Of particular concern was the difficulty of constructing objective items that reliably assess higher-learning outcomes. There was a perceived credibility gap between what CAA proponents promise and what respondents thought could be delivered; lack of support, cultural resistance and technophobia were cited less often. Related issues about usability, academics working in isolation and individual inertia were also raised. Subject-specific shared question banks and the value of exemplars were cited as important drivers for the large-scale uptake of CAA, but the provision of 'evangelists' and adherence to institutional guidelines was thought less crucial. Academic commitment was cited as an important enabler; faculty support for CAA seems limited; external funding is the principal way in which support for CAA at this level is rendered. Other important factors included the need to embed CAA within normal teaching. Effective interoperability (particularly between CAA systems and VLEs) and integration of multimedia were also cited.

Conclusion

This chapter has provided a review of current activities in the design, delivery and analysis of online assessment (see Conole and Warburton, 2005 for a broader literature review). Many of the barriers and enablers to effective implementation mirror those found in the uptake and use of other learning technologies. However, e-assessment differs because it is perceived as being of higher risk and more central to the educational process.

There are valid objections to the use of e-assessment by distance learners as their sole method of assessment. However, as a tool for encouraging student engagement throughout a course or programme, for monitoring learning and identifying weaker students, and for reducing marking and administration, it has undeniable benefits. Because of its use in providing feedback to teachers on the progress of student learning it is probably the single most important aspect of e-learning that can assist in the social inclusion agenda.

There is a general shift across education from the assessment of products or outputs to assessing the processes of learning (Edwards, 1997). New e-assessment methodologies need to be developed to meet these requirements. Similarly, issues arise from the new forms of communication and collaboration that are now possible, and which form the core of many courses where the primary study medium is a web browser. How can we measure the quality of interactions that occur within an online discussion forum and attribute this in terms of student learning? What about those who don't contribute – 'the lurkers' – are they opting out or learning differently, for example vicariously, by reading and reflecting on the postings of others? How can student weblogs be exploited for self, peer and tutor assessment?

It has been argued in this chapter that there is a bias against e-assessment among some academics for two fundamental reasons: a perceived inability to address 'deep' learning; and concerns about the authentication of students. New technologies and examples of good practice will, however, help to reduce concerns about the inadequacies of automated marking in relation to human marking. Authentication issues can be alleviated to some extent with anti-plagiarism technologies but opportunities to cheat will always remain where assessments are unsupervised (as indeed they will under exam conditions). Combining the results of e-assessment with results obtained from traditional assessment methods rather than basing certification exclusively on e-assessment taken at a distance is probably the best way forward in most situations.

While commodification in other aspects of e-learning is argued elsewhere in this book to not always be beneficial, commodification of e-assessment might actually help to address some of the inadequacies of current assessment practice. Item bank case studies show that there are benefits in institutions combining efforts to produce questions that address similar aspects of their curricula. Initiatives to produce cross-institutional item banks can encourage the production of higher-quality assessments due to their facilitation of peer reviewing and the data accrued on how students answer the questions, which can in turn be used to refine the questions. A world where banks of extremely high-quality questions are bought and sold and continually refined might be a better one than the current *ad hoc* and opaque way in which assessment (leading to certification) is carried out. Perhaps most importantly, the processes of development and refinement of questions for e-assessment can lead academics to re-evaluate their production of other course content and their teaching practice, resulting in a closer focus on learning outcome and ultimately a more effective learning experience for the students.

Chapter 11

Academic literacy in the 21st century

*Bruce Ingraham, Phil Levy, Colleen McKenna
and George Roberts*

Introduction

While much has been published on the introduction of learning technologies into traditional teaching contexts and the impact of such interventions on learning, there seems to be much less work on what happens to reading and writing in such environments and the ways in which learning technologies more broadly in society are changing notions of what it means to be literate. This chapter will initially consider the terminology surrounding literacy in online environments and go on to interrogate some of the conflicting views and ideological assumptions of the concept 'literacy'; but we begin by simply asking: What does it mean to be literate?

On the one hand everyone knows what literacy is: reading and writing. But, a journey of a thousand miles begins with a single step. This aphorism is often repeated in contexts where uncertainty is impeding progress. The phrase is popularly attributed to Mao Zedong before the Long March. The 'journey of a thousand miles' is not just about getting started; it is about the return to 'wholeness'. The single step is the first imperfect human act that breaks the perfect whole and thus necessitates the journey. As we shall see, the single step is easy; the thousand-mile journey is not.

Nevertheless, the commonsense notion of reading and writing remains helpful in understanding the issue of what it means to be literate in the context of electronically mediated education. In this chapter we focus on higher education, but the implications are, of course, much wider. In the case of higher education, literacy has always meant more than the ability to read and write. For example, it presupposes the existence of higher-level skills of reading and writing – teaching readers to be more critical and writers more articulate. Higher education also presupposes that there are discipline-specific skills of reading and writing. The notion of 'reading for a degree' reflects this sense that the higher-level skills of reading (and writing) will vary from one discipline to another. It also reflects the degree to which the activity of reading is central to higher education. Still further, being literate at this level not only means possessing the skills of reading and writing pertinent to one's discipline, it also means having the necessary skills to identify appropriate materials for study.

However, while this view of literacy is still helpful, it is only a step on a journey that is increasingly complicated by other views of what may constitute literacy today. Furthermore, this journey crosses a shifting terrain where technologies and associated practices are constantly changing. It is perhaps indicative of this sense of flux that no single name or descriptive term for contemporary literacy has gained common currency nor is there complete agreement about what the terms currently in circulation mean. A number of words and phrases have emerged to describe reading and writing activities in online environments, particularly in higher education contexts. These include information literacy, digital literacy, electronic communication, computer literacy, transliteracy, information/IT skills, etc. Shetzer and Warschauer (2000) argue for the term 'electronic literacy', which they suggest encompasses notions of 'information literacy' (involving the capacity to locate, organise, interpret and use digital information) and computer-mediated communication, knowledge construction and research (McKenna, 2002).

However, one shortcoming in many accounts of literacy in online environments is that that they tend to view acts of communicating and interpreting as neutral and transferable, rather than practices that are inscribed by power dynamics of various types (McKenna, 2005) and which rely more on socially constructed relationships rather than technological affordances (Kress, 1998; Kress, 2003).

Partly in response to this, an area of research and practice that has grown up around more traditional notions of literacy in higher education is the academic literacies work. Initiated by Lea and Street (1998) and extended by Lea and Stierer (2000), Lillis (2001) and Ivanic et al. (1999) among others, this work is beginning to have a strong influence on the way in which writing is conceptualised in higher education. For the purposes of this chapter, it is useful both because it acknowledges reading and writing in online environments as increasingly part of 'literacy' practices in higher education and because it challenges the characterisation of writing as a remedial or transferable skill and instead adopts a 'writing as social practice' (Ivanic et al., 1999) position that sees writing as shaped by disciplinary norms, institutional power dynamics, impact of audience (especially the tutor/reader–student/writer relationship) and notions of identity (and the extent to which these can be legitimately expressed in academic writing), among others (see also Chapter 5).

In this chapter we address three specific aspects of the complex issues raised above: 'information literacy', 'non-print literacies', and 'literacy and authority' in which we will return to the question of how changes in both what we choose to read and how we read may lead to fundamental changes in our understanding of authoritative scholarship. This focus reflects our view that the notion of reading critically provides a key to understanding what it means to be literate at least in the context of higher education.

Information literacy

The term 'information literacy' is currently gaining wider currency within higher education. Whether one sees information literacy as encompassing, or as encompassed by, other literacies depends on perspective. Concepts of digital literacy, cyberliteracy, electronic literacy and so on are specifically associated with technology-mediated textual, communicative and informational practices. When the focus is on interaction with digital information, information literacy then may be identified as one dimension of a larger framework: hence, Shetzer and Warshauer (2000) suggest that information literacy can be seen as one element in the broader domain of electronic literacy. Similarly, Martin (2003) suggests the term 'e-literacy' to describe an integrated form of IT literacy and information literacy. However, when the focus is on interaction with information irrespective of medium, information literacy itself may be seen as a meta-literacy that in the networked environment embraces a range of other literacies (e.g. Eisenberg et al., 2004). As defined from the perspective of information science and information professionals, information literacy refers to the capacity to find and use information in any given context, through any medium. In other words, it is applied equally to interactions with digital, print-based or human information sources.

Nevertheless, rapid and intensive developments in digital information sources and services over recent years have particular implications for information literacy development. This is not least the case in higher education, where there is increasing technological convergence between the environment for learning and teaching, and the environment for information access, use and communication. In such a context, much information use is digital information use, for purposes that include the sharing and re-use of digital learning resources and designs in virtual learning environments and repositories (Littlejohn, 2005) as well as interaction with primary and secondary sources accessed via digital

Judith Peacock (2005) offered a rallying cry from the Australian perspective, examining 'Information Literacy education in practice'. Describing the current battle over teaching and learning between pedagogists and technologists, she sees librarians as holding 'an enviable position in the conflict' (p. 154). Peacock argues that information literacy is crucial and citing Alan Bundy maintains that 'in a teaching world gone technologically mad, librarians can provide a balanced and discriminating view of the place of ICT in education'. She illustrates her points with a case study from Queensland University of Technology, but is clear that 'it is not enough ... to stand out and challenge old paradigms; they [librarians] must offer solutions and create new perceptions of information literacy education' (p. 177).

Jane Secker

libraries and collections. In this changing environment there are information literacy challenges for both students and academic staff. In particular, research in the UK and elsewhere has revealed significant limitations in students' understandings and skills in this respect (e.g. Armstrong, 2001; Rowley, 2002), attesting, for example, to the 'Googling' phenomenon whereby the search engine is the preferred means of locating academic information rather than an academic resource (Brophy *et al.*, 2004).

In the light of these considerations, there is currently a great deal of interest and activity in the academic information community in further promoting information literacy as a concept and in developing services and strategies to better support students' (and academics') information literacy development. Interest in this area is also beginning to grow in the wider educational field and in particular those interested in e-learning (e.g. Smith and Oliver, 2005), as well as an interest in promoting pedagogies that are based on active learning. For example, the Centre for Inquiry-based Learning in the Arts and Social Sciences (CILASS) based at the University of Sheffield identifies information literacy as an essential prerequisite for effective inquiry-based learning in the networked environment, and is taking forward a programme of pedagogical development and research in this area.

Definitions and standards

The roots of information science conceptions of information literacy can be traced to the 1970s, when the term was first used as a means of drawing attention to capabilities associated with participation in the information society. Since then, there has been growing international recognition of information literacy as a far-reaching economic and democratic, as well as educational, issue (e.g. Candy, 2004; Virkus, 2003; Kahn and Kellner, 2005). The ability to interact productively with information in a wide variety of formats is seen as not just important but vital for the achievement of personal, occupational, educational and societal goals (IFLA, 2005). Thus, a UNESCO-sponsored initiative summarises information literacy as follows:

> Information literacy encompasses knowledge of one's information concerns and needs, and the ability to identify, locate, evaluate, organize and effectively create, use and communicate information to address issues or problems at hand; it is a prerequisite for participating effectively in the information society, and is part of the basic human right of lifelong learning.
>
> (US National Commission on Library and Information Science, 2003)

Since the mid-1990s in particular, numerous definitions and detailed enumerations of the capabilities involved in information literacy have been put forward, many sharing a view of a number of 'core' process elements: recognising and defining an information need; locating and selecting sources; selecting and extracting information; organising and synthesising information; presenting and communicating information; and evaluating the outcome (Williams, 2005). At the same time, current definitions increasingly reflect a concern to move beyond a behaviourist, 'key skills' view of information literacy. Rather than seeing information literacy as solely a performative matter of acquiring information processing skills, a more holistic, developmental view is emerging that accords it a key role in the development of criticality and social responsibility, and in the creation and sharing of knowledge. New definitions thus tend to place greater emphasis on capabilities associated with higher-order cognition, and on values and attitudes associated with creative, responsible and ethical engagement with information. This trend suggests a need to extend beyond the existing emphasis in many practical information literacy programmes in higher education on skills associated with retrieval, evaluation and citation of information sources, important though these are.

The American Association of College and Research Libraries' Standards for the Information Literate Student (ACRL, 2000) and the Australian and New Zealand Information Literacy Framework (Bundy, 2004) are examples of particularly influential international contributions to redefining information literacy, and to establishing information literacy standards for higher education. In the UK, a consultation exercise undertaken in 1999 by the Society of College, National and University Libraries (SCONUL) led to the development of a conceptual framework – the '7 Pillars' model – that proposes learning outcomes for information literacy for UK higher education graduates (SCONUL, 1999). The model distinguishes information literacy from basic library and IT skills, and proposes a five-stage progression from novice to expert capability in seven areas, ranging from 'the ability to recognise an information need' to 'the ability to synthesise and build upon existing information, contributing to the creation of new knowledge'. It offers a tool for assessing information literacy development and support needs at the level of institutions, disciplines or programmes, and for designing information literacy curricula and performance measures.

A socio-cultural view and implications

Models and standards such as those mentioned in the previous section reflect an expanding perspective on information literacy. At the same time, as noted by Johnson and Webber (2003) and Williams (2005), they are open to critique in so far as they may continue to promote a 'tick-box' conception of information literacy capabilities and to reinforce the library and information science tradition of presenting (and teaching) information literacy as a generic phenomenon, independent of context. Another way of looking at information literacy is to see it not as a set of generic capabilities but, like any literacy, as a fundamentally situated and contextualised social process or practice (which aligns closely with the position expressed in Chapter 6 on learning theories). From a socio-cultural perspective, 'literacies are bound up with social, institutional and cultural relationships, and can only be understood when they are situated in their social, cultural and historical contexts. Moreover, they are always connected to social identities – to being particular kinds of people' (Lankshear and Knoble, 2003: 8).

From this point of view, it may be hypothesised that information literacy will be understood differently, and will take different forms, within differing communities of practice (Wenger, 1998) and in relation to differing conceptions of learning and teaching. That this is the case in higher education is borne out by the findings of a small but growing body of phenomenographic and other research that has begun to illuminate multiple ways in which information literacy is understood by academic staff and students in different disciplines, and the diverse nature of information behaviour within these contexts (e.g. Bruce, 1997; Smith and Oliver, 2005; Webber and Johnston, 2004). For example, varying conceptions held by higher education staff in Bruce's (1997) study were based on viewing information literacy primarily as using ICT, information sources, information-processing in relation to problem-solving and decision-making, controlling information, creating personal knowledge, extending knowledge or using information wisely for the benefit of others. Studies such as this suggest that strategies for both understanding and developing information literacy in higher education need to engage more deeply than is generally the case with the experience and practice of learning, teaching, scholarship and research within different disciplinary cultures and communities.

The socio-cultural view has implications for the further development of pedagogical practice. In particular, the view that higher education learning is a process of developing an identity as a member of a disciplinary community of practice implies the need for a 'situated' dimension to pedagogical design for information literacy (Smith and Oliver, 2005). Historically, primary responsibility for information literacy development in higher education has been the preserve of academic librarians rather than academic staff. Nonetheless, discipline-based integration has for many years been espoused by the academic information community as a pedagogical ideal. In practice, however, there have often been limited opportunities for librarians to provide much more than 'bolt-on' approaches to information literacy support and tuition. This situation is currently undergoing some change in many institutions, with the aim of integrating information literacy education more systematically and explicitly with the subject curriculum, leading to enhanced pedagogical collaborations between information professionals and subject experts (e.g. Freeman and Parker, 2004).

However, functional integration of information literacy teaching into the subject curriculum does not necessarily equate with 'situatedness' in terms of pedagogical approach and outcome. Whether delivered in stand-alone mode or embedded into subject curricula, approaches to information literacy support and teaching by information professionals have tended to reflect the assumptions of a generic (essentially librarian-centric) perspective on information literacy. Making this point, Williams (2005) suggests that 'integration' should be interpreted as meaning 'integration with the learner experience'. Her argument is for an information literacy pedagogy – whether stand-alone or discipline-embedded – that is grounded in close engagement with the ways in which learners conceptualise and experience their interactions with information in specific contexts, and that encourages critical reflection on differing approaches and views. From this perspective, the role of the educational designer and tutor (whether librarian or other) shifts away from direct instruction towards strategies that will facilitate those dialogical interactions between learner and tutor, and between learners, that are at the heart of constructivist and relational pedagogies.

Non-print literacies

The social 'situatedness' of the learner–tutor relationship extends beyond membership in a discipline community. Education is situated in the wider cultural community and that wider community offers information resources in many media other than print. Since the advent of printing, academic literacy skills have been focused around the reading and writing of 'printable' texts. Printed paper provided the primary means for the dissemination of literate scholarship and became the primary medium of academic communication. Even though scholarly discourse is also conducted in various face-to-face media (lectures, seminars, etc.), it is through printed books and articles that scholarly activity has been largely valorised (Ingraham, 2000). Of course, this was also largely true for the publication of non-academic information as well. Printed paper is/was the medium of popular fiction, magazines, newspapers, etc. However, for at least the last 150 years, the hegemony of printed paper has been increasingly challenged by other media (photography, sound recording, film, television, etc.). Certainly outside the scholarly arena, media such as film and television seriously challenge printed paper as the dominant means of information dissemination (Ong, 1982).

The advent of multimedia computing in the 1990s made all of these media readily available to scholarship and with that came a challenge as to how best to use this material (Ingraham, 2000; Ingraham, 2005a; Ingraham, 2005b). Essentially, this represents a challenge to academia's recognised definition of literacy. The 'new' media offer academia the opportunity not only to study evidence presented in media other than print, but also the opportunity to include such evidence in its discourse. Still further, the power of contemporary computing makes it realistic to begin creating scholarly documents in media other than print. However, if academics are to exploit this potential, they must learn both to read and to write in multiple and/or other media (c.f. Scollon, 1998; Levine and Scollon, 2004). They must develop the higher-level literacy skills of each medium that they use. For example, they must learn to analyse and understand the significance of visual images (still or moving) with the same degree of care that they would a printed argument and the old saying that 'a picture is worth a thousand words' should serve as warning of just how complex this task may be.

Case Study

'I can almost see the lights of home' (Hardy and Portelli, 1999) is one of very few examples of a fully featured scholarly article presented primarily through a medium other than print. It is an essay in music history presented in what is essentially the format of a radio documentary. By adopting this format the authors, at least implicitly, acknowledge that for music historians, if not musicologists, actually hearing the music under examination must positively contribute to the force of their arguments. 'I can almost see the lights of home' differs from a conventional radio documentary in three important ways:

- It is controllable by the 'auditor' – paused, rewound, etc.
- The discourse is conducted at a level of scholarship that in no sense 'popularises' the subject matter even though the particular subject might lend itself to such a presentation.
- The audio essay is accompanied by a full transcript through which the full panoply of scholarly referencing, etc. can be accessed.

Perhaps this transcript slightly undermines the claim that the essay is primarily mediated other than through text, but as evidenced by the increasing number of audio-enhanced PowerPoint presentations appearing as learning resources, it is easy to see how references and so forth could be displayed simultaneously with an audio or video stream that acted as the primary carrier medium.

Similarly, as academics begin to include evidence in media other than print or to construct their discourse in alternative media, they must understand how to 'write' articulately in those media. They must learn how to create convincing arguments using the techniques of a particular medium or combination of media. Ingraham (2005b), for example, examined television documentary as a possible model for the structure of multimedia academic discourse. In this particular case it was recognised that a filmic (not to mention melodramatic) narrative could be key to structuring an educational discourse. The point being not that narrative, or even the melodrama, should be excluded from the discourse, but rather that it had to be understood and used purposefully if it were to be used 'literately'.

However, contemporary technology not only provides access to 'new' media, it also has profound implications for text itself. Even very traditional academic discourse conducted through printable text may be better disseminated electronically (Ingraham, 2005b), but if so there will be significant design changes required to make such text readable and accessible (see also Chapter 8). Still further, the advent of hypertext challenges academia to reconsider in very complex ways the whole question of reading and writing text (c.f. Bolter, 2001; Burbules, 1998; Kolb, 1997; Kolb, 2000; Landow, 1997). Even at what one might see as the most trivial level the primary tools of writing are increasingly not pens, pencils and paper, but word processors, html editors, and, ironically perhaps, the resurrection of the stylus and tablet (PC). Couple to this postmodernism's concern with reading as a 'writerly' activity through which individual readers 'inscribe' (Foucault, 1977) their own meaning in the traces (Derrida, 1974) left on the page or screen, and, as we shall see at the end of the chapter, it is evident that the technology is placing new and greater demands on the literacy of both readers and writers in identifying both the limits of critical interpretation (Eco, 1990) and the articulation of evidence that lies at the heart of scholarly activity.

Finally, the sheer volume of information available in all these media further complicates the problem of needing multiple literacies to deal with the variety of media now available. The advent of the internet has provided access to so much and such varied information that the task of managing that in a critical and 'literate' manner has become almost insurmountable. For Eco (2001),

> It is the fundamental problem of the web. The whole of the history of culture has consisted in the establishment of filters. Culture transmits memory, but not all memory: it filters ... Moreover, the filters we resort to result from our having trusted what we call 'the community of learning' that, throughout the centuries, through debate and discussion, gives the guarantee, if anything else, that the filtering is reasonable ...

Perhaps unsurprisingly for a medievalist, Eco's remark retains the locus of power that has typified the essentially medieval apprenticeship system (Ingraham and Ingraham, 2006) that has dominated academia for the last 600 years as one generation of authorities trained the next. Certainly academia will have to generate filters with which to deal with the information resources available to it, but it is by no means clear that existing print-oriented filters are appropriate to the task. Indeed, it is far more likely that the process of discussion and debate will lead to radically different filters than are currently being applied. Still further, the 'web' also opens the discussion and debate to a potentially wider audience and it is by no means certain that the locus of authority for the process of filtering will remain where it is. As responsibility for meaning becomes more clearly situated in the wider arena of debate and discussion, so the locus of an authority of the 'community of learning' may become situated in a wider and more genuinely democratised community of the electronically literate.

Literacy and authority: a journey of a thousand miles

At the beginning of the chapter we noted that in Daoist thought the journey of a thousand miles is a return to wholeness. The story of Adam and Eve is an analogue. The single step is the temptation and fall; the journey is the search for redemption. The fragmenting of wholeness into a myriad of parts and the search for a new whole bring us to the problem of literacy, ideology and authority, manifested in part in the debate over multi-literacies. There is a perceptible divide between those who speak of multiple literacies and those who prefer to retain the term 'literacy' for its most commonsense and etymological core meaning of reading and writing using a restricted set of technologies (natural language, traditional alphabets and more or less traditional implements: pens and pencils, paper and – probably ducking the implications these days – keyboards and word processors). Although Kress argues that there is no need to make literacy plural because 'it is a normal and fundamental characteristic of language and literacy to be constantly remade in relation to the needs of the moment' (Kress, 1997), the step from literacy to literacies is easy.

As we have seen, there are many ways of making and communicating meaning in the world today. While there may well be some primacy given to speaking, listening, reading and writing, there are so many contexts, genres, media, representations and modes of communication that it can be an aid to understanding to break them down into convenient categories and address each category separately. But the journey back to one whole literacy is hard. The path is full of obstacles, for literacy is highly politicised in our world: 'a visiting Martian might be surprised at the extent to which arcane debates about literacy, language and learning appear in the public domain in contemporary British and American society' (Street, 1997). But literacy is, and arguably always has been (see, for example, Godman, 1990), tightly bound together with belief systems, senses of identity, power and authority (c.f. Chapter 2). It is perhaps best understood if we see literacy as the original human technology, the technology that makes all other technologies possible and, fundamentally, the original source of all human power.

Abstractions have equal weight in discourse as concrete things (Holquist, 1997). More importantly, abstractions are artefacts of technology. The technology for handling symbolic systems is as important as that for handling concrete artefacts. With the development of narrative technique and the *aides memoires* of oral poetics, language became technologised. This technologisation of language has proceeded rapidly, producing many tools for the ordering of symbolic systems, from call and response singing to income tax forms. For Fairclough (2001), these technologies are the means by which bureaucracies shape and order discourse for the perpetuation or extension of control. Information and communication technology has greatly extended the reach of discourse technologies. However, if we are to return to one 'whole' literacy, whose or what literacy would it be? Fairclough puts language at the centre of today's globalised political economics:

> Language is doubly involved in the struggle to impose the new neo-liberal order. First, the new ways of being and acting entailed are partly new ways of using language. Second, an important part of imposing the new order is winning acceptance for particular representations of change. And struggles against the new order resist both new ways of using language and new representations.
>
> (Fairclough, 2001)

Discourses on globalisation are typically oriented in one of two ways. One posits globalisation as an inevitable part of the historical process over which we have no control but to which we must adapt or be swept aside, while the other asserts that globalisation is the aim or result of consciously implemented policies promoted by those who most benefit from globalisation. It is a characteristic of the education and employment debate that globalisation is presented as inevitable. According to Esland (1996a; 1996b), if globalisation is accepted as an inevitable part of the historical process then there is little that a nation can do to plan its internal economics. As Carnoy (1997) suggests, all the state can do is best prepare individuals to operate within a paradigm, a paradigm where the education system can be understood 'as a field of competition for the legitimate exercise of symbolic violence', that is, a locus of conflict between rival principles of legitimacy and competition for the power to grant cultural consecration (Bourdieu, 1993: 121).

Hoggart provides a detailed and affecting account of the effects of popular literature, made available through near-universal literacy, on working-class attitudes in the 1950s, but neglects the purposeful intent behind the sedating, valuelessness of 'reading cut off from any serious suggestion of responsibility and commitment' (Hoggart 1958: 232). As is implicit in Eco's view, literacy and the teaching of literacy is a system for reproducing actors who are both producers of certain cultural goods as well as consumers of those goods. As with all social practice, learning participates in the ongoing discourses of emancipation and subordination. Through learning technologies the frontiers of education are made extremely permeable, and the most disputed frontier is the one that separates education from the field of power; 'the boundary of the field is a stake of struggles' (Bourdieu, 1993: 42). As Freire puts it:

> Dialogue is the encounter between men, mediated by the world, in order to name the world. Hence dialogue cannot occur between those who want to name the world and those who do not wish this naming – between those who deny others the right to speak their word and those whose right to speak has been denied them. Those who have been denied their primordial right to speak their word must first reclaim this right and prevent the continuation of this dehumanizing aggression.

> (Freire, 1996)

According to Jones:

> The critics of computer literacy accuse educators of buying into the notion that computers are an inexorable condition of the future ... and accepting the concomitant notion that the majority of the population have no control over shaping this force. ... The deeper criticism that is offered in answer is that there seems to be little conflict between the widely accepted goals of education – the development of 'concrete-operational skills of technical reason coupled with functional, utilitarian language skills' ... – and computer use –

cost cutting in educational institutions by the institutionalization of the computer as *deus ex machina*, coming to solve the difficulties education faces, usually through CAI activities instead of human teachers.

(Jones, 1991)

Educational policy has encouraged the adoption of an instrumentalist, competency-based curriculum intended to be closely aligned to the needs of industry. This has been presented as a solution to relative economic decline in the face of 'inevitable' globalisation (Field, 1995). The positivist rigour of competency frameworks makes them uniquely suited as components of technology-assisted learning programmes, which in turn lend themselves readily to a managerial agenda. Technology-assisted learning also supports the move to an administered market in education (c.f. Ranson, 1994). By increasing the granularity of 'education consumables' learners are able to buy ever-smaller 'chunks' (DfEE, 1999: 66). The impact of policy on practice is discused in more detail in Chapter 3.

But how are we to understand, to read, what we buy? Taylor (1993) addresses key issues of critical theory. 'Society', says Taylor, 'requires literacy (which is literacy rather than a literate person) because in the power–knowledge relationship of the modern world, literacy defines who controls the means of production, that is the means to produce wealth (industry) and the means to reproduce knowledge (education)' (Taylor, 1993: 139). Education policies adopted by successive British governments in response to globalisation have been focused in two conflicting directions: the desire to stimulate the growth of autonomous, entrepreneurial, IT-literate, multi-skilled individuals capable of creating and taking advantage of the opportunities inherent in a post-Fordist economy; and the desire to create a compliant, low-expectation labour force inured to the demands of flexibilisation in order to attract inward investment not on the basis of high skills available but on the basis of low costs.

Taylor goes on to say: 'If this is true, then the very nature of literacy has changed and we are forced to consider the possibility that literacy cannot combat oppression, precisely because it is literacy which gives Oppression its voice' (Taylor, 1993: 139). What, then, can be a different literacy – a literacy of liberation? Taylor distinguishes between the literacy of reading, which 'creates the possibility of consensus or convergence ... [that] educate[s] the citizen into orthodoxy, into that governability, even that vulnerability to governance and to media and myth, which are the signs of an "educated person"', and the literacy of writing that 'raises ... the possibility that something can be "said against" ... it is the creating of a response which is counter-hegemonic ... fundamentally iconoclastic ... that encourages heresy, even deviance ...' (Taylor, 1993: 146). But he only touches on the problem at the heart of writing. He says: 'The paradox of writing, which is one of the most refined symbolic systems created by humankind, is that it has the power to be anti-symbolic ...'. He doesn't explore this dilemma. But Kristeva (1989: 23–30) does, introducing a discussion of the characteristics of writing by stating that 'current science has not yet proposed a satisfactory theory of writing'. For Kristeva, 'writing is an act of differentiation and of participation with respect to reality ...'. She illustrates the inadequate state of writing theory and observes: 'The science of writing seems therefore the prisoner of a conception that confuses language with spoken language, which is articulated according to the rules of a certain grammar.' She concludes:

> In our time, under the influence of philosophical research and the knowledge of the logic of the unconscious, some researchers consider the various types of writings as languages that don't necessarily 'need' 'phonic expression' ... They thus represent particular signifying practices that have disappeared or been transformed in the life of modern man. The science of writing as a new realm ... of linguistic operation; of writing as language, but not as vocal speech or grammatical chain; of writing as a specific signifying practice that enables us to perceive unknown regions in the vast universe of language – this science of writing has yet to be developed.
>
> (Kristeva, 1989: 30)

This is the science of writing we need in order to discover Taylor's anti-symbolic, iconoclastic writing-as-liberation, and, arguably, also to engage through learning technology with literacy in its widest sense. As Fairclough says:

> I am not suggesting that power is *just* a matter of language. There is always a danger in focussing upon one aspect of a social relation or process, of being tempted to reduce it to that aspect alone ... Power exists in various modalities.
>
> (Fairclough, 2001).

But, as Jones has observed:

> Given the power that the market exerts in the daily lives of people in the US, if someone has something to sell and it necessitates the use of a computer to sell it, someone will create a software and hardware package that makes it possible to sell that product to the functionally illiterate. A good example of this is the 'Lotto' machines of the California State Lottery. Anyone with the most rudimentary reading skills can buy all the Lotto tickets they want. Given that 'citizens' are really more consumers of politics than they are participants in political process means that they are in the same camp as consumers of goods when it comes to worrying about their computer literacy.
>
> (Jones, 1991)

We are still fragmented, at the beginning of our thousand-mile journey, but to understand that beginning is, perhaps, the first step back. Literacy in its broadest sense, 'constantly remade in relation to the needs of the moment' (Kress, 1997), is the source of human power. The harnessing of that power provides the means of both oppression and liberation; the means to be told and the means to tell; the means to bring our world into existence and to defend it. Ultimately literacy in this widest sense is the means by which we define ourselves and our communities. It is in this sense that computer literacy, media literacy, information literacy, academic literacy, visual literacy and all the multi-literacies begin to re-unite through discourse technologies and communication, back to the whole of signifying practice in the vast universe of language.

Chapter 12

Collaboration

Chris Jones, John Cook, Ann Jones and Maarten De Laat

Introduction

This chapter explores one of the most central terms used in relation to online and networked learning: collaboration. The term is closely associated with a wide range of social and situated theories of learning and this review can provide only a brief introduction to what can be a complex area. An underlying assumption made here is that it is unproductive to search for one correct definition of collaboration; rather we need to understand how collaboration is used in current debates about education, learning and new digital technologies.

Our account of the usage of the term collaboration begins by examining how two closely associated terms – cooperation and collaboration – have been used and trying to draw out what might be thought of as family resemblances in these terms (Wittgenstein, 2001). The definitions of these terms have often overlapped. In a review of the literature on cooperative learning and peer tutoring, Topping defined cooperation by studying its roots.

> CO- means together in company, jointly, in common, equally, mutually, reciprocally, while -OPERATE means to work, act, influence, effect, accomplish, cause or carry out.
>
> (Topping, 1992: 151)

At about the same time Kaye defined collaborate in a remarkably similar way.

> Etymologically, to collaborate (co-labore) means work together, which implies a concept of shared goals, and an explicit attempt to 'add value' – to create something new or different through the collaboration as opposed to simply exchanging information or passing instructions.
>
> (Kaye, 1992: 2)

In as far as a distinction between the two terms can be maintained, cooperate has been applied more to a division of labour in which individuals achieve their aims by mutual assistance, whereas collaborate has implied a stronger commitment to joint aims as well as mutual assistance. Readers may prefer to use the terms largely inter-changeably, as we do in this chapter, or keep them separate (e.g. Crook, 1994; Lehtinen *et al.*, 1999). The important point for researchers and users is that, like many other factors discussed in this book in relation to e-learning, the terms cannot be defined clearly and reliably and much of their meaning relies on current usage (see, for example, Chapter 2 and the discussion in Chapter 7 on folksonomies).

A further factor used to distinguish between the two approaches has been the role of a person in authority. McConnell argues that cooperative learning situa-tions can be divided between those where an external authority, usually the teacher, enforces cooperation by structure and rewards, and those where the learn-ers choose cooperation without external intervention (McConnell, 2000: 7). He uses this basic distinction to summarise two views of cooperative learning posed as opposite ends of a spectrum. Each view is composed of a number of dimen-sions including structure, teacher control, moderation of learning, learner motivation, learning content, and assessment. At one end of the spectrum McConnell places the view found 'in the cooperative learning movement in com-pulsory school education in the USA and Israel' (McConnell, 2000: 16).

This view is at the 'external authority' end of the spectrum in which 'coopera-tion is structured and policed by a teacher' (ibid.: 21). Two reviews of theory and research from the early 1990s are examples of this school of thought (Slavin, 1990; Sharan, 1990).

At the other end, McConnell places the practice of liberal school education more prevalent in the UK. He characterised the UK approach as: 'problem or issue based. Learners learn through intrinsic motivation and rewards are largely intrinsic. There is little if any "policing" by a teacher or tutor' (McConnell, 2000: 19).

Topping (1992) also noted that some UK teachers would find the stress on team competition and individual accountability found in the US model alien, comment-ing that: 'British approaches, whilst warm, fuzzy and comfortable, demonstrate an organisational looseness bordering on chaos' (Topping, 1992: 153).

Cowie noted that such chaotic organisation could be found on both sides of the Atlantic (Cowie, 1992). Generally cooperation is more often used where the organisation of a group and its tasks is determined by a tutor, teacher or modera-tor who has some structural basis for their authority whereas, in this usage, collaboration identifies group work amongst peers with little or no direction from someone in a position of power. It should be clear how difficult this can be to apply in an educational setting in which grading and assessment are key drivers. Power is never fully absent and the distinction is not an absolute one. For recent empirical studies that cast light on these issues by examining peer and collabora-tive assessment, see Trehan and Reynolds (2002) and Hodgson (2005).

The area of cooperative or collaborative learning set out in the early 1990s has not been clarified by more recent discussion. One of the most quoted attempts to clarify usage has been that of Dillenbourg, who set out to provide a common frame-work for collaboration (1999). First he provided a simple definition of collaboration, which he then elaborated by developing a variety of meanings organised into four

One aspect of collaborative learning not addressed in this chapter is assessment. Assessment processes act to inform students of what is important to learn and what is not (e.g. see McConnell, 2006). Collaborative assessment is particularly important in the context of e-learning communities, where an ethos of collaboration and cooperation exists. In this context, the expectation is for students to engage in helping each other develop, review and assess each other's course work. It is the collaborative learning and assessment process itself that signals to the students what form of learning is expected of them (McConnell, 2002). In using collaborative learning, practitioners should consider the importance of assessment processes. We need to help students and teachers understand what collaborative learning is, why it is important and why it is being used in any particular circumstance. We need to help them understand the potential benefits to learning of collaboration. Students and teachers should be provided with opportunities for the development of collaborative learning skills, and for gaining understandings of cognitive and emotional development in group processes related to collaborative learning. An understanding of the dynamics of collaborative learning is important for students to be able to participate in group-work and 'survive' the experience. We need to provide an appropriate context for collaboration to take place. Collaborative learning has to be integrated into learning in ways that are meaningful and that are clearly understood by students. Learning environments have to be designed as part of this wider context. Reward systems that support and sustain collaborative efforts, and which allow students to take control of rewards to a large degree, have to be provided. These may include *intrinsic reward systems*, in which students play an active part in developing criteria for judging their own and each other's participation in the collaborative learning process. Assessment has to include some self–peer–tutor (collaborative) processes aimed at motivating students and ensuring their participation in the collaborative learning processes. Also included are *extrinsic reward systems*, such as institutional assessment processes or assessment systems imposed by teachers: these have to be designed in ways that support collaboration and which indicate to students that their collaborative efforts will be seriously taken into consideration. Power and control are at the heart of reward systems. Teachers have to withdraw (some of) their power as unilateral assessors in order to allow students to practise collaborative learning. By practice, I mean students' ability to live with and learn from collaboration and to take a high degree of control of the collaborative learning process, including making judgements about its intentions, processes and outcomes.

David McConnell

aspects of learning. The simple definition of collaborative learning that Dillenbourg began with was: 'a *situation* in which *two or more* people *learn* or attempt to learn something *together*' (Dillenbourg, 1999: 2 – emphasis in original).

Dillenbourg noted at the outset that each of the italicised terms in this definition can be interpreted differently, and went on to identify four aspects of learning related to collaboration (which have parallels with the definitions given in Chapter 7) and how each one of these is problematic in its own right:

- The situation – which can be characterised as more or less collaborative.
- The interactions – between pairs or in groups, which can be more or less collaborative.
- The mechanisms – claiming that some mechanisms are more intrinsically collaborative.
- The measurement of effects.

(adapted from Dillenbourg, 1999: 9)

Despite Dillenbourg's best efforts, the idea of collaborative learning is still unclear and indeed his clarification can be seen as being located within one tradition of collaborative learning. Dillenbourg's explicit aim was to bring together research from psychology and computer science, an aim not related to social and situated accounts of learning. Collaborative learning has another large source constituency, one that derives its strength from a social critique of cognition and is related to the cultural turn in the social sciences (Jameson, 1998).

Social and situated views of learning have no single source but organise around a set of complementary and contending theories. This is discussed in more detail in Chapter 6. An accessible introduction to these theories can be found in Lea and Nicoll (2002). Perhaps the most commonly referenced sources include:

- Socio-cultural theories – originating in the early Soviet theorist Vygotsky, who popularised the idea of Zone of Proximal Development (ZPD) and the idea that learning was a process of internalisation of practices emerging in the social and material world. The key idea from this school in relation to new technologies was that of a cultural tool and the mediating role given to material and cultural artefacts in learning.

  The inclusion of a tool in the process of behaviour (a) introduces several new functions connected with the use of the given tool and with its control; (b) abolishes and makes unnecessary several natural processes, whose work is accomplished by the tool; and alters the course and individual features (the intensity, duration, sequence, etc.) of all the mental processes that enter into the composition of the instrumental act, replacing some functions with others (i.e., it re-creates and reorganizes the whole structure of behaviour just as a technical tool re-creates the whole structure of labour operations).

(Vygotsky, 1986: 139–40)

There has been a growth from this root of a number of theories applied to learning, including cultural historical activity theory (CHAT) (Engeström, 1987; Cole, 1996) and activity theory (Nardi, 1996).

- Situated learning – emerging from an anthropological approach and most closely associated with the work of Lave and Wenger (1991) and the idea of apprenticeship or more generally legitimate peripheral participation. This set of theories can also be traced back to a foundational article by Brown *et al.* (1989). It has developed in a number of ways, most notably in Wenger's idea of Communities of Practice (CoPs):

     Being alive as human beings means that we are constantly engaging in the pursuit of enterprises of all kinds, from ensuring our physical survival to seeking the most lofty pleasures. As we define these enterprises and engage in their pursuit together, we interact with each other and with the world and we tune our relations with each other and with the words accordingly. In other words we learn. Over time, this collective learning results in practices that reflect both the pursuit of our enterprise and the attendant social relations. These practices are thus the property of a kind of community created over time by the sustained pursuit of a shared enterprise. It makes sense, therefore, to call these kinds of communities *communities of practice.*

     (Wenger, 1998: 45)

- Distributed cognition – most associated with the work of Hutchins, this bridging theory sets out a claim that cognition is not a localised individual phenomena but rather it is best understood as distributed across individuals, artefacts and representations (Salomon, 1993; Hutchins, 1995).
- Social constructivism – constructivism has a long history in educational theory and has been strongly associated with Piaget. Constructivism stresses the active role of knowledge construction and can take an individual or social form. For Piaget, though it is often associated with individual approaches, peer interaction was a key activity and for Piaget and those influenced by him the role of conflict both within the individual and between individuals was an important process in learning (Doise and Mugny, 1984; Dillenbourg, 1999). Social constructivism provides another link to the ideas of Vygotsky.

As was noted above, the development of social and situated views of learning is closely related to what has been called the cultural turn in the social sciences (Jameson, 1998). The key feature of this re-orientation of the social sciences has been the central focus on social and cultural factors rather than the individual and their psychology or the biological bases of learning, factors that were strongly emphasised in behaviourist and cognitivist theories of learning. The above list of social and situated theories could be organised in a variety of different ways and a search on any one of these terms will often yield overlaps in authors and central ideas. The key point is that collaborative learning is loosely related to a broader set of ideas that emphasises a distinctively social and situated approach to learning, a point echoed in Chapter 6.

Philosophical and organisational roots

Researchers in this community have explicitly drawn on a number of key thinkers including Hegel, Marx, Dewey, Bahktin and Heidegger (Koschmann, 1996; Koschmann, 2001; Stahl, 2003; Stahl, 2004). In some part these discussions relate to the essential focus on meaning-making that the authors propose as central to computer supported cooperative/collaborative learning (CSCL). Koschmann for example states that:

> CSCL is a field of study centrally concerned with meaning and the practices of meaning-making in the context of joint activity, and the ways in which these practices are mediated through designed artefacts.
>
> (Koschmann, 2002: 20)

Stahl states that:

> meaning-making can be treated as an essentially social activity and that it is conducted jointly – collaboratively – by a community, rather than by individuals who happen to be co-located.
>
> (Stahl, 2003: 523)

The strong case that Stahl argues is that meaning-making takes place not just in the context of social practices and mediation through artefacts – it *is* those practices. The point being made here is not that readers need to be well versed in these philosophical debates but that they need to be aware that what might appear to be simple or slight disagreements can at times rest on significant differences at deep theoretical and philosophical levels between divergent disciplinary cultures in psychology, social sciences and computer science and in different philosophical traditions. Collaborative learning is a contentious and problematic area.

Collaborative learning can be taken to mean learning at the small-group level, but there are readings of collaboration that situate collaborative learning in wider social conditions. Modern social organisations are characterised by cooperative and collaborative applications of many types of specialised labour. Education in this regard is reflective of general social organisation. Current concerns with making education directly relevant to employment have emphasised teamwork and cooperative and collaborative approaches to teaching and learning (Wolf, 2002). The curriculum has come under pressure to become more relevant to current working practices and collaborative learning can be seen as a means of developing students' teamworking skills.

This vocationalist (Goodyear, 1999) or technical-rationalist view (Ashwin and McClean, 2005) is also taken up by Kirschner *et al.* (2004), who emphasise the relationship between both the vocationalist and reflexive views of learning posited by Goodyear (1999) and a need for collaborative learning. The vocationalist view attends to the needs of employers and the kinds of graduates that they wish to recruit, whilst the reflexive view considers that higher education has a role in equipping students with an understanding, a self-reflexive critical awareness and a capacity to take informed but critical action in the world (Barnett, 1997). Kirschner *et al.* make the claim that these two views of learning cannot be responded to by 'traditional contiguous didactic (academic) teaching and learning settings that are more often than not both individual and competitive in nature' (Kirschner *et al.*, 2004: 4) and go on to claim that collaborative or cooperative learning settings are the only way to achieve the goals of both outlooks.

While collaborative learning often has a focus on the micro analysis of group interaction, there are strong links with organisational and broad social issues. The theoretical perspective of cultural historical activity theory has been one of the more active in pursuing such broader organisational issues; see, for example, Engeström (1999; 2001). More recently there have been developments in the CSCL tradition that call for a greater emphasis on infrastructural, institutional and meso-level factors (Arnseth and Ludvigsen, 2004; Guriby, 2005; Jones *et al.*, 2006). Collaborative learning takes place in organisational contexts that set the parameters for what is possible. The interactions in a collaborative course or programme take place within the confines of validation criteria for courses and programmes and the institutional requirements for assessment, and they make use of technological infrastructures, such as virtual learning environments, that are contextual givens, out of the immediate control of the participants in the collaborative process.

Why collaborate?

A number of answers can be found in recent literature and they indicate widely divergent views about what sorts of measures, if any, could be used to assess collaborative or cooperative learning. Koschmann and Stahl argue that learning is essentially about meaning-making. In their view, any attempt to measure success in terms of outcome is profoundly mistaken. Koschmann, for example, argues that:

> Traditional theories of learning treat learning as a concealed and inferred process, something that 'takes place inside the learner and only inside the learner' (Simon, 2001: 210). CSCL research has the advantage of studying learning in settings in which learning is observably and accountably embedded in collaborative activity. Our concern, therefore, is with the unfolding process of meaning-making within these settings, not so-called 'learning outcomes'.
>
> (Koschmann, 2001: 19)

What follows must then be treated with care. Advocates of collaborative learning such as Koschmann and Stahl do not believe it can be supported by claims that it is more efficient or more effective as a learning process; rather they believe either:

- that collaboration is justifiable on other grounds; or
- that collaborative learning is more of a descriptive enterprise than it is a moral or ethical advocacy.

This point is closely related to the close association between social and situated views of learning and collaboration or cooperation. For some writers collaboration loses its particular character and it comes to mean something general, like social activity. In this reading, collaborative learning means something close to social learning or learning in general as all learning can be described as a social activity. Collaborative learning understood in this way, as social learning, is not an approach that can be argued for; it is more like a descriptive enterprise setting out how people learn *in* and *through* social activity. Other approaches see collaborative learning as better than other forms of learning in ways unconnected to measured learning outcomes. For example, Yates identifies a 'democratic theory' when discussing computer-mediated communication (CMC) (Yates, 1997). In such approaches the benefits of collaborative learning are not simply measured by learning outcomes; they are related to a view of social and democratic development.

Such benefits have been noted for over 15 years. Cowie remarked in 1992 that cooperative learning was supported by a variety of pressures. She noted a concern with enterprise drawn from an industrial practice focused on job satisfaction and commitment that demanded a workforce capable of a reflective practice in pursuit of improved products. Cooperative learning was seen as a corrective to existing social divisions of power: 'Cooperative learning in this sense opens up the possibility of a different balance of power in the classroom where pupils can explore their own meanings and may challenge those of others in a supportive community of peers' (Cowie, 1992: 158).

The pressure for a more vocational approach in higher education and the possibility that collaborative and cooperative approaches could mitigate this social pressure has been a recurrent theme. More recently the trend towards networked individualism (Wellman *et al.*, 2003) in what has been described as a networked society (Castells, 2000; Castells, 2001) has provided a contrast with collaborative learning (Jones, 2004; Jones *et al.*, 2006). It is an interesting question for CSCL, and collaborative learning approaches more generally, whether this approach to learning is intended to *fit in* with modern social trends or to act as a *counterweight* to them. It is the position of the authors that in terms of educational research we should not adopt a moral stance either for or against collaboration as an ethical choice.

More popularising texts list the benefits perceived to stem from collaborative learning in a series of bullet points under headings such as academic, social and psychological benefits (see, for example, Roberts, 2005: 2–4). Based on earlier work by Panitz (2001), the benefits set out are supported by a large reference list pointing to supporting studies. The academic benefits suggested by Roberts include: the promotion of critical thinking, involving students in the learning process, improving classroom results, and involving students in appropriate problem-solving techniques. Social benefits include: developing a social support system for students, building a diversity of understanding, and establishing a positive atmosphere for modelling and practising cooperation. The psychological benefits claimed include increasing student esteem and developing positive attitudes towards teachers.

It is not possible in a short chapter to comment on the range of supporting research drawn upon by this popular literature. In consequence we focus here on an example that comes from the teacher-focused US school of cooperative learning. The example we have chosen comes from the highly contested area dealing with learning outcomes (see also Chapter 7). While research on collaborative and cooperative learning has claimed a number of wider social benefits, the central claim was one of academic achievement (Johnson and Johnson, 1989; Johnson *et al.*, 2000; Sharan, 1990; Slavin, 1990).

As Slavin states:

> In summary, cooperative learning has been shown in a wide variety of studies to positively influence a host of important noncognitive variables. Although not every study has found positive effects on every noncognitive outcome, the overall effects of cooperative learning on student self-esteem, peer support for achievement, internal locus of control, time on-task, liking of class and classmates, cooperativeness, and other variables are positive and robust.
>
> (Slavin, 1990: 53)

Johnson and Johnson reviewed over 323 studies conducted over 90 years, comparing cooperative, competitive and individualistic learning situations. They concluded that:

> generally achievement is higher in cooperative situations rather than competitive or individualistic ones and that cooperative effort results in more frequent use of higher-level reasoning strategies, more frequent process gain and collective induction, and higher performance on subsequent tests taken individually (group-to-individual transfer) than do competitive or individualistic efforts.
>
> (Johnson and Johnson, 1989: 33)

The claim is that cooperative learning is the technique that stands out:

> students in the 50th percentile in a cooperative learning situation will perform at the 75th percentile of students learning in a competitive learning

situation and at the 77th percentile of students learning in an individualistic situation.

(Johnson and Johnson, 1989: 24)

Johnson and Johnson claim that if the lower quality-studies are removed (that is, studies with a lower degree of experimental controls and rigour), the effects are even more marked. In the more recent meta-review of cooperative learning methods Johnson *et al.* (2000) conclude on an equally positive note:

> The current research findings present a promise that if cooperative learning is implemented effectively, the likelihood of positive results is quite high. Results, however, are not guaranteed. The results of this meta-analysis provide evidence that considerable research has been conducted on cooperative learning methods, that eight diverse methods have been researched, all methods have produced higher achievement than competitive and individualistic learning ...

Research into cooperative learning is driven by a formal scientific method that requires measurement and specification of outcomes. It is largely comparative and short term and assumes that we already know what the phenomenon is in order to investigate it.

Despite the earlier comments with regard to measured learning outcomes and meaning-making, the research into the learning outcomes of cooperative learning has been widely used to support the introduction of CSCL (see, for example, Kaye, 1992; Kaye, 1995; McConnell, 2000; Crook, 1994; Jonassen, 1996; Roberts 2005).

Why collaborate? The technological imperative

The debate about technology and learning has often had a technological determinist impulse behind it. The technology deployed in society either necessitates or encourages particular types of education and learning. Such an approach has been widespread, appearing in both policy statements and in academic discourse (Jones, 2002; Clegg *et al.*, 2003; Pelletier 2005). At a more specific level, text-based computer conferencing has been identified as a technology that inclines its users towards cooperative or collaborative learning techniques (Kaye, 1992; Kaye, 1995; McConnell, 2000; O'Malley, 1995). In two complementary texts issued as part of the NATO ASI series, conferencing was identified as a key area for research into collaborative methods with its own specific design issues based on its asynchronous nature (Kaye, 1992; O'Malley, 1995).

> the features of asynchronous conferencing systems which seem particularly suited to distance education are overcoming space/time/access constraints; the text-based nature of the medium is consonant with the skills of textual analysis and composition which are part key features of the distance learner's

repertoire; messages or parts of them can be re-used in many ways; it provides facilities for self-help and cooperative working.

(O'Malley, 1995: vi)

The emphasis on distance in this approach is refined elsewhere to indicate any kind of separation, through distance or:

separated more by the conventions of their everyday work-lives than by any major physical barrier.

(McConnell, 2000: 1)

The key areas of agreement are that computer conferencing has definite characteristics that incline its users towards cooperative and collaborative methods. More recently, work has been undertaken examining collaborative learning supported by synchronous and mobile technologies; examples of this research can be found in recent CSCL conference proceedings (Wasson *et al.*, 2003; Koschmann *et al.*, 2005). The key question for research into CSCL is in determining the character of the relationship between tools and artefacts and social and organisational forms. A key finding of CSCL research is that the technical is not an independent factor and that technology does not in any simple sense cause educational effects or any particular social or pedagogical responses.

Individuals, classrooms and computers

Sharan (1990), outlining the reasons for the rapid dissemination of cooperative learning, noted that: 'Classrooms are, first and foremost, social settings inhabited by relatively large groups of students.' He goes on to outline cooperation as a form of classroom management: 'By basing the learning process on the interaction among small groups of students formed within existing classrooms, cooperative learning incorporates the social dimension of the classroom as a component of its basic procedures' (Sharan, 1990: 286).

The basic structure of a computer network separates students and teachers by time or by distance and situates them in relation to individual machines. Even where special designs have been made for Collaborative Learning Laboratories – see for example Koschmann *et al.* (1996: 107) – the machine remains an individual work area. Crook roughly divides the use of computers for learning by examining the social configurations through which computers enter into learning activities. His approach is explicitly related to a concern that computers may isolate learners. The social configurations he outlines are often reduced to four main categories – learning *with*, *at*, *around* and *through* the computer (Crook, 1994). These social configurations are not necessary outcomes of the technology and the technology could facilitate an extension of the idea of distance and open learners as individual and autonomous rather than cooperative and collaborative (Thomson, 1998). Collaborative and cooperative learning in a computer-supported setting begins from a less intuitively strong position in relation to work as a social activity than cooperative learning in the traditional classroom.

Working together using computer-mediated communication is done apart and, as Kaye explains, it is contrary to many common educational practices.

> One reason why collaborative learning appears to be more commonplace in the work environment than in many parts of the formal educational system may be because, in our culture, the latter is mainly based on recognition of individual achievement within an essentially competitive environment (collaboration between schoolchildren, in certain circumstances, is still sometimes labelled as 'cheating').
>
> (Kaye, 1992: 3)

The process of education has long been recognised as an encouragement to learner isolation:

> What is learned, then, is passivity and alienation from oneself and others, and that the most fruitful relationships with people will be as passive and impersonal as the solitary interaction with the computer.
>
> (Kreuger *et al.*, 1989: 114)

Higher education, without even considering computers, is still organised with lectures as the dominant mode of teaching in many disciplines. The physical space defined in most lecture theatres is one that suggests an individual relationship to the speaker and doesn't allow for easy social interaction and collaboration amongst peers. Assessment is organised to generate individual grades within each course unit, level and eventually the degree class, and collaboration can be seen by students focused on their grades as unproductive, threatening to achieving students and an unnecessary burden.

The individual or isolating possibilities of computer-based learning have also been noted as a factor in teacher resistance to the introduction of new technologies (Cuban, 1986; Cuban, 2001; Crook, 1994). The use of CMC has two apparent disadvantages, in that it takes place outside of the social context of the classroom, 'apart' from others, and it takes place in relation to a device or machine. The claims for computer conferencing as a cooperative or collaborative medium have to be assessed against their use within an existing individualised practice, where communication takes place between separated learners in a process with machines that may incline the user towards isolation.

Recent research in CSCL

In recent years the developing field of CSCL has grown into an international movement with its own conference series and from early 2006 a new international journal (see Box 12.1).

Box 12.1: Finding out more about CSCL

Conferences and professional associations supporting CSCL:
The most important of these is the International Society for the Learning Sciences.
Membership of this body carries with it subscription to the new International
Journal of Computer-Supported Collaborative Learning: http://www.isls.org/.
A related international conference in the UK is the Networked Learning
Conference series. Papers from previous conferences can be accessed from this
site: http://www.networkedlearningconference.org.uk/.

Book series
The Computer Supported Collaborative Learning Series published by Kluwer
Academic Publishers is a good source of current material.
Related work, including some focused explicitly on education, can be found in the
CSCW Series published by Springer.

Website
The website of the Collaborative Learning Project, linked to Tom S. Roberts at
Central Queensland University, provides a good and quite comprehensive introduction to the CSCL area in higher education. It includes maintained links to online
papers and conferences: http://clp.cqu.edu.au.

Several reviews of CSCL have taken place in Europe and these can provide an
overview of both the pedagogical roots of collaborative learning and the technological tools applied in this area (Lehtinen *et al.*, 1999; Lehtinen, 2003; Lakkala *et
al.*, 2001). The current state of theory is still that CSCL is an emergent paradigm.

> In sum, even if the stress in CSCL research is on socially oriented theories of
> learning, there is still no unifying and established theoretical framework, no
> agreed objects of study, no methodological consensus, or agreement about
> the unit of analysis. Positively considered, this ambiguity can be seen as
> reflecting the richness or diversity of the field. Negatively interpreted, it
> seems that the field is proceeding along increasingly divergent lines.
>
> (Lakkala *et al.*, 2001: 8)

This is not only at a scientific or theoretical level; it is also reflected in practitioners' accounts in the UK (Jones *et al.*, 2000; Jones and Asensio, 2001).

> Overall practitioners identified collaboration as an aim but were concerned
> that it was difficult to achieve and difficult to conceptualise. Collaboration
> and participation were both features that exemplify the gap that practitioners
> experienced between expectations and outcomes.
>
> (Jones *et al.*, 2000: 25)

CSCL is a field that still needs a great deal of development before it becomes a common practice in education.

Strijbos *et al.* (2004) provide an overview of CSCL in higher education. Perhaps a particularly useful chapter is the conclusion, which summarises 'What we know about CSCL and what we don't (but need to) know about CSCL'. The headings with which they summarise what we know include the following:

- *It's all about learning* – the authors argue for what they call a 'probabilistic perspective' on design. That is, they argue that we know that causal approaches to design do not work but that design is still possible in CSCL environments. Other authors have pointed to the problem of unpredictability in collaborative environments and in conducting collaborative tasks (e.g. Jones, 1999b). Jones reports students simulating collaboration online whilst co-present and seated around four computers. We know that design of CSCL, whilst necessary and achievable, is complex and emergent rather than deterministic and predictable.

Are we limiting our ability to reach aspired goals by our own terminology, one that effectively obscures many of the elements that desperately need to be addressed by policy? Whereas education is by definition a multi-faceted activity understood to involve a variety of players and activities – teachers and teaching; students and studying; institutions and structures; information, knowledge and, it is hoped, learning – e-learning is a term comprising one letter representing a physical property of technology (e for electronic) and the hoped-for outcome (learning) for one participant in the interaction. Given the power of language to constrain our thinking, is our current circumscribed terminology making it increasingly difficult to keep in mind and focus on elements of this expanding activity that, while not readily apparent in the term 'e-learning' itself, must be understood and included when establishing policy and researching the phenomenon? In the US a number of public and private organisations have addressed quality issues through the development of guidelines relating to design, instruction, student support, faculty devlopment, etc. At the same time that US educational researchers are expanding their repertoire of methodological tools for studying an increasingly multi-faceted educational environment, many funders of research – most notably the federal government, but others as well – are narrowing their focus to 'scientific research', which can answer some questions very well but many questions poorly. Although presumably done with the best of intentions in the name of 'accountability', this trend has the potential to greatly hamper e-learning research efforts by excluding many of the methods best suited to answering the important questions associated with this incredibly complex phenomenon.

Melody Thompson

- *Learning, collaboration and assessment* – the probabilistic nature of design carries over into assessment and the understanding, sharing of knowledge and learning that takes place. This approach is supported by research in a UK context. For example, Jones and Asensio report the unpredictability of students' understandings of written assessment instructions for a collaborative task (Jones and Asensio, 2001).
- *What is meant by 'support'* – the overall claim is that we know that: 'CSCL implementation is not limited to introducing a new technological environment, but rather that it requires the alignment of technology with learning/teaching objectives which is not readily accomplished in technical environments used by higher education institutes' (Strijbos *et al.*, 2004: 250).
- *Technology and interaction* – the focus of design requires a shift from interface design to interaction design, and the focus on usability may need to expand to include the utility of a system in a specific setting.
- *Learning through collaboration supported by computers* – the aim should be to increase the alignment of the various elements in a CSCL setting by systematic design so that the *probability* of desired outcomes is increased.

The list of things we do not know but need to know includes:

- *Face-to-face versus computer mediated?* – research too often remains in the rut of comparing face-to-face with computer-mediated communication. Increasingly, students experience an educational environment that is interpenetrated with technology at all levels and it remains true that for some purposes face-to-face is the best option. Research needs to provide a basis for good choices of when to use different technologies and how to use them to achieve particular ends.
- *Retrospective versus prospective analysis?* – Strijbos *et al.* make a claim for what they call prospective analysis, the testing of falsifiable hypotheses, rather than a reliance on 'retrospective' analysis of events that are 'usually *not planned*' (Strijbos *et al.*, 2004: 254). We would disagree with this analysis because we still know *too little* about what happens in the day-to-day practice of teaching and learning. However, we think Strijbos *et al.* are right to focus on this issue as the underlying question motivates both of our responses – how can good research inform practice so that we can achieve more predictable/reproducible results?
- *Small groups and group dynamics?* – the authors call for CSCL to revisit social psychology as they suggest it is a valuable resource for understanding small group dynamics that are essential to CSCL. We would add to that the need for incorporating understandings of practice and meaning-making, often informed by ethnomethodology – an approach focused on 'making the learning visible' (Stahl, 2003, 2004).
- *Analysis of communication and interaction?* – the changing styles of research into communication and interaction are noted with a move from surface

analysis of content to a need for a deeper understanding of the nature of communication. Both quantitative and qualitative approaches are identified as possible approaches but the key for Strijbos *et al.* (2004) is that reliability remains a prerequisite for drawing conclusions and replicating experiments. We agree that the issue raised is important to CSCL but disagree with the solution offered. The positivist stress on reliable and replicable results sits uneasily with the probabilistic and complex nature of CSCL described by the same authors. We argue that we need to have an emphasis on developing new methods of research and analysis for complex and emergent systems.

Conclusion

In conclusion, this discussion about collaboration takes place at a time when two fundamentally different views of the internet and the web are reflected in views about e-learning. These can be characterised as the broadcast and the discussion perspectives.[1] For those concerned that e-learning might assist in the de-professionalisation, commercialisation and commodification of learning, the new networked technologies are yet another broadcast medium. Content is king in this view and the key technologies involve individualisation, delivery, re-use and the packaging of materials as learning 'objects'. The network is important in this view as a cost-effective delivery mechanism. In contrast, the discussion perspective that emerges out of the cooperative and collaborative learning tradition we have discussed in this chapter sees the network as primarily a communication medium. The key feature of the new technology in this view is its capacity for interactivity, understood as allowing for communication between two or more participants in a dialogue or conversation. The classic components of cooperation and collaboration, discussion, dialogue and community are now possible without the traditional constraints of time and place. The potential for collaborative learning is extended by new technologies to a broad new constituency. The discussion around networked technology naturally mirrors the long-standing division between instructivist or transmission approaches and constructivist or situated views of learning. These viewpoints lead to profoundly different approaches as to how and to what extent networked technologies are employed in education. Our hope is that this chapter has provided its readers with a solid basis on which to evaluate the contribution of a cooperative or collaborative approach.

Note

1   We are grateful to Martin Weller for this formulation, which can be found in an internal Open University Virtual Learning Environment Report on Phase 1, November 2004.

Chapter 13

Learning technologies

Affective and social issues

Ann Jones and Kim Issroff

One perennial issue in the area of learning technologies that is a major theme of this book is whether and how the use of learning technologies will enable us to *re-think* how we teach. In this chapter the focus of that debate is how we might approach teaching and learning with technologies in order to address social and affective issues – particularly student engagement. We are using the term affective in the same way as described by Oatley and Nundy (1996: 258) as a general term covering concepts such as emotion, mood, attitude and value.

Overview of the chapter

The chapter starts with a brief review of some relevant theoretical approaches to motivation. This leads us to consider features that are likely to increase motivation and we discuss these largely in the context of research into collaborative 'side-by-side' learning and collaborative learning online. Collaborative learning is a major theme in this chapter and this is both because of the particularly social nature of collaborative learning (Jones and Issroff, 2005) – which means that social and affective factors have had more attention in this area than in many others – and also because we consider Crook's (2000) argument, that collaboration is particularly motivating, to be compelling. Informal settings are also of particular interest, partly because learner engagement is usually high in these contexts and also because of the increasing emphasis on lifelong learning. Another related area that we consider is that of play – a context that has high engagement but until recently has been rarely considered in the context of adult learning.

Finally we draw the chapter together with a discussion of an area in which we think learning technologies can really make a difference to learning and where social and affective factors are of particular importance: mobile learning.

Motivation

There has been a concern with understanding student motivation in the context of learning technologies for some time but there is still relatively little work in this area. Some uses of learning technologies are often perceived to be highly motivating, so one line of interest has been in finding out why this might be. For example, in early seminal work on computer games (Malone, 1981; Malone and Lepper, 1987) the question 'What makes computer games fun?' was posed. This had little follow-up until relatively recently, when computer games have once again become a 'hot' research topic (see, for example, Kirriemuir and McFarlane, 2004), along with informal contexts and the role of play. Researchers and practitioners have also looked for relevant theories and models of motivation that can help to inform the design of learning technologies or our understanding of what it is that is motivating. One model that is widely referred to in this context is Keller's ARCS (attention, relevance, confidence and satisfaction) model (Keller and Suzuki, 1988), which synthesised existing psychological research on motivation.

Another line of interest is to exploit the properties of learning technologies in order to enhance the learner's motivation. This is the starting point for Issroff and del Soldato (1996). Four motivational factors emerge from their review of the literature on motivation and learning: curiosity, challenge, confidence and control. Briefly, it is suggested that it is important to arouse the learner's curiosity; to provide the right level of challenge (material that is neither too easy nor too difficult); to build the learner's confidence (again through judicious selection of tasks relating to prior achievements); and finally to provide the appropriate level of control.

The idea of control has often been discussed in the context of learning technologies (see, for example, Kinzie, 1990; Klein and Keller, 1990; Seaton, 1993; Freitag and Sullivan, 1995) and was once very hotly debated. Keller argues that ideally learners should perceive themselves as being in control of their learning process and indeed, in using learning technologies, the learners' ability to negotiate their own paths through the material may be very attractive and motivating. However, it can be argued that to have such control, learners need to have at least some minimal knowledge of the system to make informed choices. So, paradoxically, guiding instructions are a way of allowing learners to exercise control. Indeed, when hypertexts were introduced, it was found that many learners often did not know where they were in the system that they were navigating through and this phenomenon became known as 'lost in hyperspace' (Edwards and Hardman, 1993). Interestingly, although hypertexts are now largely extinct as such, the phenomenon is still an issue in areas such as digital libraries (Theng, 1999).

Eales *et al.* (2002) distinguish between *authentic* motivation – related to a focus on the development of robust, long-term knowledge – and *inauthentic* motivation – focused on assessment and the tactics of schooling. They note the importance of the ownership of learning in their comparison of three different settings of computer-supported collaborative learning. They emphasise that ownership of the learning problem is a particularly powerful form of motivation – and that it often occurs outside formal educational settings. They view computer-supported collaborative learning as a way of virtually 'deschooling' education by bridging educational and outside worlds. Note that this view is in stark contrast to the argument presented in Chapter 10 that assessment is a way of motivating

Case study

A few years ago one of the authors and a colleague ran a course (largely online) for other colleagues in our HE institution. They were asked to work in pairs near the beginning of the course and to discuss their own good and bad learning experiences. This then formed the starting point for an online discussion.

Two particular things struck us about what was reported back. The first relates to the content. The most frequent feature of a good learning experience was having an 'inspirational' teacher who was often described as 'passionate' about the subject area, or who 'brought the subject alive'. Sometimes people referred to teachers with whom they had developed a very good relationship. The second thing we noted was that it really mattered that this exercise was done in pairs. Often the partners initially reported quite different experiences and features, but some people also recognised something familiar in their partner's experience even though they had not identified it initially. For others, the experience they heard was not one that they could relate to themselves, but it did, they reported, give them further insight into what made for a good learning experience. We need to be careful about what we can claim about this positive learning experience and its relationship to its setting and the setting's social dynamics. Arguably a similar kind of insight might be achieved by students working alone with print or other media resources and using the experiences of 'virtual colleagues' presented there as a stimulus to reflection and comparison. And indeed – as discussed elsewhere in the chapter – it clearly matters with whom you are paired: pairing of itself is no guarantee of added value.

But the example serves as an illustration of the potential of social and cultural factors for shaping students' learning experiences in positive ways. For instance, students would have found it difficult to bypass the activity completely by ignoring their partner without appearing rude – compare this with a 'private' self-learning context. And once embarked on an exchange of personal histories, as students' comments revealed, there seems little doubt that this created an affective synergy that was both personally and intellectually rewarding. So it turns out that the social context of the exercise is really important.

What interested us about this exercise is that what was most often reported as mattering were *affective* factors – how the learners *felt* about the experience: they were inspired, or they felt passionate. Conversely, and perhaps not surprisingly, affective issues were also present in bad learning experiences, where people were, for example, not motivated or being taught by someone who did not appear very interested themselves. Similarly we should bear in mind that activities in a social setting do not appeal to us all: for some (for example those with low self-esteem), activities with an interpersonal element are not an a priori 'good thing' with congenial associations; rather they represent dangerous public contexts that involve considerable personal risk-taking (see, for example, Joinson, 2003). Given the choice, students with such personality traits will tend to choose the more self-protecting media such as email or online discussions in preference to face-to-face contexts. Clearly, affective factors matter.

students to do particular things – such as using learning technologies. Indeed, as educational technologists we often advise authors that in order to ensure that students use particular resources or read particular parts of a course, they need to be integrated into the assessment.

Such 'inauthentic' motivation clearly works to an extent, in that learners try to learn what is assessed. But perhaps Eales *et al.*'s argument suggests that such learning will not be as robust and embedded as we would wish.

In reviewing the motivation literature more generally, it is important to consider how motivation is currently viewed. Whilst motivation has always been a focus of research, it is only during the last thirty years that attention has been focused on the relationship between motivation and learning. In the 1960s and 1970s motivation was contrasted with cognitive processes and generally studied in laboratories. However, since the 1980s, research on motivation has been carried out in real contexts, signifying the recognition that learning is a situated activity. As Järvelä points out:

> Through the influence of sociocultural and situated cognition theories, it has been recognized that motivation of individual learners is also influenced by social value and by the context in which the learning takes place. Motivation is no longer a separate variable or a distinct factor, which can be applied in explanations of an individual's readiness to act or learn – but it is reflective of the social and cultural environment.
>
> (Järvelä, 2001: 4)

This has led to an emphasis on the situated nature of learning, with less attention being paid to the design of software and hardware. Collaborations are crucial when considering situated learning, as illustrated in the case study that follows on page 192, and this is discussed in the next section.

None of this should surprise us. We are all aware of the importance of such factors in our own learning – the effect of being tired or uninterested, and the excitement and motivation of working in a team that 'gels' and throws up exciting ideas. Yet, social and affective issues have to date received little attention in studying learning – whether in the field of learning technologies or more generally. However, this is starting to change, and this is partly to do with gradual changes in theoretical perspectives on learning. For example, the social constructivist approach, which is currently influential, emphasises the importance of the social context of learning, as do contemporary theoretical approaches to adult learning (see, for example, Lea and Nicoll, 2002).

Collaborative learning and motivation

Collaborative learning has already been discussed in Chapter 12. Here, the focus is somewhat different. Collaborative learning is an area where social and affective factors have received the most attention. This is partly because of its nature: working

How should this perspective be taken into account in research on collaborative learning, and when it is supported by technology especially? Earlier research on collaborative learning has not seen motivation as a part of the collaboration process – but rather as a possible motivating variable. New technology-based learning environments in education and work contexts emphasise the social nature of learning and are often based on the principles of shared cognition and collaboration. Inevitably, the new social and collaborative practices challenge traditional motivation research to locate goals and engagement in the dynamic activities of social systems or communities of learners. In these settings, individuals mutually influence each other and the construction of motivational meanings reflects individuals' motivational beliefs, prior experience and subjective appraisals of the affordances and constraints of the current situation (Järvelä and Volet, 2004). Researchers have produced new concepts related to collaborative learning, such as involvement, engagement, mutual understanding and ownership, which have implicitly been linked to motivation, but not empirically analysed nor conceptually defined. We need more precise ideas about how to conceptualize shared and social processes of collaboration in terms of their motivational meanings.

Sanna Järvelä

collaboratively with others involves groups of learners, often small groups or pairs who are specifically working in a social context, and so this forces attention on social issues. Crook (2000), however, argues that collaboration and motivation are *strongly* related: collaboration is a *motivated* activity because it has a distinct, important emotional dimension – collaborative settings evoke affective responses. He cites evidence from developmental psychology of the importance and the attraction for the child (and its partner) of engaging in joint interaction. What is so motivating in collaboration, according to Crook, is 'shared meaning' – both the sense of shared histories, which learners build up in collaborative activities, and also that the shared history is unique to this particular group.

In the next two sections we consider the features likely to increase such motivation, and the role of other social and affective factors in collaborative learning, first in settings where the learners are in the same location and then where they are geographically separate and collaborating through their use of the computer.

The role of affective factors in collaborative learning (side by side)

Much of the current work and interest in collaborative learning is on collaboration *through* computers (where computers provide the method of communication) and we will consider this area later, but here we are concerned with groups of learners who are physically located together and using a computer to work on a particular task. In this section in particular, much of the research concerns children but most of the issues discussed also apply to adult learning.

Issroff and del Soldato (1996) define *social affinity between partners* as 'a level of respect and a willingness to work together'. Interestingly, although there is a wealth of literature on computer-supported collaborative learning using pairs of students, few of these studies have either taken this issue into account or focused on it. Issroff and del Soldato argue that social affinity will always have a significant effect on the nature and effectiveness of a collaborative interaction. In practice, teachers are well aware of its importance, and very often choose *not* to pair up children who are friends in case they are distracted from their work. However, research in this area (mainly on children rather than adults) suggests that such affinity has a positive effect on collaborative work. Jones and Pellegrini's work (1996) showed the benefits of working collaboratively with a friend in a collaborative setting when the task relies on the use of metacognitive skills. Vass (2002; 2004) has built on this work in a detailed longitudinal study of the impact of friendship on the task of creative collaborative writing. She found that friends did not need to negotiate the rules of collaboration, and furthermore, that they had established ways of working which were implicitly understood rather than explicitly discussed. Vass discovered a further 'bonus' for her friendship pairs: that they were in the habit of 'mucking about' together; *play* was an important feature of their relationship. Her work shows how this ease with each other is harnessed in their creative work. It also raises the issue of social and affective factors in informal contexts: the friendship pairs drew activities that they engaged in out of school into their work *in* school.

Another important issue is the *distribution of control*. A collaborative learning environment often needs to be managed to ensure a balance of control amongst students so that some do not dominate. This can be achieved in several ways – for example, the students can be allocated tasks or the software can be used to artificially manipulate control. However, there are two different aspects of control in relation to computer-supported collaborative learning: control of one's own learning and control of the tool (e.g. the mouse). These two aspects affect each other (the control of the system's interface has an effect on the accomplishment of the learning activity) but they are not interchangeable. For example, in studying pair collaboration, Issroff (1994) found that there was strong hardware dominance by one member of a pair studied and this boy initially appeared to be controlling the interaction. Further investigation of the pair's discussion, however, revealed that the other member of the pair, a girl, was controlling the entire interaction.

Although most collaborative work involves pairs of learners sharing one input device, there has been some work on the use of multiple input devices. For example, Stanton *et al.* (2002) specifically investigated the impact of multiple input devices in the KidStory project. The research team on this project worked with young children (aged 5–6) to developed KidPad, a drawing and zooming tool to be used with one or more mice to support side-by-side collaboration at the computer.

They found that the quality of the stories produced was higher for those children using two mice, on the whole, although gender also played a significant role.

The role of affective factors in collaborative learning online

Issues such as social affinity apply equally well to online collaboration. Much of the literature and practice on the *affective* impact of being part of an online learning community originated in the field of distance education, which experimented with computer mediated communication (CMC). The convergence of telecommunications and computers in the 1980s allowed a way of addressing a problem that had long been recognised in distance education – learners' isolation. The Open University was an early user of CMC and applied it initially in the 1980s to address learners' isolation and to supplement students' learning experiences. Although affective issues were not to the fore at the time, CMC did force attention on at least some of these, as it became clear that this medium, for some learners at least, afforded less emotional restraint and led to flaming. It also quickly became clear that, in order to make such ventures successful, the social aspects of building up relationships online needed to be considered. Participants needed to feel *safe* enough to enter what could feel like a strange community. For example, Wegerif (1998) found that individual success or failure on one online course depended upon the extent to which students were able to cross a threshold from feeling like outsiders to feeling like insiders.

In trying to understand when and why online learning becomes productive and what makes online communities work, focused investigations into particular aspects of use are needed. Examples of such work include how best to motivate and engage students and keep them online (e.g. Thomas and Carswell, 2000; Mason and Weller, 2000), the impact of CMC on the role of teaching staff (Jelfs and Colbourn, 2002; Light *et al.*, 2000), and factors that influence its success (Tolmie and Boyle, 2000). The issue of the tutor role has received much emphasis in the discussion of CMC, with predictions and accounts of CMC allowing a shift from leading the teaching to a much more 'equal' and 'peer-like' position. Light *et al.* (2000) provide a helpful summary of this debate and illustrate the *social* role of the tutor. Whilst early advocates envisaged peer-learning as the dominant mode, too little input from the tutor can also be problematic, both for the quality of the outcome and also because there is a need for intervention if the social dynamics become problematic – where flaming occurs for example.

Tolmie and Boyle (2000) review the factors influencing the success of CMC environments in university teaching. Some of these are affective factors, and others involve affective considerations. These include: the size of group; knowledge of other participants; student experience; ownership of task; and the need for/function of CMC. An over-large group size may make it difficult for learners to get to know each other sufficiently for enough trust to develop, and developing a community where participants feel safe and trust each other is crucial. Knowledge of other participants is a central part of such a venture. The role of ownership of the task has already been identified, and the importance of having a positive student experience is well known from other contexts (e.g. Issroff, 1994). What might be less obvious is that a clear need for CMC (as with other learning technologies) is necessary for learner engagement, otherwise, for time-poor learners, other demands on their time will win out.

Online *learning* communities usually congregate around formally organised learning activities but there is also interest in online communities more generally. New technologies can enable 'virtual' communities of practice to develop, and students can access communities of experts who are operating in 'real-world' contexts outside education. In science teaching, for example, students might have access to practising scientists and be able to discuss their projects with them as part of *learning* communities (Scanlon, 1998). Preece (2000) documents and discusses the phenomenal growth of online communities more generally, their nature and how best to support them and pays considerable attention to social and affective aspects. She argues for the importance of sociability in communities that depend on trust, collaboration and appropriate styles of communication. Preece has a particular concern with empathy and has analysed the nature of empathic support across a number of online communities.

This kind of technology use allows learning to take place in contexts other than educational institutions. For many learners this means that they are more likely to be genuinely engaged – because they are learning *in context* and will have the 'authentic' motivation discussed by Eales *et al.* (2002).

Play and informal learning

At various points in this chapter we have alluded to the motivation and engagement that is inherent in play. How can we capitalise on this in the context of learning?

Although play is widely acknowledged as a context for children's learning it has rarely been explicitly considered as a fruitful context for adult learning. Yet its potency and potential were noticed in the early 1980s by Malone and more recently there has been a renewed interest in the potential of computer games for learning because of their motivational power (see Kirriemuir and McFarlarne, 2004, for an introduction to current thinking on the role of computer games in supporting children's learning). However, there has been little theoretical investigation of this area.

As we have seen, most theoretical approaches to motivation have focused on analysing the different *cognitive* components of motivation (reference above), although some of the factors identified (such as curiosity) have an emotional quality. A few years ago a very different approach by Csikszentmihalyi (1999) gained some ground in the context of work on creativity. Csikszentmihalyi refers to 'flow' – a type of concentrated timeless activity. He describes flow as 'being completely involved in an activity for its own sake. The ego falls away. Time flies. Every action, movement, and thought follows inevitably from the previous one,

Digital gaming is now recognised as offering significant opportunities for learning, and indeed that much of the learning associated with such play is social (McFarlane *et al.*, 2002; Gee, 2003) . Social learning associated with digital gaming is particularly evident in a range of online contexts. The game-related online communities where learning is clearly evident fall into three categories: in game, for example in MMOGs (massively multiplayer online games); in game support sites where the key purpose of the site is to share expertise associated with game play; and in fiction sites where creative output inspired by favourite games (and other media) is shared, critiqued and developed within a supportive community of fellow enthusiasts. In each form of these communities there is a level of engagement, commitment, and genuinely collaborative learning that would be the envy of any e-moderator in a formal learning context (McFarlane, 2007). The last of these perhaps offers a model that can most obviously hold up a mirror to the equivalent activities in formal learning. Fan fiction is a creative genre that has been around for a long time. Inspired by books, film, or more recently digital games, fans create their own productions. These might be poems, short stories, paintings, even novels. Some of these are even great works; Tennyson's *Mort D'Arthur* inspired by Arthurian legend, and Waterhouse's *The Lady of Shalot* inspired by another of Tennyson's poems could be viewed as examples of fan fiction. But less famous works are also important, and internet technologies have ensured that these too may also have a global audience. There are a number of websites, some started and run by fans, that offer a place for fan fiction to be shared and celebrated. The volume and sophistication of some of the work that appears is impressive and much of it comes from young people in many parts of the world. Whole novels, published chapter by chapter, are not uncommon. Collaboration is also rife. This can range from constructive critical comment on a piece of writing, to the composition of music, to a poem posted by another fan, or the re-working of a pen-and-ink image to include colour. All of this is achieved in a spirit of celebration of a shared love of the original inspiring texts, and of support for fellow contributors. Purely negative responses are rare, and receive a fast and furious reaction from community members. The level of creativity and collaborative learning seen in these sites would be the envy of any e-learning course developer. And one thing we can be sure of is that the resulting content, and the learning resulting from the development of this work, are both highly personalised. So how might the experience of being a member of such a learning community compare to being signed up to an institutional VLE? Do these webspaces offer the same opportunities for posting drafts, getting feedback from a range of readers, and re-drafting? Does this form of collaboration on or offline have a place in the formal curriculum? Or will we continue to see the kind of product that has dogged FE and HE, which is basically an online filing cabinet with some rather poor communication tools that are used reluctantly and with little impact on learning in most cases? If so we will have missed a real opportunity to use technology to give learners a voice and an audience, to make the processes of creation, reflection and development key to learning.

Angela McFarlane

like playing jazz. Your whole being is involved, and you're using your skills to the utmost' (http://www.brainchannels.com/thinker/mihaly.html). Katzeff (2003) suggests that play as a context for learning may provide conditions that evoke flow. She has extracted some key features from the literature on play that are likely to be relevant for adults:

- Play is likely to motivate if it provides complex and challenging experiences and immediate feedback.
- Play supports the competence of improvisation.
- Play may stimulate novel lines of thinking through arousing functions within Vygotsky's zone of proximal development (Vygotsky, 1978).

This view of play resonates most closely with socio-constructivist approaches to learning and Katzeff draws attention to the relationship between work in this area and many of the central features of play. She argues that play as a rich context for learning should be taken into account when designing digital learning environments and draws particular attention to the power of simulations and role play.

A similar approach is often adopted in the development of informal learning environments such as those found in contemporary museums. For example, Hawkey (2002) discusses learning with ICT in one particular informal environment. The UK Natural History Museum is an example of this, and see Hawkey (2004) for a review that includes informal learning both in museums and online. Whilst the earlier section on online learning focused on *dialogue* as the main tool for learning, the sites discussed by Hawkey are intended to allow users to engage, explore and build. They do this through the provision of interactive resources such as QUEST. In this resource, the home page depicts photographs of a number of natural objects such as lichen on a tree and a butterfly. Visitors to the site are invited to explore the objects through tools such as a ruler for measuring, scales, etc.

This approach shares some features with the online communities discussed earlier. Users of these resources choose the activities that they want to engage in, so they have ownership of their learning (within the constraints of what is available). Resources such as QUEST are also designed to simulate the role of the scientist – in particular focusing on investigation. So this approach is very much in the spirit of Wenger's view of learning induction into a community of practice (1998); here it is a community of scientists. One might argue that this is overstating the case, and it is true that the users in this resource do not have contact with working scientists. However, there is a facility to post messages – which is well used – and in other similar approaches to learning science, learners can indeed contact scientists and ask them questions (e.g. Scanlon, 1998).

Informal learning and mobile technologies

At various points in this chapter we have referred to learning in *informal contexts* – i.e. learning that takes place outside institutions such as schools and universities. In discussing motivation, we noted the importance of learners being in control of their learning.

In this section we consider the use of mobile technologies for informal learning. We believe that mobile devices have two features that connect strongly with affective factors and particularly with motivation.

The first feature is the context of use. There has been phenomenal adoption and growth of mobile phone use, especially by teenage groups. These were not designed as learning devices although institutions have tried to capitalise on their success and to use them in supporting 'institutional learning' in various ways e.g. to remind students of assignments. Even so, most uses of mobile devices occur outside conventional educational contexts in informal settings. Interestingly, the vast majority of lifelong learning is in exactly such informal settings; see, for example, Vavoula and Sharples (2003) and Clough (2005). What we do know about learners in such settings is that they are strongly motivated.

The second feature is an aspect of learner control: ownership. Mobile devices seem to give their users a very strong sense of control and ownership – and as we saw earlier this was highlighted as a key motivational factor, and its importance was confirmed by Twining and Evans' recent study (Twining and Evans, 2005) on the use of Tablet PCs in schools (in press).

Given this resonance with affect it is worth considering mobile learning further. Sharples (2003) notes that in formal settings such as the classroom, the use of mobile devices is often viewed as a disruptive influence. He argues for a more positive approach where the use of mobile devices is harnessed for education and advocates the development of mobile technologies to support learning both within and outside the formal classroom. Such technologies should allow lifelong learning; for example, what has been captured on one device should be easily transported to another – not made redundant with the obsolescence of the technology.

Sharples also comments on how control – an important factor in successful learning – may be distributed between learners who are working together. This view of the role of technology as providing a pervasive conversational learning space is powerful. Such a mobile learning device, he argues: 'can assist conversational learning by integrating learning descriptions across different locations, for example by making connections between exhibits in a museum and by holding the results of learning actions for later retrieval and reflection. It can also provide tools for learning in contexts such as electronic measuring instruments, maps and reference guides' (Sharples, 2003: 509).

We are struck by how many of the requirements that Sharples outlines for mobile devices resonate with the factors involved in motivation. *Highly portable* devices, *available anywhere* can be used in the most relevant contexts and carried with the learner, which should support ownership of the learning problem, identified earlier as a particularly powerful form of motivation. *Individual* devices will also support ownership and control, and also an additional 'motivational feature' that has not been explicitly discussed, but which has been implicit in much of the discussion (especially in the idea of control) – relevance. The task must have strong relevance to the learner's goals and interests.

Concluding remarks and future research

Mobile technologies are an example of powerful motivational forces that we have not yet started to really understand. Their impact on how people communicate and structure their lives is constantly evolving. If we are to harness some of this impact for learning, we need to understand how people engage with these technologies in their everyday lives and why they have been appropriated so enthusiastically. We would argue that we particularly need to understand the affective factors around the use of technologies such as mobile devices, outside educational institutions, in order to harness this understanding and apply it to a number of contexts.

In thinking about future research, there are two important aspects. First, from an evaluation perspective, we need to understand what the desired affective outcomes are from the use of technology. There may be instances where there is a conflict between desired cognitive outcomes and affective outcomes. For example, it is easy to think of a situation in which there is a tension between students feeling confident about their own abilities *and making progress on a particular task.* We also need to understand more about how teachers perceive learning situations and their intended affective outcomes.

Second, we need to understand which aspects of learning situations influence students' affections. For example, what is the impact of the way in which an activity is introduced to a student? It may be that the ways in which the teacher/course designer presents the activity are more important than the design of the activity and/or the design of the technology that supports the activity. There is, after all, clear evidence that assessment has an enormous impact on the ways in which students engage with learning resources and this may override all other design considerations.

Turning to the themes that run right through the book, the notion of learning technologies as an interdisciplinary area has been illustrated in most if not all the chapters and this is no exception. Research on affect and in particular emotion takes place mainly within psychology and in particular developmental psychology. This field has had a large theoretical influence on learning technologies: for example, the socio-constructivist approach that has been a dominant theory in learning technology for some time has its roots in developmental psychology, and its influence is also clear in education and HCI – both fields related to learning technology. Research on motivation takes place mainly in psychology but also in educational research. One reason why we are arguing for the need to consider the role of affect in learning technology at this point in time is that from being a neglected area in psychology, there has been much more attention on affect over the last twenty-five years and a recognition of its importance alongside cognition. Indeed it can be argued that it is very hard to separate the two.

Considering affect is also important in one of the other themes that run throughout the book, that of access and inclusion. This may not be so immediately evident, but one argument for why learning technologies might allow us to rethink how we learn and teach lies in their emotional power. In the last section we argued that mobile technologies seem to have a particular attraction for many people, especially young people. This can lead to opening up access and widening participation; by harnessing such technologies we may draw in learners who have hitherto felt excluded and have been difficult to reach in more traditional ways. Examples of how such technologies have been used in this way can be found in JISC's good practice guide *Innovative Practice with E-learning* (JISC, 2005a). We would argue that there is an emotional perspective to this widening access. Conversely, however, we also need to recognise that new technologies also increase barriers for some learners. Barriers such as access and the digital divide are well documented: there is less documentation, although there is research evidence, on what we might call affective barriers such as perceptions about the technology, anxieties about using it and bad emotional experiences. We therefore need to continue our work in this area so that we can harness the positive, as much as possible, whilst understanding and reducing the affective barriers that learning technologies can also bring.

Chapter 14

Evaluation

Martin Oliver, Jen Harvey, Gráinne Conole and Ann Jones

The importance of evaluation has grown in recent years so that this topic has become the focus of considerable policy and research interest (Oliver, 2000). As new learning technologies emerge there is a need to evaluate how these are used to support an increasingly diverse student population. All staff are now expected to carry out evaluations to account for resources or to justify strategic initiatives. Additionally, for individuals trying to instigate change, evaluation data can be important in providing relevant information to initiate, support and empower change by the 'production of knowledge that makes a difference' (Patton, 1997).

Evaluation is not a simple, standardised practice; it has evolved to meet the needs of many different groups. Consequently, it can be hard to define, although a common definition involves both describing and judging in terms of both merit and worth (Guba and Lincoln, 1989).

Furthermore, the relationship between evaluation and research more generally remains contested. Evaluation can, in fact, contribute to research as well as providing feedback for a changing teaching and learning practice. Both processes may use the same methods and study the same things. However, one way to distinguish them is to consider how findings are used. If they are interpreted by an immediate, local audience and used to support decision-making, the study was probably an evaluation; if findings are interpreted in terms of theories and are presented as a contribution to knowledge, it was probably research.

> This emphasis on judging may be typical, but it is not universal. Not all evaluators feel that evaluation should both describe and judge; those who position themselves in the ethnographic tradition, for example, argue that their work should be non-judgemental, concentrating instead on providing credible and plausible accounts of observed practice
>
> **C. Jones**

Values

The concepts introduced above need explanation. As described by Guba and Lincoln (1989), 'merit' and 'worth' are conceived of as part of a broader concept of 'value'. 'Merit' refers to intrinsic qualities, whilst 'worth' refers to extrinsic or contextual value. These definitions are rendered problematic by the critiques discussed in Chapter 2, and the shift in knowledge production away from positivism. The alternative to talking about these as intrinsic properties is to treat value and worth as socially constructed. This renders all aspects of an object's value extrinsic and contextual. For this reason, it makes sense to talk in a less precise but more intuitive way about things having worth if their value can be determined in terms of input/output efficiency (e.g. if they are financially effective) and merit if their value arises from moral or philosophical positions (e.g. if a particular initiative encourages qualities that society thinks are 'good', such as reflection, whether or not it is cost effective).

This perspective highlights the political nature of evaluation, and calls into question whether evaluators can ever be objective. While studies might seek to help individuals by developing shared understanding of how the world works, information can also be used by policy-makers to control processes and make the world work more effectively. There are, however, clear links between these two processes: both are empirical, leading to the construction of models and judgements about practice (Oliver, 2000).

Finally, although the process may be value-driven, it is possible to reframe evaluation so that it is not primarily judgemental, but instead focuses upon helping people to see the values in something, enabling them to become judges for themselves: 'If connoisseurship is the art of appreciation, criticism is the art of disclosure' (Eisner, 1998).

Changing approaches and different schools

Broadly, approaches in evaluation range from positivist approaches focused upon objective data collection (typically using quantitative methods) to interpretivist ones more rooted in constructivism (typically using qualitative methodologies). Guba and Lincoln (1989) chart a brief history of educational evaluation from the use of achievement tests in the 1890s onwards. Initially, 'evaluation' was a subsidiary concept to measurement and the emphasis was on the scientific testing of individual differences using standardised tests, often with little reference to the curriculum (or wider context) from which the students were drawn.

However, in the early 1960s, educational evaluators began expressing dissatisfaction with this approach, arguing that studies needed to support refinement and improvement, not simply provide judgements that endorsed or condemned courses. There was an important shift during the 1970s with the rejection of the established evaluation format (which was described rather scathingly as the 'agricultural-botany paradigm', reflecting the idea that curricula were 'applied to' students like chemical fertilisers on plant crops) as being unable to meet its own criteria of objectivity or to help educational practitioners. Importantly, this shift in emphasis led to the distinction between *formative* (shaping) and *summative* (judgemental) evaluations still recognised today.

Interest currently lies in the development of systems that minimise additional data collection but which still provide adequate information to make informed judgements about an institution's procedures. Unlike action research, in which judgements arise from iterative cycles of study and reflection of local contexts, the models underpinning quality assurance are typically imposed, and this can limit the usefulness of the study for understanding or improving things (Chelimsky, 1997). Although quality systems within UK higher education are now moving away from the data-heavy processes of the 1990s, the principle of accountability that resulted in the introduction of such systems remains strong in both the UK and America (Davies *et al.*, 2000; Feuer *et al.*, 2002). In America, these calls have already been followed through, with the 'No Child Left Behind' Act advocating in law that educational research should use quantitative approaches to implement evidence-based practice (Feuer *et al.*, 2002).

The rise of a new approach did not lead to the old being abandoned; indeed, both remain visible in educational research today, and the controversies over method and meaning that led to the split remain unresolved (Hammersley, 1997). There have been numerous attempts to unify the two schools; although none has been successful, these attempts have given rise to yet other approaches. Patton (1997), for example, has suggested that the argument between the two traditions has distracted evaluators from a more important issue: that no matter how closely a study adheres to the principles of its tradition, if the report that is produced sits on a shelf unread then the investigation was pointless.

These controversies make it clear that methods are not neutral; there is no single approach that all evaluators would agree is 'good'. Moreover, any method can be used inappropriately. As a result, it is important to understand the limitations of each approach in order to ensure that any conclusions that are drawn are warranted. A series of methods currently used to evaluate e-learning is discussed below.

Experimental methods

Within the experimental tradition, studies are often based upon comparisons between conditions in order to demonstrate improvement or identify differences. Studies also rely on the ability to control the 'noise' introduced by the complexity found in the classroom so as to focus on the effects of just a handful of variables. Educational resources can be trialled in this way as part of the design process, especially when determining usability issues. Early evaluations also attempted to use this approach to demonstrate the effectiveness of computer-based approaches (Gunn, 1997). There was an emphasis on quantitative data collections, benchmarked ratings of courseware or the production of statistics to show one method was better than or equivalent to another (e.g. that software was 'better' in some absolute sense than a chapter of a book; see the WinEcon evaluation – Allen *et al.*, 1996 – for example).

However, numerous researchers have argued that hypothesis testing was simply not the best way to understand the complex real-world situations where the materials would be used which, unlike laboratory settings, were not amenable to control and causality was difficult to demonstrate (see, for example, Oliver and Conole, 1998). The use of a control group is also ethically problematic (denying access to potentially beneficial opportunities), and intervention studies introduce issues of authenticity and transferability of findings. Contextual elements (such as access to supportive peers, parents or paid tutors) were seen to affect performance in unexpected but powerful ways; changes to computing access policies, teaching staff or resources and infrastructure can all change the nature of an innovation as it is studied; students who experience bad teaching often work harder as a result, hiding possible negative effects; and, of course, educational contexts are social settings, so there is often nothing to stop those with access to an innovation sharing with those who do not. Unpredicted but beneficial outcomes emerge that are not part of the study. Experiments can happen only when the research process interferes with this social setting (for example, by taking people out of it and placing them in a lab) – although experimental researchers do recognise that the relationship between their findings and classroom practice ('ecological validity') may be problematic.

Illuminative evaluation

Illuminative methodologies developed in response to experimental approaches by adopting ethnographic strategies. This provided a more open-ended, exploratory approach to evaluation (Parlett and Hamilton, 1972), emphasising the need to follow up unanticipated developments, to show an awareness of the influence of context (which traditional methods sought to eradicate through controlled experiments) and thus to 'illuminate' the focus of the study. Evaluators took a 'neutral outsider' stance in order to observe practices as they happened. Adopting such an approach was possible only on a small scale, which contrasted with the apparent need for increasingly larger-scale experimental methods, but also made this process both time-intensive and costly. Such a 'value free' approach sometimes results in a mismatch between the sponsor's expectations and study outcomes.

Systems approaches

The systems approach model emerged during the 1970s as a way of providing evaluation feedback linked to learning outcomes. This approach also aimed to move away from scientific methods, as formative feedback linked to learning would help inform ongoing judgements as well as contributing to a body of knowledge about education and training (Hamblin, 1974). Many studies are intended to improve students' learning, even if only indirectly.

Such an outcomes-focused approach was sometimes criticised as being mechanistic and limited, and almost positivist in style. There were also issues about whose objectives were being addressed and how this information would be fed back to policy-makers. There is also a perceived risk – shared with quality assurance systems – that asking questions about achieving particular goals changes practice rather than describing it (Blalock, 1999).

Goal-free evaluation

Rather than focusing upon stated intentions and to help eliminate the bias of stakeholders, goal-free evaluation (Scriven, 1972) takes a more constructivist approach, pursuing issues that emerge as having significance rather than pre-determining the study focus. Potentially, this provides a broader perspective, exploring unanticipated outcomes through working and spending time with the various stakeholder groups. This approach also differs from the research-like illuminative approach in that its purpose is to help make informed decisions about practice (rather than just describe it) through its interventionist use of dialogue between stakeholders.

Action research

The rise of action research models marked an important trend in educational evaluation, producing a new body of educational research knowledge as well as influencing evaluation methodologies. Action research has its roots in the work of the psychologist Lewin, who sought to understand and model how individuals acted in society (Lewin, 1952). He emphasised the importance of working with the people being studied in order to effect change, an approach that resonated with the problems facing teachers who sought to evaluate what took place in their own classrooms (McNiff, 1988). Action research has developed into a movement within education that places value on the ideas of democracy, emancipation and collaboration; within action research, it is argued that evaluation should not be something done to subjects, but something done *with* participants (Kemmis, 1996). The evaluation process thus develops iteratively: it moves through cycles of planning, acting, observing and reflecting that build upon each other, sometimes progressing (for example, by developing and refining a model of classroom practice, or taking an increasingly detailed focus on a particular issue), sometimes diverging (for example, by highlighting an important but previously neglected issue that the evaluator considers worthy of investigation), depending on the interests and values of those involved (McNiff, 1988).

However, it should be noted that – in spite of their similarities, such as a concern with generating locally meaningful understanding – there are important differences between action research and evaluation. Evaluation does not always share the democratising agenda; action research may be relatively unconcerned with judging; and action researchers usually study their own practices whilst evaluators typically study other people's.

Responsive and utilisation-focused evaluation schools

These are approaches that adopt a pragmatic focus towards educational evaluation. They involve tailoring an evaluation so that it will 'make a difference' (Patton, 1997), which inevitably involves taking into account the viewpoints of various stakeholder groups. The popularity of this method reflects evaluators who seek to act as change agents; using evaluation helps initiate this change.

Different approaches utilise different ways of integrating stakeholder involvement. Stake's responsive evaluation (1980), for example, structures activities in a way that is responsive to the various stakeholder groups' needs. Guba and Lincoln's fourth-generation evaluation approach (1989) seeks to identify stakeholder groups' concerns and negotiate a strategy before data are collected, thereby taking into account a range of different values and perspectives.

Patton (1997) starts from the premise that a good evaluation is one that enables people to do things. Usefulness is thus privileged over rigour, and any method can be used so long as the audience of the report will find it credible. The importance of rigour is not ignored, however; utilisation-focused evaluators still aspire towards it. The focus on use means that evaluations have to be timely ('quick and dirty' is preferred to 'perfect but late') and informative – and importantly, they must inform someone who can act. In contrast to the democratising principles of action research, say, this approach emphasises rhetorical persuasion, with powerful stakeholders as an audience.

The utlisation-focused school of evaluation can be seen as a good example of ways in which processes have become commodified. Because this approach is organised around the notion that studies should be 'consumed', it can simply serve those who have power (for example, those who can afford to commission studies). As a result, it is important that utilisation-focused evaluators remain sensitive to issues of audience and politics so that they can take a radical position rather than reinforcing inequality (c.f. Freire, 1993).

Integrative evaluation

The integrative evaluation model was proposed by Draper et al. (1994) as a way to evaluate resources within a broader education context by placing the audience and their needs above methodology. It proposes the use of a barrage of data collection techniques to provide a rounded picture of students' and teachers' practice with technology. Issues and anomalies can then be remedied, until the use of technology becomes seen as a normal and natural part of the course.

Evidence-based practice

Whilst these different schools of thought seem to imply that educational evaluation has moved steadily away from its roots in experimentation, this is not entirely true. Particular forms of evaluation rooted in quantitative methods and aspiring to scientific status have gained prominence in the current era of educational accountability, even though it has been noted that policy-based, outcomes-driven audits of practice run the risk of distorting rather than reporting the practice they seek to describe (Blalock, 1999). Additionally, there have been calls from policy-makers in the UK to adopt the idea of evidence-based practice developed in medicine for use in education (Davies *et al.*, 2000; Fitz-Gibbon, 2000). In America, these calls have led to the 'No Child Left Behind' Act, which advocates in law that educational research should implement evidence-based practice by using quantitative approaches (Feuer *et al.*, 2002), ignoring widespread criticisms that the approach is methodologically and ethically inappropriate (e.g. Hammersley, 2001; Oliver and Conole, 2003; St Pierre, 2002).

As part of the medical model, a hierarchy of evidence has been drawn up that states explicitly the degree of faith placed on different kinds of study. Randomised control trials, following the classic experimental model, sit at the top of the hierarchy as a gold standard, with qualitative methods (such as all those described above) relegated to the level of anecdotal evidence, either discounted entirely or at best given a role in supporting the findings from favoured types of study. As a reaction against 'unsystematic' research, it appears that educational evaluation has come full circle.

The ethics and politics of evaluation

The process of evaluation cannot be separated from 'issues of power, politics, value judgements and human interests' (Esterby-Smith, 1994). Evaluation is intended to improve, make changes or allocate resources. As a consequence, the communication and negotiation process is one that needs to be handled carefully.

Research into ethical issues in the evaluation of learning technology is not common, but should underpin evaluation. Cohen and Manion (1994) provide a thorough guide to the ethical issues associated with educational research; these are echoed in the guides to ethical conduct produced by groups such as the British Educational Research Association (BERA, n.d.). These include, for example: getting access and gaining acceptance; privacy; anonymity; confidentiality; and deception. The cornerstone of addressing these issues, argue Cohen and Manion (1994), is informed consent. This is the principle that each individual has the right to freedom and self-determination; participants in research should thus have the right to understand what they are taking part in and to end their involvement at any point. However, as they point out, there are many problems with this principle: in some studies where deception is necessary (such as those involving covert observation), providing a full explanation is impractical; there is an inevitable tension between providing an audience with enough information about research participants and ensuring that they cannot be identified; there are also many debates about whether the rights of individuals can ever be compromised to further the good of the many. Because these tensions are complex, they must be interpreted on a case-by-case basis. As a result, it is important that educational research studies discuss these issues; in particularly complex cases, the whole purpose of a paper might be to explore such issues as a case study.

Issues in evaluating learning technology

The messiness of e-learning

As described in Chapter 1, there is considerable confusion about what 'counts' as e-learning, and also what terms should be used to describe it. This is a particular problem for evaluation. Many of the approaches described above emphasise the need for dialogue between stakeholders; in e-learning, this may prove particularly difficult since each may have different – even contradictory – assumptions about what e-learning is and how it works. This makes the initial scoping phase of work particularly important.

Doing evaluation

A recurrent issue in e-learning is that practitioners are expected to evaluate their own initiatives – even though academics have rarely received training to do this, see no particular benefits and have other priorities (Harvey *et al.*, 2002). As a consequence, efforts have been made to support academics with guidance, tools and models.

A number of evaluation frameworks have been developed that articulate the process of evaluating e-learning, such as the CIAO! framework (Jones *et al.*, 1996), the integrative approach (Draper *et al.*, 1994), the SECAL method (Gunn, 1997) and the ELT framework (Oliver *et al.*, 2002). Conole and Oliver (2002), for example, have attempted to model the process of evaluation based on studies of practice. This model splits the process into a sequence of steps. Of course, this is an idealised representation of practice; in reality, progress through these is unlikely to be linear, and not all studies or evaluators will follow every step. By starting from studies of practice, this research assumes that evaluation is a socially constructed practice. An alternative approach would be to work out the 'essence' that defines 'evaluation' as a concept, perhaps through philosophical enquiry.

According to this model, evaluation consists of the following stages:

1. Identification of the audience(s) for the evaluation
2. Selection of an evaluation question
3. Choice of an evaluation methodology
4. Choice of data collection methods
5. Choice of data analysis methods
6. Selection of the most appropriate format(s) for reporting the findings to the audience.

These steps can be thought of as a combination of contextual (1, 2 and 6) and mechanical (3, 4 and 5), or alternatively as strategic and tactical choices. A similar distinction is advocated by Draper *et al.* (1994).

Placing the audience and its needs above methodology locates such models firmly within the school of utilisation-focused evaluation; in other traditions, the methodology would influence the kinds of questions that were considered to be acceptable – so, for example, experimental studies would require well-defined hypotheses, whereas illuminative studies would typically involve open-ended questions.

Tools to help with evaluation

A number of projects have used the kinds of models outlined above to develop tools for novice evaluators. Ehrmann (1999), for example, complemented a model of the process with a data bank of survey questions. Other researchers have pursued more flexible developments – for example, the online evaluation toolkit (Conole and Oliver, 2002). Such developments use the model to form an interactive resource that prompts reflection, records decisions and provides advice on the options available at each point in the process. However, to date, the evidence that these tools change practice is limited. They have been shown to change evaluation *plans*, but the longitudinal studies needed to demonstrate an impact on practice are lacking (Oliver *et al.*, 2002).

A number of other peculiarities influence data collection around e-learning. Much useful data can be captured, including transcriptions of online dialogues. Nonetheless, researchers must be cautious not to place too much faith in such records, since they portray only part of the picture – the social contexts that surround such data may be completely hidden (Jones, 1998b). Further complications arise from the distance that often exists between evaluator and participants: methods such as interviews, which rely on face-to-face contact, may be impractical where participants are geographically dispersed, and will need to be rethought if conducted using new technologies since participants' responses differ (Oliver, 2001). The same is true even for online surveys, which tend to attract responses from different groups than paper-based surveys, changing the impression given by the data.

Issues of method

Although whole texts have been written on issues of methods, there are several particular difficulties for e-learning evaluation. One recurrent issue, for example, concerns drawing comparisons. Experimental studies rely on the ability to draw comparisons between conditions – however, since educational innovations such as the introduction of technology may change the nature of what is learned, any comparison between this and previous practice must be viewed with scepticism. It has been argued (Oliver and Conole, 1998), however, that actually this happens all the time; what is important is not whether or not comparisons can be drawn (you could ask, for example, 'how do these two groups perform on this exam?'), but what they *mean* (for example, 'have these two groups learned different things?'). Such a change of emphasis echoes practices within qualitative traditions of research, where case studies are important. Although these are the study of particular cases, either authors or readers often feel the need to compare what is reported with other reports or with personal experience (Stake, 1994). Here, questions are not about whether such comparisons are valid but whether they are educative. Thus the issue of comparisons now covers a range of emphases, from the technical problems of valid inference about models (or the world) to a social or psychological focus on meaning-making.

Another issue facing evaluation is the question of authenticity. It is well established that people involved in studies perform differently from those who are not. This phenomenon is known as the Hawthorne effect. It is also recognised that the presence of an observer (for example, in a classroom) changes the way in which people interact. For studies in education, these problems are extremely important because they imply that the process of doing research changes what it is you are researching (Kvale, 1996). Some traditions have embraced this issue – it is, for example, the whole point of action research that such studies *should* change, not just comment upon, the world (Kemmis, 1996). Other evaluators try to overcome this issue by trying to blend in (for example, following the ethnographic tradition; c.f. Jones, 1998b) or by seeking to study day-to-day activities in an unobtrusive manner for at least some small part of their process (for example, the CIAO! framework; Jones *et al.*, 1996).

Causes are also hard to determine within education, since contextual elements (such as access to supportive peers, parents or paid tutors) can affect performance in unexpected but powerful ways; changes to computing access policies, teaching staff or resources and infrastructure can all change the nature of an innovation as it is studied; students who experience bad teaching often work harder as a result, hiding possible negative effects; and, of course, educational contexts are social settings, so there is often nothing to stop those with access to an innovation sharing with those who do not (Oliver and Harvey, 2002). This has implications for experiments, which are possible only *because* the research process interferes with this social setting (for example, by taking people out of it and placing them in a lab), inevitably causing problems for the relationship between their findings and classroom practice ('ecological validity').

Any study is only as good as the data that it draws upon (Patton, 1997). This observation is particularly important in the context of studies involving children, although some researchers would argue that the same concerns hold true for data concerning any individual's experience of education. In addition to pragmatic problems such as participants who seek to please the researcher (telling them what they want to hear) or subvert the process in some way, there is also the educational problem that people cannot always articulate what they have learned. Some knowledge, it is argued, is tacit; although we have learned something, we cannot put it into words (McMahon, 2000). Similarly, we may have learned how to do something, but this is no guarantee that we will choose to do it (Barnett, 1997). Thus studies can provide only partial accounts; as a consequence, it is important for the evaluator to appreciate what the limits on their data are.

With any study, irrespective of methodology, the question of how widely the conclusions can be generalised must be considered. Again, qualitative methods often make this concern explicit, valuing 'rich' descriptions of contexts so that the reader can decide upon the extent to which this case resembles their own (Stake, 1994). In experimental studies, however, the reader must infer from any demographic information given whether or not the participants in the research are in any way similar to the pupils who might be involved in some learning development. These demographic data represent a model of what the researcher believes is significant: for example, that the important variation between individuals can be described in terms of classification according to age and gender. Since students vary from year to year and from institution to institution (let alone country to country), as well as in terms of what might be described as their social class, a model such as this can easily be argued to neglect important variables. Even the decade in which the study took place has been shown to have an important influence on the design and interpretation of studies (Berliner, 2002). If the model is incomplete in these potentially important ways, then the confidence with which conclusions can be generalised must be called into doubt. And, of course, all models are incomplete; they are selective representations, emphasising some features and ignoring others. This makes it important to recognise the rhetorical way in which they operate. Indeed, it has been argued that, rather than trusting the general conclusions of experiments over the provisional conclusions of case studies, experiments ought to be doubted and questioned in exactly the same way as the tentative findings of qualitative studies (Holt and Oliver, 2002).

There are ethical as well as technical issues associated with comparative evaluations. Can one group be denied access to a new form of education – particularly if the researchers suspect it might be more effective and hence give an advantage on formally assessed work? One solution to this problem involves piloting initiatives within non-assessed areas of the curriculum. This remains problematic, however, because assessment has such a profound effect on how pupils act (Biggs, 1999); the situation may thus change dramatically once assessment is reintroduced. Other alternatives include crossover designs, in which the group experiencing the innovation swaps with the group which does not have access to it after some mid-point measurement or observation, or simply providing access to the resources for revision purposes once the study is complete.

The role of the evaluator

The role of the evaluator is one that necessarily changes with each different methodology. For some this might mean acting as a neutral outsider or administrator of predefined tests while for others this involves becoming a 'critical friend', educator, advocate or even lobbyist (see, for example, Patton, 1997). As the level of participation increases within the process, so their role becomes more influential in determining both evaluation process and product. Besides methodological and technical competency based on their training in systematic inquiry and analysis, evaluators are likely to need skills in communication and team building, group process and negotiation (Guba and Lincoln, 1989).

This may imply that the evaluator is (initially) separate to the stakeholders, being brought in to undertake an evaluation study. This might be possible in funded projects but for day-to-day practice it is likely that one of the key stakeholders will have to take on the role of evaluator. Both options introduce issues. How will personal interest and investment influence data collection methodologies? How easily can the roles of (say) assessor and evaluator be moved between? By comparison, which factors will influence the selection of an external evaluator, and how much of an impact does their possession of 'evaluation skills' or personal goals have upon the resultant process?

The influence of context

Earlier, the process of evaluation was described as starting from an awareness of different audiences and their concerns. Designing studies around the interests of such audiences positions evaluation as being a practical and political activity. As Weiss (1993) argues, 'evaluation is a rational enterprise that takes place in a political context', which 'by its nature makes implicit political statements about such issues as the problematic nature of some programs'. Unlike illuminative or experimental studies, this kind of evaluation cannot be a search for 'truth' in some positivist, revealed sense. Instead, it is a process that seeks to inform and educate in order to inform subsequent action (Patton, 1997). This raises important ethical questions for evaluators. If evaluation enables action, whose actions will be supported? Whose agendas will be served? Who is paying for the evaluation?

The concept of educational evaluation, like the studies it involves, critically depends on context, and some contexts are more regulated than others. Regulation can provide useful guidelines or a rod for stakeholders' backs. The key is to offer tangible benefits to learners, teachers and institutions, preferably in that order. Prescribed methods are not always conducive to this aim, as common (ab)use of student evaluation of teaching questionnaires shows. Used well they provide one source of feedback to guide improvement; used badly they become an obstacle course around exam time and a whip to spur teachers on through the tenure track. A truly authentic evaluation involves collaboration among teachers, developers and learners using existing knowledge, experience and impact analysis, to create quality learning opportunities in a given context. Knowledge of established theory and methodology may be limited, but the 'common sense' 'grass roots' 'design-based research' approach still works well. It may not produce generalisable results, but then neither do many other 'approved' methods.

Cathy Gunn

Traditionally, those who are served are those who commission the study; the people in the study are positioned as research subjects and treated as sources of data. Other forms of evaluation (such as action research or utilisation-focused evaluation) have tried to subvert this situation, treating people as research participants or collaborators, rather than subjects to be 'treated'. In some cases, the process of evaluation alters to reflect this new mindset. Participants can redesign the study; they can conduct their own, independent enquiries that are incorporated into the design; they may provide points of view not invited by the study; they can be invited to discuss the agenda of the study and the appropriateness of the methods used; and they may be reporting the findings directly to the funders rather than having their stories re-interpreted by evaluators. Whether any of this is a useful or important thing to do will depend on the specific situation being evaluated. What is important is that the evaluator should remain aware of the different political agendas that their study might be used to support so that they can take a principled position about which groups' agendas they will work to support (Oliver and Harvey, 2002).

Broad stakeholder involvement can make the evaluation process extremely complex. To address this, some approaches use the negotiation of concerns between evaluator and stakeholder groups as part of the process (e.g. Guba and Lincoln, 1989). The process of clarifying the purpose of an evaluation or confronting the data generated can help stakeholders to appreciate each other's relative values (Eisner, 1998) as well as realise the educational value inherent in that experience (Patton, 1997). Conflict between stakeholder groups may also result, however, in which case the evaluator must act as a facilitator, negotiating outcomes and the implications of decision-making. In order to fulfil such a facilitative role effectively involves gaining stakeholders' cooperation and trust, then sustaining their interest and involvement over an extended period of time (Guba and Lincoln, 1989). However, such involvement is not without its cost: the evaluator's perceived loss of 'objectivity' may result in reduced trust or value from other quarters; this can reduce the impact of their findings or hinder access to sources of quality data since they are no longer viewed as neutral.

Conclusions

Evaluation may be seen as an increasingly important part of educational practice, but the research effort that has been invested in this topic has served to complicate, not simplify, its practice. Evaluation remains problematic and contested conceptually, technically and philosophically. Within such a complex area, it becomes increasingly important for individual researchers and practitioners to be clear about their assumptions and their theoretical commitments.

Evaluation also serves to illustrate the politics that surround e-learning. The explicit consideration of stakeholders and their agendas foregrounds the issues that can arise. Provision of evidence may serve the interests of sponsors or it may be challenging, radical or educative. Stylistic decisions about whether a study is an intervention, a judgement or a description reveal how evaluation plays a part in this book's themes of interactivity and of change. Fundamentally, the idea that evaluations should lead to use – a tenet of utilisation-focused approaches – illustrates the process of the commodification of knowledge.

Because of these complications, it has become impossible to advocate 'good practice' in any simple or generic way (although the development of models and toolkits may allow practitioners to follow accepted practice amongst the community of evaluators). Raising awareness of these issues amongst researchers and practitioners is thus increasingly important; this, together with efforts to understand the process and significance of evaluation in ever greater depth, represents important directions for future research in this area.

Chapter 15

Conclusion

Martin Oliver and Gráinne Conole

The aim of producing a book that reflected the dialogues and debates within the field of e-learning, as outlined in Chapters 1 and 2, causes particular problems when producing a closing chapter. It would be wrong to end with neat conclusions, just as it would be wrong to end without any conclusions at all. Instead of trying to produce a single, authoritative vision of the field, then, what we will do here is highlight shared issues and areas of difference. To focus this discussion, we will draw first upon the themes identified in Chapter 1 as a background that shapes work in this area, and then follow this with issues that characterise e-learning research itself.

Revisiting the themes of this book

In Chapter 1, six themes were identified that ran throughout the book. Each of these will be reviewed, briefly, to summarise the ways in which they influence work on e-learning.

Interdisciplinarity

The failure of any school of thought to dominate e-learning leads to benefits and problems. The difficulties are readily apparent across this book: research cannot be readily synthesised, since studies begin from different (even incompatible) assumptions and adopt different approaches. This was particularly evident in the discussion of methodology in Chapter 2, but can be seen, for example, in the discussions of what learning is in Chapter 6 or what motivation is in Chapter 13.

The positive aspect of this situation is the level of awareness that these problems engender. When assumptions are not shared and perspectives cannot be taken for granted, it is necessary to rethink the fundamentals of research on a regular basis. This kind of rethinking can be seen, for example, in the best of the debates around naming the area (see below).

However, this does pose practical problems for those engaged in researching the field. Balancing different perspectives and interpreting particular studies in terms of the traditions of research that led to them is a demanding and time-consuming process. The consequent risk is that interdisciplinary engagement will remain superficial, rather than fulfilling its potential.

Access and inclusion

Issues of inclusion are addressed in particular in Chapter 8, but access and inclusion is a recurrent theme across the other chapters as well. This theme can be interpreted from a technological perspective (Chapters 4, 7, 8 and 9) in terms of how the design and management of educational resources and software influence or impact on how accessible they then are for different audiences. It can also be viewed from a pedagogical and organisational perspective (Chapters 5 and 6) in terms of how different pedagogical approaches and means of implementing technologies enable access.

This diversity of perspectives reveals a more complex picture of inclusion than is usually adopted. Instead of a simple binary of haves and have-nots, it shows how individuals can have access in one way and lack it in another. Rather than being 'types', people should be understood as having a complex profile of engagement with technology, with others and with ideas.

This complexity makes action difficult, however. Deciding which kind of inclusion it is most important to consider or to act upon is a political act. Additionally, there can be no simple answers in such a complex situation.

Change

Most of the chapters in this book concern change. In some cases this is primarily an historical account, as with the review of policies in Chapter 3. In others, such as in Chapters 7 and 8, the emphasis is more on creating change – Chapter 8 argues for particular perspectives that designers could or should take. (This also illustrates one aspect of the politics of e-learning.) Other chapters have explored the consequences of change. In Chapter 11, for example, it is clear that researchers are trying to understand what new kinds of text production and consumption mean in terms of our understanding of literacy.

None of this is surprising, given that technology itself is constantly changing. What is interesting, however, is that changes in technology are positioned both as a cause (as with literacy) and as an effect (as with design). This complex relationship between technology and people warrants further exploration, particularly if positions such as technological determinism – which treats technology as the cause of change – are to be resisted. A more sophisticated account of this relationship is needed so that research in the field can develop.

Commodification

Within this book, the theme of commodification arose from Lyotard's discussion of the exteriorisation of knowledge (Chapter 2). The more obvious illustrations of this can be seen in the discussions of how best to organise content for learners (see, for example, Chapter 8) or how to get learners to perform their knowledge in a way that can be assessed – usually by creating some kind of artefact, such as a sequence of multiple choices (Chapter 10) or equally the creation of various kinds of texts (Chapter 11).

Perhaps less obvious, but at least as powerful, is the way in which knowledge is represented in technology. Chapter 4 provides many examples of this – such as the historical case of Bush's Memex, which instantiated in a technical design an understanding of how people learn; or the discussion of visualisation technologies, which are designed to reveal particular representations of knowledge to learners.

It is important to recognise this tendency within the field to view knowledge as something distinct from people, rather than as a quality they possess. The desire to design technology can be understood in terms of commodification, with the value of technology being judged performatively, in terms of its use. This is reflected in the prevalence of studies intended to improve the use of technology, as opposed to critiques of why technology is adopted in the first place. This imbalance limits the kinds of progress that researchers in the field are currently able to make.

Interactivity and social interaction

Irrespective of the position taken on knowledge, interactivity is important. Whether this be in the form of feedback on test performance (e.g. Chapter 10) or the co-construction of knowledge (Chapter 12), interactivity has been shown to be fundamental to the process of learning.

This might seem to undermine the importance of the concept: if it is always required, it is not a discriminating concept, and therefore lacks analytic value. However, what these chapters have shown is that different kinds of interactivity can be valuable depending on the circumstances of use – and the decision as to which are most important to foster will be influenced by behaviourist or social perspectives on learning.

This is not a simple case of discussion falling into social conceptions of learning and materials into positivist ones. As Chapter 8 illustrated, if the designer views their materials as an opportunity for mediated discussion with the learner, a social perspective on learning is being enacted. If a positivist views a discussion as an opportunity to correct misconceptions (i.e. to control, rather than to generate, understanding), then a behaviourist model would serve to explain the role of feedback.

Moreover, collaboration does not just affect the acquisition of concepts. As Chapter 13 demonstrated, the motivational effects of working with others cannot be underestimated. To neglect the effect of interactivity and interaction on learners' activities is to take an inappropriately narrow focus on the outcomes, rather than the process, of learning.

Political aspects

The influence and presence of political decisions was foregrounded in the book in Chapters 3 (where priorities are expressed through policies), 5 (where power is codified through institutional structures) and 14 (where evaluators have to decide which agendas to serve). However, the decision to invest resources – either financial or in terms of personal time – in a particular activity is inherently political, and is equally present in terms of the design of curricula and forms of assessment (Chapters 7 and 10) as it is in terms of the creation of policies.

Although the term 'stakeholder' is over-used, it is an unavoidable conclusion that an array of individuals has different vested interests in higher education, from the commercial desire to see education produce employable graduates (see Chapter 2) to the liberal desire for individuals to be able to express themselves in a variety of ways (see Chapter 11). Organisationally, as Chapter 5 showed, learners, teachers, librarians, learning technologists, technical experts and managers are all involved in creating and judging education. The best way for these relationships to be configured continues to be debated – typically by subsets of those involved rather than involving everyone. It seems unlikely that the political tensions visible in e-learning will be resolved in the near future.

Issues and tensions

The initial themes that were used to frame the work form a background to this area of research. They may be visible within e-learning, but they are not unique to it. However, a series of issues and tensions can be identified that characterise the current state of this area of research.

The contested nature of the area

Given that e-learning is both interdisciplinary and political, as outlined above, it is inevitable that it remains contested. The continuing changes in terminology (Chapter 1), in policy emphasis (Chapter 3) and so on illustrate this struggle in motion. Each discipline emphasises different aspects of e-learning; and even within one specific area, such as how to design learning materials, different perspectives on learning can lead to contradictory recommendations.

What does this mean for researchers, practitioners and policy-makers? Simply, that no work in e-learning is 'neutral'. Any design, claims and practices involve taking a position on what e-learning is, how it should be done, and which aspects of it are important. As argued in Chapter 2, this makes naïve positions where these decisions are left tacit – a problem for the field. Without understanding why someone has acted as they have, it is difficult to imagine how best to interpret or respond to their actions.

As Chapter 1 illustrated, nascent disciplines are characterised by turmoil and insecurity. Ongoing attempts to establish consensus on terminology, methodology and so on are evidence of this. Rather than attempting to ignore, down-play or 'solve' this situation, as so often happens now, it may be more productive to accept it, to recognise differences (and in some cases, incompatibilities) between areas of research and to see whether constructive dialogues between these positions can be established.

The complexity of context

Each of the chapters has shown how e-learning is understood differently depending on which aspects of its context are taken into account. Organisational contexts, theoretical contexts, social (and motivational) contexts, assessment frameworks – each of these is present in the book precisely because it influences how e-learning takes place. The same is true of each of the topics covered here. How, then, can we cope with the complexity of the concept of context? It seems unlikely that a complete account can be provided. Instead, it may be more productive to consider which contextual elements are of importance (or interest), and to focus on them. Activity theory, with its Marxist roots (Kuutti, 1996), frames actions in terms of communities with rules and divisions of labour, viewing activity as a process of production. Its growing popularity within the field reflects the fact that many researchers have found these to be useful elements to consider. Similarly, Biggs' theory of constructive alignment (1999) focuses on the curriculum as a context; its popularity arises from the perception that assessment does have a powerful influence on students' actions.

Neither of these positions is complete: each, however, is valuable. Moving towards a fuller, better integrated account of context may be possible in the future; but for now, greater awareness of its role, and greater openness about which aspects of it are deemed to be important, seem like necessary steps for researchers working in the field.

Outcomes vs. process

E-learning makes teaching, learning and assessment processes more explicit. Implementing these within systems, rules or artefacts codifies processes that might otherwise remain tacit or be socially negotiated.

Unfortunately, this means that the kinds of data that can be considered are often reduced to easily computable forms. Within assessment, this would typically be multiple-choice input; within evaluation or the framing of a research method, it might be the number of messages a student posts. The process leading to a button click or a message being sent cannot be taken into account.

Such developments do have advantages – particularly in terms of automating what would otherwise be extremely time-consuming processes, particularly when faced with increasing numbers of students and a widespread move towards monitoring and accountability. In many situations, it is a necessary response to practical problems, even if it is not an ideal one. However, the growing interest in attempting to map processes – for example, studying users' trails through learning object repositories as a way to map out learning 'trajectories' – reflects a growing dissatisfaction with the adequacy of outcome-oriented interpretations.

Content vs. communication

Although 'e-learning' is the dominant term in current research in this area, the older term 'Information and Communication Technology' is useful in highlighting two different uses of technology. On the one hand, there is information management: an individual process, often involving databases of some sort. On the other, there is communication: a social process, where the only 'resources' that might be created are ephemeral and fleeting, and what is important is the way these are created, rather than managed. Clearly, both of these form part of the process of learning – however, it is apparent from the preceding chapters that some areas of research value one above the other, resulting in a tension over which to prioritise.

However, it should also be kept in mind that content *is* a form of communication. The selection of particular ideas, the emphasis of features or concepts through a specific design – all of these can be interpreted semiotically, as an attempt to share meaning and understanding with others (or, at least, to help them construct meaning from their experience of this thing).

Summary

The purpose of this book was not to provide simple answers. It was not intended to say how to 'do' e-learning (either as policy or practice), nor to establish any single hegemonic position on how to research it. Instead, its purpose was to inform, to challenge and to sensitise. Drawing together research on this series of topics has provided a point of departure for anyone seeking to engage with e-learning. We have avoided claims of being authoritative, but have sought to be wide-ranging in this process, so that a better-informed position can be taken.

We have sought to challenge through the use of contrasting perspectives, recognising the importance of these as a way of stimulating debate and progress within e-learning. No matter what a reader's view on the field, it is our hope that they will find something to disagree with here because, without such disagreement, the field would be lifeless and sterile. We have attempted to sensitise by highlighting issues that might otherwise remain unknown to anyone but small groups of specialist researchers and showing how important they can be to e-learning.

The only indication of our success in this is if readers find things that are unexpected or surprising in these chapters, and then take greater care to attend to them in the future. Certainly, the process of producing this book has changed the way in which many of its writers view e-learning and how some of us will go about researching it; we can but hope the same is true for readers more generally.

E-learning remains complicated, fast-moving and important. We cannot change that; nor can we 'solve' it. This is why it is a complicated but also such a fascinating, exciting area to be involved in – it is its blessing and its curse. What we have attempted to do here is to hold it in focus, to reveal and illuminate facets of this complex phenomenon that we are involved in both studying and producing. Its name may change; its characteristics might vary; different technologies and different practices might fall within its purview. This should not worry us; it is the hallmark of a vibrant, living field of research and practice. We do not fully understand it, and we will not fully understand it; but this should not stop us from trying to, nor from taking delight in the pursuit of understanding it.

References

Abel, R. (2005) *Will Open Source Software Become an Important Institutional Strategy in Higher Education?*, Alliance for Higher Education Competitiveness Inc. Available online at: www.a-hec.org.

ACRL (2000) *Academic Library Trends and Statistics.* Available online at: http://www.ala.org/ala/acrlbucket/nonserialtitles/acrl2000academic.htm, last accessed 31 March 2006.

Agger, B. (2004) *The Virtual Self: A Contemporary Sociology*, Oxford: Blackwell.

Alexander, D. (2003) 'Redesign of the Monash University web site: a case study in user-centred design methods', *Paper presented at AusWeb03.* Available online at: http://ausweb.scu.edu.au/aw03/papers/alexander/paper.html, last accessed 5 October 2005.

Allen, P., Booth, S., Crompton, P. and Timms, D. (1996) 'An evaluation of the WinEcon software', in Allen, P., Booth, S., Crompton, P. and Timms, D. (eds), *Case Studies: Integrating Learning with Technology*, 51–66, TLTP Project Varsetile, http://annick.stir.ac.uk/, University of Stirling, Scotland.

APIS-MS (2005) *APIS Marking Service.* Available online at: http://www.jisc.ac.uk/index.cfm?name=toolkit_strath, last accessed 30 March 2006.

Armstrong, C. (2001) 'A study of the use of electronic information systems by higher education students in the UK', *Program*, 35(3), 241–62.

Arnseth, H.C. and Ludvigsen, S.R. (2004) 'Systemic versus interpretative approaches to CSCL research: findings and future steps', *CSCL SIG Symposium*, Lausanne 7–9 October 2004. Available online at: http://www.pfi.uio.no/KIM–prosjektet/Innhold/CSCL_lausanne_HCA_SLv2.doc, last accessed 2 December 2005.

Ashton, H.S., Schofield, D.K. and Woodgar, S.C. (2003) 'Piloting summative web assessment in secondary education', in Christie, J. (ed.), *Proceedings of the 7th International Computer-Assisted Assessment Conference*, Loughborough: Loughborough University.

Ashton, H.S., Beavers, C.E., Schofield, D.K. and Youngson, M.A. (2004) 'Informative reports – experiences from the Pass-IT project', in Ashby, M. and Wilson, R. (eds), *Proceedings of the 8th International Computer-Assisted Assessment Conference*, Loughborough: Loughborough University.

Ashwin, P. and McLean, M. (2005) 'Towards an integration of the "approaches to learning" and "critical pedagogy" perspectives in higher education through a focus on academic engagement', in Rust, C. (ed.) *Improving Student Learning: Diversity and Inclusivity*, Proceedings of the 12th Improving Student Learning symposium, Birmingham 2004, Oxford: Oxford Centre for Staff and Learning Development (OCSLD).

Bacsich, P., Ash, C. and Heginbotham, S. (2001) *The Cost of Networked Learning, Phase Two*, Sheffield: Sheffield University.

Bailey, C., Fill, K., Zalfan, M.T., Davis, H.C., Conole, G. and Olivier, B. (2006) 'Panning for gold: designing pedagogically-inspired learning nuggets', *Educational Technology and Society – Special Issue (January 2006), Theme: Learning Design.* Available online at: http://www.ifets.info/journals/9_1/10.pdf, last accessed 30 March 2006.

Baker, M.J. (2000) 'The roles of models in artificial intelligence and education research: a prospective view', *International Journal of Artificial Intelligence in Education*, 11, 122–43.

Baker, M., Hansen, T., Joiner, R. and Traum, D. (1999) 'The role of grounding in collaborative learning tasks', in Dillenbourg, P. (ed.), *Collaborative Learning: Computational and Cognitive Approaches*, 31–63, Amsterdam: Elsevier.

Barnard, A.G. (1970) 'Teaching Computing in Universities', Report of the joint working party, UGC/CBURC.

Barnett, R. (1990) *The Idea of Higher Education*, Buckingham: Open University Press.

Barnett, R. (1994) *The Limits of Competence*, Buckingham: Open University Press.

Barnett, R. (1997) *Higher Education: A Critical Business*, Buckingham: Open University Press.

Bauman, Z. (2000) *Liquid Modernity*, Cambridge: Polity Press.

Bauman, Z. (2002) *Society Under Siege*, Cambridge: Polity Press.

Beaty, L. (2006) 'Towards professional teaching in higher education: the role of accreditation', in Ashwin, P. (ed.), *Changing Higher Education: The Development of Learning and Teaching*, London: Routledge.

Becher, T. and Trowler, P. (2001). *Academic Tribes and Territories*, Buckingham, UK: Society for Research into Higher Education and Open University Press.

Beck, U. (1992) *Risk Society Towards a New Modernity*, London: Sage.

Beetham, H. (2002a) 'The Learning Technology Career Development Scoping Study'. Available online at: http://www.jisc.ac.uk/index.cfm?name=project_career, last accessed 29 July 2003.

Beetham, H. (2002b) 'Developing learning technology networks through shared representations of practice', *Proceedings of the 9th International Improving Student Learning Symposium*, 421–34, Oxford: OCSLD.

Beetham, H. (2004) 'Review: Developing e-learning models for the JISC practitioner communities', *A Report for the JISC E-pedagogy Programme*, JISC. Available online at: http://www.jisc.ac.uk/uploaded_documents/Review%20models.doc, last accessed 24 July 2006.

Beetham, H. (2005) 'What is learning and how do we learn? Introduction to three types of learning theory'. In Beetham, H. and Roberts, G. (eds) *Introduction to Learning Theory and Design for Learning*, Oxford: ALT.

Beetham, H., Jones, S. and Gornall, L. (2001) 'Career Development of Learning Technology Staff: Scoping Study Final Report', *JISC Committee for Awareness Liaison and Training.* Available online at: http://www.jisc.ac.uk/index.cfm?name=project_career, last accessed 6 August 2003.

BERA – British Educational Research Association (n.d.) *Ethical Guidelines.* Available online at: http://www.bera.ac.uk/guidelines, last accessed 11 October 2005.

Berliner, D. (2002) 'Educational research: the hardest science of all', *Educational Researcher*, 31(8), 18–20.

Biggs, J. (1999) *Teaching for Quality Learning at University*, Buckingham: Society for Research in Higher Education, Open University Press.

Blalock, A. (1999) 'Evaluation research and the performance management movement: from estrangement to useful integration?', *Evaluation*, 5(2), 117–49.

Bloom, B.S. (1956) *Taxonomy of Educational Objectives*, London: Longman.

Bloom, B., Engelhart, M., Furst, E., Hill, W. and Krathwohl, D. (1956) *Taxonomy of Educational Objectives: The Classification of Educational Goals. Handbook 1: Cognitive Domain*, London: Longman.

Blunkett, D. (2000) Speech given at the University of Greenwich, 15 February 2000. Available online at: http://cms1.gre.ac.uk/dfee/#speech, last accessed 16 December 2005.

Bohman, P. (2003a) 'Introduction to web accessibility'. Available online at: http://www.webaim.org/intro/, last accessed 5 October 2005.

Bohman, P. (2003b) 'Visual vs cognitive disabilities'. Available online at: http://www. webaim.org/techniques/articles/vis_vs_cog?templatetype=3, last accessed 5 October 2005.

Bologna Working Group on Qualifications Frameworks (2005) 'A framework for qualifications for the European higher education area', *Bologna Working Group on Qualifications Frameworks*, Copenhagen: Ministry of Science and Innovation. Available online at: http://wwwbologna-bergen2005.no/Docs/00-Main.doc/050218_QF_EHEA.pdf, last accessed 20 March 2006.

Bolter, J.D. (2001) *Writing Space: Computers, Hypertext, and the Remediation of Print*, 2nd edn, Mahwah, NJ: Lawrence Erlbaum Associates.

Booth, C. (1998) 'Accreditation and teaching in Higher Education', final report to the Committee of Vice-Chancellors and Principals of the Universities of the United Kingdom, London: Committee of Vice-Chancellors and Principals.

Boud, D. (2000) 'Sustainable assessment: rethinking assessment for the learning society', *Studies in Continuing Education*, 22(2), 151–67.

Boud, D., Cohen, R. and Walker, D. (eds) (1993) *Using Experience for Learning*, Buckingham: The Society for Research into Higher Education and Open University Press.

Bourdieu, P. (1993) *The Field of Cultural Production*, Cambridge: Polity Press.

Boyle, A. and O'Hare, D. (2003) 'Assuring quality computer-based assessment development in UK higher education', in Christie, J. (ed.), *7th International CAA Conference*, Loughborough: Loughborough University.

Boyle, A., Hutchison, D., O'Hare, D. and Patterson, A. (2002) 'Item selection and application in higher education', in Danson, M. (ed.), *6th International CAA Conference*, Loughborough: Loughborough University.

Boyle, T. (2003) 'Design principles for authoring dynamic, reusable learning objects', *Australian Journal of Educational Technology*, 19(1), 46–58.

Boyle, T. and Cook, J. (2001) 'Towards a pedagogically sound basis for learning object portability and re-use', in Kennedy, G., Keppell, M., McNaught, C. and Petrovic, T., *Proceedings of ASCILITE 2001*, 101–9. Available online at: http://www.medfac. unimelb.edu.au/ascilite2001/pdf/papers/boylet.pdf, last accessed 23 August 2004.

Boyle, T. and Cook, J. (2003) 'Learning objects, pedagogy and reuse', in Seale, J.K. (ed.), *Learning Technology in Transition: From Individual Enthusiasm to Institutional Implementation*, Lisse: Swets and Zeitlinger.

Boyle, T., Bradley, C., Chalk, P., Jones, R., Haynes, R. and Pickard, P. (2003) 'Can learning objects contribute to pedagogical improvement in higher education: lessons from a case study?', submitted to *Computers and Education*, based on a talk given at CAL 2003, April, Belfast.

Boys, J. (2002a) 'Learning lessons from MLE development projects – A review of the 7/99 JISC-funded projects', Commissioned JISC report. Available online at: http://www.jisc.ac.uk/index.cfm?name=mle_799_review, last accessed 30 March 2006.

Boys, J. (2002b) 'Managed Learning Environments, joined up systems and the problems of organisational change'. Available online at: http://www.jisc.ac.uk/index.cfm?name=mle_related_joined, last accessed 30 March 2006.

Bradley, C. and Boyle, T. (2004) 'The design, development and use of multimedia learning objects', *Journal of Educational Multimedia and Hypermedia, Special Edition on Learning Objects*, 13(4), 371–89.

Britain, S. (2004) 'A Review of Learning Design: Concept, Specifications and Tools', a report for the JISC E-learning Pedagogy Programme, JISC. Available online at: http://www.jisc.ac.uk/uploaded_documents/ACF83C.doc, last accessed 30 March 2006.

Britain, S. and Liber, O. (2004) *A Framework for the Pedagogical Evaluation of Virtual Learning Environments*, JISC commissioned review. Available online at: http://www.jisc.ac.uk/uploaded_documents/VLE%20Full%20Report%2006.doc, last accessed 30 March 2006.

Brookfield, S. (2001) 'Through the lens of learning: how the visceral experience of learning reframes teaching', in Paechter, C., Edwards, R., Harrison, R. and Twining, P. (eds), *Learning, Space and Identity*, 67–78, London: Paul Chapman, SAGE Publications in association with the Open University.

Brophy, P., Markland, M. and Jones, C.R. (2004) EDNER+: Final Report, Manchester: Centre for Research in Library and Information Management. Available online at: http://www.cerlim.ac.uk/projects/iee/reports/final_report.doc, last accessed 30 March 2006.

Brown, J.S., Collins, A. and Duguid, P. (1989) 'Situated cognition and the culture of learning', *Educational Researcher*, 18(1), 32–42.

Bruce, C. (1997) 'The relational approach: a new model for information literacy', *The New Review of Library and Information Research*, 3, 1–22.

Bruner, J.S. (1975) 'The ontogenesis of speech acts', *Journal of Child Language*, 2, 1–19.

BSI (2002) 'BS 7988:2002 code of practice for the use of information technology (IT) in the delivery of assessments', London: BSI.

Buckingham Shum, S. and Sunner, T. (2001) 'JIME: an interactive journal for interactive media'. Available online at: http://firstmonday.org/issues/issue6_2/buckingham_shum/, *First Monday*, 6(2), last accessed 23 March 2006.

Bull, J. (2001) 'TLTP85 implementation and evaluation of computer-assisted assessment: final report'. Available online at: http://www.caacentre.ac.uk/dldocs/final_report.pdf, last accessed 30 March 2006.

Bull, J. and Hesketh, I. (2001) 'Computer-Assisted Assessment Centre update', in Danson, M. and Eabry, C. (eds), *5th International CAA Conference*, Loughborough: Loughborough University.

Bull, J. and McKenna, C. (2004) *Blueprint for Computer-assisted Assessment*, London: RoutledgeFalmer.

Bundy, A. (ed.) (2004) *Australian and New Zealand Information Literacy Framework*, 2nd edn, Adelaide: Australian and New Zealand Institute for Information Literacy (ANZIL). Available online at: http://www.caul.edu.au/info-literacy/InfoLiteracyFramework.pdf, last accessed 30 March 2006.

Burbules, N. (1998) 'Rhetorics of the web: hyperreading and critical literacy', in Snyder, I. (ed.), *Page to Screen: Taking Literacy into the Electronic Era*, 102–22, London: Routledge.

Burgstahler, S. (2002) 'Distance learning: universal design, universal access', *Educational Technology Review*, 10, 1. Available online at: http://www.aace.org/pubs/etr/issue2/burgstahler.cfm, last accessed 5 October 2005.

Bush, V. (1945) 'As we may think', *The Atlantic Monthly*. Available online at: http://www.theatlantic.com/doc/194507/bush, last accessed 24 March 2006.

Caldwell, B., Chisholm, W., Vanderheiden, G. and White, J. (2004) 'Web Content Accessibility Guidelines 2.0', *W3C Working Draft*, 19 November 2004. Available online at: http://www.w3.org/TR/WCAG20/, last accessed 5 October 2005.

Campbell, L. (2003), 'Engaging with the learning object economy' in Littlejohn, A. (ed.), *Reusing Online Resources: A Sustainable Approach to E-learning*, 35–45, London: Kogan Page.

Candy, P. (2004) *Linking Thinking: Self-directed Learning in the Digital Age*, Canberra: Department for Education, Science and Training. Available online at: www.dest.gov.au/research/publications/linking_thinking/default.htm, last accessed 30 March 2006.

Carbonell, J.R. (1970) 'AI in CAI: an artificial intelligence aproach to computer-aided instruction', *IEEE Transactions on Man-machine Systems*, MMS-11(4), 190–202.

Carnoy, M. (1997) 'The great work dilemma: education, employment and wages in the new global economy', *Economics of Education Review*, 16(3), 247–54.

Caroll, J. (2002) *A Handbook for Deterring Plagiarism in Higher Education*, OCSD, Oxford: Oxford Brookes University.

Carr, W. and Kemmis, S. (1986) *Becoming Critical: Knowing Through Action Research*, London: Falmer Press.

Carr-Chellman, A. (2005) *Global Perspectives on E-learning: Rhetoric and Reality*, London: Sage.

Carrington, V. and Luke, A. (1997) 'Literacy and Bourdieu's sociological theory: a reframing'. *Language and Education*, 11(2), 96–112.

Castells, M. (1996) *The Information Age: Economy, Society and Culture – Volume 1, The Rise of the Networked Society*, Oxford: Blackwell.

Castells, M. (1999) 'Flows, networks, identities', in Castells, M., Flecha, R., Freire, P., Giroux, H., Macedo, D. and Willis, P. (eds) *Critical Education in the New Information Age,* Lanham, MD: Rowman and Littlefield.

Castells, M. (2000) *The Rise of the Network Society*, Oxford: Blackwell.

Castells, M. (2001) *The Internet Galaxy: Reflections on the Internet, Business, and Society*, Oxford: Oxford University Press.

CBURC (1968–1991) *Reports of the Computer Board for Universities and Research Councils*, London: HMSO.

Chartrand, H. (1989) 'University research in the information economy: a clash of cultures', *Cultural Economics – The Collected Works of H. Chartrand*. Available online at: http://www.culturaleconomics.atfreeweb.com/University.htm, last accessed 30 March 2006.

Chelimsky, E. (1997) 'Thoughts for a new evaluation society', *Evaluation*, 6(1), 7–21.

Cheng, C. and McFarlane, A. (2006) 'Gaming culture and digital literacy: Inspiration and audience', *Nordic Journal of Digital Literacy*, 2(1), Universitetsforlaget, Oslo.

Chisholm, W., Vanderheiden, G. and Jacobs, I. (1999) 'Web Content Accessibility Guidelines 1.0', *W3C Recommendation 5-May-1999*. Available online at: http://www.org/TR/WAI-WEBCONTENT/, last accessed 5 October 2005.

Chouliaraki, L. (2002) 'The contingency of universality: some thoughts on Discourse and Realism', *Social Semiotics*, 12(1), 83–114.

Clancy, W.J. (1987) *Knowledge-based Tutoring: The GUIDON Program*, Cambridge, MA: MIR Press.

Clark, R. (1983) 'Reconsidering research on learning from media', *Review of Educational Research*, 53, 445–59.

Clegg, S., Hudson, A. and Steele, J. (2003) 'The emperor's new clothes: globalisation and e-learning in higher education', *British Journal of Sociology of Education*, 24(1), 39–53.

Clough, G. (2005) *Informal Learning, PDAs and Mobile Phones*, MSc thesis, IET, Open University, United Kingdom.

Cohen, L. and Manion, L. (1994) *Research Methods in Education*, 4th edn, London: Routledge.

Cohen, L., Manion, L. and Morrison, K. (2000) *Research Methods in Education*, 5th edn, London: RoutledgeFalmer.

Cole, M. (1996) *Cultural Psychology: A Once and Future Discipline*, Cambridge, MA: Harvard University Press.

Colley, H., Hodkinson, P. and Malcom, J. (2002) *Non-Formal Learning: Mapping the Conceptual Terrain. A Consultation Report*, Lifelong Learning Institute, University of Leeds, November 2002.

Collins, A. (1977) 'Processes in acquiring knowledge', in Anderson, R.C., Spiro, R.J. and Montague, M.E. (eds), *Schooling and the Acquisition of Knowledge*, 339–63, Hillsdale, NJ: Lawrence-Erlbaum.

Collins, A., Brown, J.S. and Newman, S.E. (1989) 'Cognitive apprenticeship: teaching the crafts of reading, writing, and mathematics', in Resnick, L.B. (ed.), *Knowing, Learning, and Instruction: Essays in Honor of Robert Glaser*, 453–94, Hillsdale, NJ: Lawrence-Erlbaum.

Condron, F. and Sutherland, S. (2002) 'Learning environments support in the UK further and higher education communities', commissioned JISC report. Available online at: http://www.jisc.ac.uk/index.cfm?name=mle_related_les, last accessed 30 March 2006.

Conole, G. (2002) 'The evolving landscape of learning technology', *ALT-J*, 10(3) 4–18.

Conole, G. (2003) 'Research questions and methodological issues'. Unpublished ELRC report, University of Southampton.

Conole, G. (2005) 'Mediating artefacts to guide choice in creating and undertaking learning activities', presentation at CALRG seminar, Open University, 1 November 2005.

Conole, G. (2006) 'What impact are technologies having and how are they changing practice?', in McNay, I. (ed.), *From Mass to Universal HE: Building on Experience*, Buckingham: Society for Research in Higher Education, Open University Press.

Conole, G. (forthcoming) 'Relationship between policy and practice – the gap between rhetoric and reality', in Andrews, R. and Haythornthwaite, C. (eds), *E-learning Research Handbook,* London: Sage.

Conole, G. and Oliver, M. (2002) 'Embedding theory into learning technology practice with toolkits', *Journal of Interactive Educational Media*, 8. Available online at: http://www.jime-open.ac.uk/2002/8/, last accessed 30 March 2006.

Conole, G. and Dyke, M. (2004) 'What are the affordances of information and communication technologies?', *ALT-J*, 12(2), 113–124.

Conole, G. and Fill, K. (2005) 'A learning design toolkit to create pedagogically effective learning activities', *Journal of Interactive Multimedia Education, special issue on learning design*, Tattersall, C. (ed.).

Conole, G., and Sclater, N. (2005) 'Using evaluation to inform the development of a user-focused assessment engine', *Proceedings of the Ninth International Computer Assisted Assessment Conference*, Loughborough University, England, 5–6 July 2005.

Conole, G., Dyke, M., Oliver, M. and Seale, J. (2004) 'Mapping pedagogy and tools for effective learning design', *Computers and Education*, 43(1–2), 17–33.

Conole, G., Littlejohn, A. Falconer, I., and Jeffery, A. (2005) 'Pedagogical review of learning activities and use cases', *LADIE project report*, JISC funded project under the e-Frameworks programme, Bristol: JISC.

Conole, G., Carusi, A., de Laat, M., Wilcox, P. and Darby, J. (2006) 'Learning from the UKeU experience', Special issue in Studies in Continuing Education, 28(2), 135–50.

Cook, J. (2002) 'The role of dialogue in computer-based learning and observing learning: an evolutionary approach to theory', *Journal of Interactive Media in Education*, 5. Available online at: http://www-jime.open.ac.uk/2002/5, last accessed 30 March 2006.

Coopers and Lybrand/Tavistock Institute (1996) *Evaluation of the Teaching and Learning Technology Programmes*, Coopers and Lybrand report, HEFCE commissioned report M21/96, Bristol: Higher Education Funding Council for England.

Cortez, C., Nussbaum, M., López, X., Rodríguez, P., Santelices, R., Rosas, R. and Marianov, V. (2005) 'Teachers' support with ad-hoc collaborative networks', *Journal of Computer Assisted Learning*, 21(3) 171–180.

Cowan, J. (2002) 'The impact of pedagogy on skills development in higher education – or – should we facilitate the Kolb cycle constructively or socio-constructively?' Keynote paper. *Skills Development in Higher Education: Forging Links*, Hatfield: University of Hertfordshire, Hatfield.

Cowie, H. (1992) 'Peer commentaries on Keith Topping's overview of cooperative learning and peer tutoring', *The Psychologist: Bulletin of the British Psychological Society*, 5, 158–9.

Cowley, L. and Wesson, J. (2000) 'Design patterns for web-based instruction', in Bourdeau, J. and Heller, R. (eds) *Proceedings of Ed-Media 2000, World Conference on Educational Multimedia, Hypermedia and Telecommunications*, Montreal, Canada: 26 June –1 July , 2000.

Crook, C.K. (1994) *Computers and the Collaborative Experience of Learning*, New York: Routledge.

Crook, C.K. (2000) 'Motivation and the ecology of collaborative learning', in Joiner, R., Miell, D., Littleton, D. and Faulkner, D. (eds), *Rethinking Collaborative Learning*, 161–78, London: Free Association Press.

Csikszentmihalyi, M. (1999) 'Implications of a systems perspective for the study of creativity', in Sternberg, R. (ed.), *Handbook of Creativity*, 312–35, Cambridge, MA: Cambridge University Press.

Cuban, L. (1986) *Teachers and Machines*, New York: Teachers College Press.

Cuban, L. (2001) *Oversold and Underused: Computers in the Classroom*, Cambridge, MA: Harvard University Press.

Currier, S., Campbell, L. and Beetham, H. (2006) 'JISC Pedagogical Vocabularies Project, *Report 1:* Pedagogical Vocabularies Review', *JISC commissioned report.*

Available online at: http://www.jisc.ac.uk/elp_vocabularies.html, last accessed 20 March 2006.

Currier, S., Barton J., O'Beirne, R., Ryan, B. (2004) 'Quality assurance for digital learning object repositories: issues for the metadata creation process', *ALT-J*, 12(1), 5–20.

Dalziel, J.R. (2003) 'Implementing learning design: the Learning Activity Management System (LAMS)', *Interact, Integrate, Impact*, 593–6, Proceedings of the ASCILITE conference. Available online at: http://www.ascilite.org.au/conferences/adelaide03/docs/pdf/593.pdf, last accessed 30 March 2006.

Dalziel, J. (2005) Sharing Learning Design Through the LAMS Community, Presentation for CETIS Pedagogy and Metadata Workshop, 20 September 2005. Available online at: http://metadata.cetis.ac.uk/sig_meetings/OUSept2005/jamesdalziel.lamscommunity.ppt, last accessed 30 March 2006.

Darby, J. (2001) 'Networked learning in higher education: the mule in the barn', in Steeples, C. and Jones, C.R. (eds), *Networked Learning: Perspectives and Issues*, London: Springer Verlag.

Davidov, A. (2002) 'Computer screens are not like paper: typography on the web', in Sassoon, R. (ed.), *Computers and Typography 2*, Bristol: intellect1.

Davies, H., Nutley, S. and Smith, P. (2000) 'Introducing evidence-based policy and practice in public services', in Davies, H., Nutley, S. and Smith, P. (eds), *What Works? Evidence-based Policy and Practice in Public Services*, 1–12. Bristol: Policy Press.

Davies, P. (2002) 'There's no confidence in multiple-choice testing', in Danson, M. (ed.), *6th International CAA Conference*, Loughborough: Loughborough University.

Deepwell, F. and Beaty, L. (2005) 'Moving into uncertain terrain: implementing online higher education', in Fallows, S. and Bhanot, R. (eds), *Quality Issues in ICT-based Higher Education*, London: RoutledgeFalmer.

De Laat, M., Lally, V. and Lipponen, L. (2005) 'Teaching online in networked learning communities: a multi-method approach', *Researching dialogue and communities of enquiry in elearning in HE*. ESRC E-learning seminar series, Southampton: University of Southampton. Available online at: http://www.wun.ac.uk/elearning/seminars/seminars/seminar_two/seminartwo.html, last accessed 30 March 2006.

Del Soldato, T. and Boulay, B. (1996) 'Implementation of motivational tactis in tutoring systems', *International Journal of Artificial Intelligence in Education*, 6(4), 337–78.

Derrida, J. (1974) *Of Grammatology*, London: Johns Hopkins University Press.

Dewey, J. (1933) *The Middle Works, 1899–1924*, in Boydston, J., edited collection, Carbondale: Southern Illinois University Press.

Dewey, J. (1938) *Experience and Education*, New York: Collier Books.

Dewey, J. (1949) *Experience and Existence*, in Boydston, J. (ed.), *John Dewey: The Later Works, 1949–1952, Volume 16*, Southern Illinois University Press.

DfEE (1998) *The Learning Age*, Department for Education and Employment. Available online at: http://www.lifelonglearning.co.uk/greenpaper/, last accessed 24 July 2006.

DfEE (1999) *White Paper – Learning to Succeed: A New Framework for Post-16 Learning*, Department for Education and Employment. Available online at: http://www.skills.org.uk/lts-wp.pdf, last accessed 30 March 2006.

DfES (2003) 'Widening participation in higher education'. Available online at: http://www.dfes.gov.uk/hegateway/uploads/ewparticipation.pdf, last accessed 29 March 2006.

DfES (2005) 'DfES e-learning strategy: harnessing technology – transforming learning and childrens' services'. Available online at: http://www.dfes.gov.uk/publications/e-strategy/, last accessed 30 March 2006.

Dillenbourg, P. (1999) *Collaborative-learning: Cognitive and Computational Approaches*, Oxford: Elsevier.

Djanogly (2005) 'Successful first term for Foster and Partners latest City Academy'. Available online at: http://www.fosterandpartners.com/internetsite/html/News.asp?ID=194, last accessed 28 November 2005.

Doise, W. and Mugny, W. (1984) *The Social Development of the Intellect*, Oxford: Pergamon.

Draper, S.W. and Brown, M.I. (2004) 'Increasing interactivity in lectures using an electronic voting system', *Journal of Computer Assisted Learning*, 20, 81–94.

Draper, S., Brown, M., Edgerton, E., Henderson, F., McAteer, E., Smith, E. and Watt, H. (1994) *Observing and Measuring the Performance of Educational Technology*, TILT report no. 1, University of Glasgow.

Driver, R. (1983) *The Pupil as Scientist?* Milton Keynes: Open University Press.

Drucker, P. (1994) *Knowledge Work and Knowledge Society: The Social Transformation of this Century*. 1994 Edwin L. Godkin Lecture. Transcript available online at: http://www.ksg.harvard.edu/ifactory/ksgpress/www/ksgnews/transcripts/drucklec.html.

Duffy, T.M., Jonassen, D.H. and Lowyck, J. (eds) (1993) *Designing Environments for Constructive Learning*, Berlin: Springer.

Duncan, C. (2003) 'Granularization', in A. Littlejohn (ed.) *Reusing Online Resources: A Sustainable Approach to E-learning*, 12–19, London: Page.

Dyke, M. (2001) *Reflective Learning and Reflexive Modernity as Theory Practice and Research in Post-Compulsory Education*, Educational Studies PhD Thesis, Guildford, University of Surrey.

Dyke, M. (2006) 'The role of the "Other" in reflection, knowledge formation and action in a late modernity', *International Journal of Lifelong Education*, 25(2), 105–23.

e3an (2005) *Electrical and Electronic Engineering Assesment Network*. Available online at: http://www.e3an.ac.uk/, last accessed 30 March 2006.

Eales, R.T.J., Hall, T. and Bannon, L.J. (2002) 'The motivation is the message: comparing CSCL in different settings', *Proceedings of Computer Support for Collaborative Learning 2002 (CSCL '02)*, Stahl, G. (ed.), 310–17, New Jersey: Lawrence Erlbaum Associates.

Eco, U. (1990) *The Limits of Interpretation*, Bloomington: Indiana University Press.

Eco, U. (2001) *Authors and Authority*, Bibliothèque publique d'information', Paris. Available online at: http://www.text-e.org.

Edwards, D.M. and Hardman, L. (1993) 'Lost in hyperspace: cognitive mapping and navigation in a hypertext environment', in McAleese, R. (ed.), *Hypertext: Theory Into Practice*, 90–105, Oxford: Intellect.

Edwards, R. (1997) *Changing Places? Flexibility, Lifelong Learning and Learning Society*, London: Routledge.

Ehrmann, S. (1999) 'Studying teaching, learning and technology: a tool kit from the Flashlight programme', *Active Learning*, 9, 36–9.

Eisenberg, M.B., Lowe, C.A. and Spitzer, K.L. (2004) *Information Literacy: Essential Skills for the Information Age*, 2nd edn, Westport CT and London: Libraries Unlimited.

Eisner, E. (1998) *The Kind of Schools We Need: Personal Essays*, London: Heinemann.

Elsom-Cook, M. (2001) *Principles of Interactive Multimedia*, London: McGraw Hill.

ELTI (2003) 'The JISC Embedding Learning Technologies Institutionally project'. Available online at: http://www.jisc.ac.uk/index.cfm?name=project_elti, last accessed 29 July 2003.

Elton, L. (1999) 'New ways of learning in higher education: managing the change', *Tertiary Education and Management*, 5, 207–25.

Engeström, Y. (1987) *Learning by Expanding: An Activity Theoretical Approach to Developmental Research*, Helsinki: Orienta-Konsultit Oy. Available online at: http://communication.ucsd.edu/MCA/Paper/Engeström/expanding/toc.htm, last accessed 6 November 2005.

Engeström, Y. (1999) 'Innovative learning in work teams: analyzing cycles of knowledge creation in practice', in Engeström, Y., Miettinen, R., and Punamäki, R.L. (eds), *Perspectives on Activity Theory*, 377–404, Cambridge: Cambridge University Press.

Engeström, Y. (2001) 'Expansive learning at: work: towards an activity theory reconceptualisation', *Journal of Education and Work*, 14, 133–56.

Engeström, Y., Miettinen, R. and Punamäki, R.L. (eds) (1999) *Perspectives on Activity Theory. Learning in Doing: Social, Cognitive and Computational Perspectives*, Cambridge: Cambridge University Press.

EPSRC (2003) http://www.epsrc.ac.uk/researchfunding/programmes/informationandcommunicationstechnologies/reviewsandconsultations/realisingpotentialofelearningfullreport.htm, last accessed 30 November 2005.

Esland, G. (1996a) 'Knowledge and nationhood: the new right, education and the global market', in Avis, J., Bloomer, M., Esland, G., Gleeson, D. and Hodkinson, P. (eds) *Knowledge and Nationhood: Education, Politics and Work*, London: Cassell.

Esland, G. (1996b) 'Education, training and nation-state capitalism: Britain's failing strategy', in Avis, J., Bloomer, M., Esland, G., Gleeson, D. and Hodkinson, P. (eds) *Knowledge and Nationhood: Education, Politics and Work*, London: Cassell.

Esterby-Smith, M. (1994) *Evaluation of Management, Education, Training and Development*, London: Gower.

Facer, K., Furlong, J., Furlong, R. and Sutherland, R. (2003) *Screenplay*, London: RoutledgeFalmer.

Fairclough, N. (2001) *Language and Power,* 2nd edn, Harlow: Pearson.

Feigl, H. and Brodbeck, M. (1953) *Readings in the Philosophy of Science*, New York: Appleton-Century Crofts.

Feuer, M., Towne, L. and Shavelson, R. (2002) 'Scientific culture and educational research', *Educational Researcher*, 31(8), 4–14.

Fiddes, D.J., Korabinski, A.A., McGuire, G.R., Youngson, M.A. and McMillan, D. (2002) 'Are mathematics exam results affected by the mode of delivery', *ALT-J*, 10, 61–9.

Field, J. (1995) 'Reality testing in the workplace: are NVQs 'employment-Led?', in Hodkinson, P. and Issitt, M., *The Challenge of Competence: Professionalism through Vocational Education and Training*, London: Cassell.

Fitz-Gibbon, C. (2000) 'Education: realising the potential', in Davies, H., Nutley S. and Smith, P. (eds), *What Works? Evidence-based Policy and Practice in Public Services*, 69–92, Bristol: Policy Press.

Flowers Committee (1965) 'Computers for Research', a report of a working party for the University Grants Committee, UGC 7/635, London: HMSO.

Forrester, K., Payne, J. and Ward, K. (1995) *Workplace Learning: Perspectives on Education, Training and Work*, Aldershot: Avebury.

Fosnot, C. (1996) *Constructivism: Theory, Perspectives and Practice*, New York: Teachers College Press.

Foucault, M. (1977) *Discipline and Punish: The Birth of The Prison*, London: Allen and Unwin.

Foucault, M. (1979) *Discipline and Punish: The Birth of The Prison*, Cambridge: Cambridge University Press.

Fowler, C. and Mayes, T. (2004) 'Mapping theory to practice and practice to tool functionality based on the practitioners' perspective'. Available online at: http://www.jisc.ac.uk/uploaded_documents/Stage%202%20Mapping%20(Version%20 1).pdf, last accessed 30 March 2006.

Freeman, M. and Parker, L. (2004) 'Blended learning – blended resources: a collaborative approach to supporting students', in Banks, S., Goodyear, P., Hodgson, V., Jones, C., Lally, V., McConnell, D. and Steeples, C. (eds), *Proceedings of Networked Learning 2004*, 5–7 April 2004. Lancaster University and University of Sheffield. Available online at: www.shef.ac.uk/nlc2004/Proceedings/Individual_Papers/Freeman_Parker.htm.

Freire, P. (1993) *Pedagogy of the Oppressed*, new revised 20th-anniversary edition, New York: Continuum.

Freire, P. (1996) *Pedagogy of the Oppressed*, London: Penguin.

Freitag, E.T. and Sullivan, H.J. (1995) 'Matching learner preference to amount of instruction: an alternative form of learner control', *Educational Technology Research and Development*, 43(2), 5–14.

Garfinkel, H. (1967) *Studies in Ethnomethodology*, Englewood Cliffs, NJ: Prentice-Hall.

Gee, J. P. (2003) *What Video Games Have to Teach us about Learning and Literacy*, USA: Palgrave Macmillan.

Giddens, A. (1991) *The Consequences of Modernity*, Cambridge: Polity.

Giddens, A. (1999) *Runaway World: How Globalization is Reshaping Our Lives*, London: Profile.

Glaser, B. (2002) 'Constructivist grounded theory?' *Forum: Qualitative Social Research*, 3(3). Available online at: http://www.qualitative-research.net/fqs/fqs-eng.htm.

Godman, P. (1990) 'Literary classicism and Latin erotic poetry of the twelfth century and the Renaissance', in Godman, P. and Murray, O., *Latin Poetry and the Classical Tradition: Essays in Medieval and Renaissance Literature*, 149–82, Oxford: Clarendon.

Goodman, S., Lillis, T., Maybin, J. and Mercer, N. (2003) *Language, Literacy and Education: A Reader*, Stoke on Trent: Trentham Books.

Goodyear, P. (1999) 'New technology in higher education: understanding the innovation process', in Eurlings, A., Gastkemper, F., Kommers, P., Lewis, R., van Meel, R. and Melief, B. (eds) *Integrating Information and Communication Technology in Higher Education*, Deventer: Kluwer.

Gosling, D. (2001) 'Educational development unit in the UK – what are they doing five years on?', *International Journal for Academic Development*, 6(1), 74–90.

Guba, E. and Lincoln, Y. (1989) *Fourth Generation Evaluation*, London: Sage.

Gunn, C. (1997) 'CAL evaluation: future directions', *ALT-J*, 5(1), 40–7.

Guribye, F. (2005) 'Infrastructures for Learning: Ethnographic Inquiries into the Social and Technical Conditions of Education and Training', unpublished PhD thesis, University of Bergen, Norway.

Guri-Rosenbilt, S. (2005) '"Distance education" and "e-learning": not the same thing', *Higher Education*, 49, 467–93.

Hamblin, A.C. (1974) *Evaluation and Control of Training*, Maidenhead: McGraw-Hill.

Hammersley, M. (1997) 'The relationship between qualitative and quantitative research: paradigm loyalty versus methodological eclecticism', in Richardson, J. (ed.) *Handbook of Qualitative Research Methods*, 159–74. Leicester: The British Psychological Society.

Hammersley, M. (2001) 'On "systematic" reviews of research literatures: a "narrative" response to Evans and Benfield', *British Educational Research Journal*, 27(5), 543–54.

Hammond, M. (1995) 'Learning from experience: approaching the research of CD-ROM in schools', in Tinsley, J.D. and van Weert, T.J. (eds) *World Conference on Computers in Education VI: WCCE '95 Liberating the Learner*, London: Chapman and Hall.

Hardy, C. and Portelli, A. (1999) 'I can almost see the lights of home – a field trip to Harlan County, Kentucky', *Journal for MultiMedia History*, 2. Available online at: http://www.albany.edu/jmmh/vol2no1/lights.html.

Hartley, J.R. (1998) 'Qualitative reasoning and conceptual change: computer-based support in understanding science', in Winkels, R.G.F. and Bredeweg, B. (eds), *Interactive Learning Environments: Special Issue on the Use of Qualitative Reasoning Techniques in Interactive Learning Environments*, 5, 53–64.

Hartley, R., Ravenscroft, A. and Williams, R.J. (1992) 'CACTUS: command and control training using knowledge-based simulations', *Interactive Learning International*, 8(2), 127–36.

Harvey, J., Oliver, M. and Smith, J. (2002) 'Towards effective practitioner evaluation: an exploration of issues relating to skills, motivation and evidence', *Educational Technology and Society*, 5(3), 3–10. Available online at: http://ifets.ieee.org/periodical/vol_3_2002/v_3_2002.html.

Hawkey, R. (2002) 'The lifelong learning game: season ticket or free transfer?' *Computers and Education*, 38(1–3), 5–20.

Hawkey, R. (2004) 'Learning with digital technologies in museums, science centres and galleries', NestaFutureLab Report 9. Available online at: http://www.nestafuturelab. org/download/pdfs/research/lit_reviews/futurelab_review_09.pdf.

Hayes, H. (2005) *Digital Repositories Helping Universities and Colleges*. Briefing Paper – Higher Education Sector, JISC, August 2005. Available online at: http://www.jisc.ac.uk/uploaded_documents/HE_repositories_briefing_paper_2005.pdf.

HEFCE (1997) *Teaching and Learning Technology Programme Phase 3: Invitation to Bid*, HEFCE, 14/97. Bristol: HEFCE, TLTP.

HEFCE (1998) *An Evaluation of the Computers in Teaching Initiative and Teaching and Learning Technology Support Network*, report 98/47, HEFCE.

HEFCE (2005a) HEFCE e-learning strategy. Available online at: http://www.hefce.ac.uk/pubs/hefce/2005/05_12/, last accessed 14 March 2006.

HEFCE (2005b) 'Summative evaluation of the Teaching Quality Enhancement Fund (TQEF): a report to HEFCE by The Higher Education Consultancy Group and CHEMS Consulting'. Available online at: http://www.hefce.ac.uk/Pubs/rdreports/2005/rd23_05/rd23_05.doc.

Heim, M. (1998) *Virtual Realism*, New York: Oxford University Press.

Henkel, M. (2000) *Academic Identities and Policy Change in Higher Education*, London: Jessica Kingsley.

Hodgson, V. (2005) 'Participative assessment and the learners' experience'. in Ashwin, P. (ed.) *Changing Higher Education: The Development of Learning and Teaching*, London: RoutledgeFalmer.

Hoggart, R. (1958) *The Uses of Literacy: Aspects of Working-class Life with Special Reference to Publications and Entertainments*, Harmondsworth: (Pelican) Penguin.

Holquist, M. (1997) 'The politics of representation', in Cole, M., Engeström, Y. and Vasquez, O., *Mind, Culture and Activity*, 389–408, Cambridge: Cambridge University Press.

Holt, R. and Oliver, M. (2002) 'Evaluating web-based learning modules during an MSc programme in dental public health: a case study', *British Dental Journal*, 193(5), 283–8.

Holyfield, S. (2002) 'Developing a Shared Understanding of the Managed Learning Environment – the role of diagramming and requirements gathering', commissioned JISC report. Available online at: http://www.jisc.ac.uk/index.cfm?name=mle_diagram_report.

Hoyles, C. and Noss, R. (1992) 'A pedagogy for mathematical microworlds', *Educational Studies in Mathematics*, 23, 31–57.

Hutchins, E. (1995) *Cognition in the Wild*, Cambridge, MA: The MIT Press.

IFLA (2005) *Beacons of the Information Society: The Alexandria Proclamation on Information Literacy and Lifelong Learning*, International Federation of Library Associations and Institutions. Available online at: www.ifla.org/III/wsis/Beacon InfSoc.html.

IMS (2005) 'Specifications'. Available online at: http://www.imsglobal.org/specification-download.cfm.

Ingraham, B. (2000) 'Scholarly rhetoric in digital media', *Journal of Interactive Media in Education*. Available online at: http://www-jime.open.ac.uk/00/ingraham/ingraham-t.html.

Ingraham, B. (2005a) 'Beyond Text', *Innovate*. Available online at: http://innovateonline.info/index.php?view=articleandid=28.

Ingraham, B. (2005b) 'Academic print in digital formats', in Cook, J. and Whitelock, D. (eds) *Exploring the Frontiers of E-learning: Borders, Outposts and Migration*. Research Proceedings of the 12th Association for Learning Technology Conference (ALT-J 2005), 6–8 September 2005, University of Manchester, England.

Ingraham, B. (2005c) 'Ambulating with mega-fauna', in Bayne, S. and Land, R. (eds), *Education in Cyberspace*, London: RoutledgeFalmer.

Ingraham, B. and Bradburn, E. (2003a) *Converting OLF Materials for Use Online*, London: The Open Learning Foundation.

Ingraham, B. and Bradburn, E. (2003b) *Sit Back and Relax: A Guide to Producing Readable, Accessible Onscreen Text*. Available online at: http://readability.tees.ac.uk.

Ingraham, B. and Ingraham, S. (2006) 'e-Quality: a dialogue between quality and academia', *E-learning*, 3(1). Available online (forthcoming) at: http://www.wwwords.co.uk/elea/content/pdfs/3/issue3_1.asp.

Irwin, T. (1985) *Aristotle Nicomachean Ethics*, Cambridge: Hackett Publishing Company.

Issroff, K. (1994) 'Gender and cognitive and affective aspects of cooperative learning', in Foot, H.C., Howe, C.J., Anderson, A., Tolmie, A.K. and Warden, D.A. *Group and Interactive Learning*, Southhampton and Boston: Computational Mechanics Publications.

Issroff, K. and del Soldato, T. (1996) *Incorporating Motivation into Computer-supported Collaborative Learning*. Proceedings of European Conference on Artificial Intelligence in Education, Ficha Tecnica, Lisbon.

Issroff, K. and Scanlon, E. (2001) 'Case studies revisited: what can activity theory offer?' *Proceedings of International Conference on Computer Supported Collaborative Learning 2001 (CSCL 2001)*, Maastricht, Netherlands, 22–24 March 2001.

Ivanic, R., Barton, D. and Hamilton, M. (1999) *Situated Literacies: Reading and Writing in Context*, London: Routledge.

Jacko, J.A. and Hanson, V.L. (2002) 'Universal access and inclusion in design', *Universal Access to the Information Society*, 2, 1–2.

Jameson, F. (1998) *The Cultural Turn: Selected Writings on the Postmodern 1983–1998*, London: Verso.

Järvelä, S. (2001) 'Shifting research on motivation and cognition to an integrated approach on learning and motivation in context', in Volet, S. and Järvelä, S. (eds) *Motivation in Learning Contexts: Theoretical Advances and Methodological Implications*. The Netherlands: Pergamon.

Järvelä, S. and Volet, S. (2004) 'Motivation in real-life, dynamic and interactive learning environments: stretching constructs and methodologies', *European Psychologist*, 9(4), 193–7.

Jarvis, P. (1987) *Adult Learning in a Social Context*, London: Croom Helm.

Jarvis, P., Holford, J., Griffin, C. (1998) *The Theory and Practice of Learning*, London: Kogan Page.

Jarvis, P. (2004) *Adult Education and Lifelong Learning*, London: RoutledgeFalmer.

Jelfs, A. and Colbourn, C. (2002) 'Virtual seminars and their input on the role of the teaching staff', *Computers and Education*, 38, 127–36.

JISC (2001) *Five-year Strategy 2001–2005*, Bristol: JISC.

JISC (2005a) 'Innovative practice with e-learning', Bristol: JISC. Available online at: www.jisc.ac.uk/elearning_innovation.html, last accessed 27 March 2006.

JISC (2005b) 'Effective practice with e-learning – a good practice guide in designing for learning', Bristol: JISC. Available online at: http://www.jisc.ac.uk/uploaded_documents/ACF5DO.pdf, last accessed 14 March 2006.

JISCInfoNet (2003) 'Creating a Managed Learning Environment (or MLE) infoKit'. Available online at: http://www.jiscinfonet.ac.uk, last accessed 29 July 2003.

Jochems, W., Van Merrienboer, J.D. and Koper, K. (2004) *Integrated E-learning – Implications for Pedagogy, Technology and Organization*, London: RoutledgeFalmer.

Johnson, B. and Webber, S. (2003) 'Information literacy in higher education: a review and case study', *Studies in Higher Education*, 28(3), 335–52.

Johnson, D.W. and Johnson, R.T. (1989) *Cooperation and Competition: Theory and Research*, Edina, MN: Interactive Book Co.

Johnson, D.W., Johnson, R.T. and Stanne, M.B. (2000) *Cooperative Learning Methods: A Meta-Analysis*. Available online at: http://www.co-operation.org/pages/cl-methods.html, last accessed 16 November 2005.

Joinson, A.N. (2003) *Understanding the Psychology of Internet Behaviour: Virtual Worlds, Real Lives*, Basingstoke and New York: Palgrave Macmillan.

Jonassen, D.H. (1996) *Computers in the Classroom: Mindtools for Critical Thinking*, Englewood Cliffs, NJ: Merrill, Prentice Hall.

Jonassen, D., Mayes, T. and McAleese, R. (1993) 'A manifesto for a constructivist approach to technology in higher education', in Duffy, T., Jonassen, D. and Lowyck, J. (eds), *Designing Constructivist Learning Environments*. Available online at: http://www.dfes.gov.uk/publications/e-strategy/.

Jones, A. and Issroff, K. (2005) 'Learning technologies: affective and social issues in computer supported collaborative learning, *Computers and Education*, 44(4), 395–408.

Jones, A., Scanlon, E., Tosunoglu, C., Ross, S., Butcher, P., Murphy, P. and Greenberg, J. (1996) 'Evaluating CAL at the Open University: 15 years on', *Computers in Education*, 26(1–3), 5–15.

Jones, B. (1991) *Critical Computer Literacy* (originally submitted in partial fulfilment of the PhD in Communication), University of California at San Diego. Available online at: http://communication.ucsd.edu/bjones/comp_lit.html.

Jones, C. (1998a) 'Evaluating a collaborative online learning environment', *Active Learning*, 9, 31–5. Available online at: http://www.ilt.ac.uk/public/cti/ActiveLearning/al9pdf/jones.pdf, last accessed 23 September 2002.

Jones, C. (1998b) 'Evaluation using ethnography: context, content and collaboration', in Oliver, M. (ed.), *Innovation in the Evaluation of Learning Technology*, 87–100, London: University of North London Press.

Jones, C. (1999a) 'Co-operating to collaborate: course delivery using computer conferencing in higher education', in Eurlings, A. *et al.* (eds) *Integrating Information and Communication Technology in Higher Education*, 271–89, Kluwer: Deventer.

Jones, C. (1999b), 'From the sage on the stage to what exactly?', *ALT-J*, 7(2), 27–36.

Jones, C. (2002) 'Is there a policy for networked learning?' In Banks, S., Goodyear, P., Hodgson, V. and McConnell, D. *Networked Learning 2002: A research based conference on e-learning in Higher Education and Lifelong Learning*, Sheffield: University of Sheffield. Available online at: http://www.networkedlearningconference.org.uk/, last accessed 6 September 2006.

Jones, C. (2004) 'Networks and learning: communities, practices and the metaphor of networks', *ALT-J*, 12(1), 82–93.

Jones, C. and Asensio, M. (2001) 'Experiences of assessment: using phenomenography for evaluation', *ALT-J*, 17(3), 314–21.

Jones, C., Asensio, M. and Goodyear, P. (2000) 'Networked learning in higher education: practitioners' perspectives', *The Association for Learning Technology Journal*, 8(2) 18–28.

Jones, C., Dirckinck-Holmfeld, L. and Lindström, B. (2006) 'A relational, indirect, meso-level approach to CSCL design in the next decade', *Ijcscl International Journal of Computer Supported Collaborative Learning*, 1(1), 35–56.

Jones, I. and Pellegrini, A.D. (1996) 'The effects of social relationships, writing media and microgenetic development on first-grade students' written narratives', *American Educational Research Journal*, 33(3), 691–718.

Jones, S. (1999) *Doing Internet Research – Critical Issues and Methods for Examining the Net*, London: Sage.

Kahn, R. and Kellner, D. (2005) 'Reconstructing technoliteracy: a multiple literacies approach', *E-learning*, 2(3), 238–51. Available online at: http://www.wwwords.co.uk/ELEA/content/pdfs/2/issue2_3.asp#4.

Kant, I. (1781) *Critique of Pure Reason*, in translation by POLITIS, V 1993, London: Everyman.

Katzeff, C. (2003) 'Capturing playfulness in the design of digital learning environments for adults'. Available online at: http://www.tii.se/share/downloads/Prestudy_Play Design.pdf.

Kay, A. (1972) *A Personal Computer for Children of All Ages*, Xerox Palo Alto Research Centre. Available online at: http://www.mprove.de/diplom/gui/Kay72a.pdf, last accessed 20 November 2005.

Kaye, A.R. (ed.) (1992) *Collaborative Learning through Computer Conferencing: The Najdeen Papers*, Berlin: Springer-Verlag.

Kaye, A. (1995) 'Computer supported collaborative learning', in Heap, N., Thomas, R., Einon, G., Mason, R. and Mackay, H. (eds), *Information Technology and Society*, London: Sage.

Keller, J.M. and Suzuki, K. (1988) 'Use of the ARCS Motivation Model in courseware design', in Jonassen, D.H. (ed.), *Instructional Designs for Microcomputer Courseware*, Hillsdale, NJ: Lawrence Erlbaum.

Kelly, B., Phipps, L. and Swift, E. (2004) 'Developing a holistic approach for e-learning accessibility', *Canadian Journal of Learning and Technology*, 30, 3. Available online at: http://www.cjlt.ca/content/vol30.3/kelly.html, last accessed 5 October 2005.

Kemmis, S. (1996) 'Emancipatory aspirations in a postmodern era', in Zuber-Skerritt, O. (ed.), *New Directions in Action Research*, 199–242. London: Falmer Press.

Kennedy, H. (1998) *Learning Works (The Kennedy Report)*. Available online at: http://www.niace.org.uk/Organisation/advocacy/Archive/kennedybriefing.htm, last accessed 24 July 2006.

Kennedy, N. (1998) *Experiences of assessing LMU students over the web*, Leeds: Leeds Metropolitan University.

Kinzie, M.B. (1990) 'Requirements and benefits of effective interactive instruction: learner control, self-regulation and continuing motivation', *Educational Technology, Research and Development*, 38(1), 5–21.

Kirriemuir, J and McFarlane, A (2004) *A Literature Review on Computer Games and Learning*, Report 7, Nesta Futurelab Bristol. Available online at: www.nestafuture lab.org.

Kirriemuir, K. and McFarlarne, A. (2004) *Literature Review in Games and Learning*, Report 8, Nesta Futurelab. Available online at: http://www.nestafuturelab.org/research/reviews/08_01.htm.

Kirschner, P.A., Martens, R.L. and Strijbos, J.-W. (2004) 'CSCL in higher education?' in Strijbos, J.-W., Kirschner, P. and Martens, R. (eds) *What We Know About CSCL: And Implementing it in Higher Education*, Boston, MA: Kluwer Academic Publishers.

Klein, J.D. and Keller, J.M. (1990) 'Influence of student ability, locus of control, and type of instructional control on performance and confidence', *Journal of Educational Research*, 83(3), 140–6.

Kolb, D. (1984) *Experiential Learning; Experience as the Source of Learning and Development*, Englewood Cliffs, NJ: Prentice Hall.

Kolb, D. (1997) 'Scholarly hypertext: self-represented complexity', *Hypertext 97*, ACM, New York.

Kolb, D. (2000) 'Hypertext as subversive', *Culture Machine*. Available online at: http://culturemachine.tees.ac.uk/Cmach/Backissues/j002/Articles/art_kolb/Introduction_143.html.

Koper, R. (2003) 'Combining reusable learning resources and services with pedagogically purposeful units of learning', in Littlejohn, A. (ed.) *Reusing Online Resources: A Sustainable Approach to eLearning*, 46–59, London: Kogan Page.

Koper, R. (2004) 'Editorial: technology and lifelong learning', *British Journal of Educational Technology*, 35(6), 675–8.

Koper, R. and Olivier, B. (2004) 'Representing the learning design of units of learning', *Education, Technology and Society*, 7(3), 97–111.

Koschmann, T. (ed.) (1996) *CSCL: Theory and Practice of an Emerging Paradigm*, Mahwah, NJ: Lawrence Erlbaum Associates.

Koschmann, T. (2001) 'Revisiting the paradigms of instructional technology', in Kennedy, G., Keppell, M., McNaught, C. and Petrovic, T. (eds), *Meeting at the Crossroads. Proceedings of the 18th Annual Conference of the Australian Society for Computers in*

Learning in Tertiary Education, 15–22, Melbourne: Biomedical Multimedia Unit, The University of Melbourne. Available online at: http://www.ascilite.org.au/conferences/melbourne01/pdf/papers/koschmannt.pdf, last accessed 2 December 2005.

Koschmann, T. (2002) 'Dewey's contribution to the foundations of CSCL research', in Stahl, G. (ed.), *Computer Support for Collaborative Learning: Foundations for a CSCL community*, proceedings of CSCL 2002, Boulder, Colorado, USA. 7–11 January, 2002.

Koschmann, T., Chai, T.-W. and Suthers, D.D. (eds) (2005) 'CSCL 2005 the next ten years!', *Proceedings of the International Conference on Computer Supported Collaborative Learning*, Taipei, Taiwan.

Koschmann, T., Kelson, A.C., Feltovich, P.J., Barrows, H.S. (1996) 'Computer-Supported Problem-Based Learning: A principled approach to the use of computers in the collaborative learning', in Koschmann, T. (ed.) *CSCL: Theory and Practice of an Emerging Paradigm*. Mahwah, NJ: Lawrence Erlbaum Associates.

Koschmann, T., Suthers, D. and Chan, T.-W. (eds) (2005) *Computer Supported Collaborative Learning 2005: The Next Ten Years!* Mahwah, NJ: Lawrence Erlbaum Associates.

Kress, G. (1997) *Before writing: rethinking the paths to literacy*, London: Routledge.

Kress, G. (1998) 'Visual and verbal modes of representation in electronically mediated communication: the potentials of new forms of text', in Snyder, I. (ed.), *Page to Screen: Taking Literacy into the Electronic Era*, 53–79, London: Routledge.

Kress, G. (2003) *Literacy in the New Media Age*, London: Routledge.

Kreuger, L.W., Karger, H. and Barwick, A. (1989) 'A critical look at children and microcomputers: some phenomenological observations', in Pardeck, J.T. and Murphy, J.W. (eds), *Microcomputers in Early Childhood Education*, New York: Gordon and Breach.

Kristeva, J. (1989) *Language, the Unknown: An Initiation into Linguistics*, New York: Columbia University Press.

Kukulska-Hulme, A. and Traxler, J. (2005) *Mobile Learning: A Handbook for Educators and Trainers*, London: Routledge.

Kumar, K. (1995) *From Post-industrial to Post-modern Society: New Theories of the Contemporary World*, Oxford: Blackwell.

Kuutti, K. (1996) 'Activity theory as a potential framework for human-computer interaction research', in Nardi, B.A. (ed.), *Context and Consciousness: Activity Theory and Human-Computer Interaction*, Cambridge, MA: MIT.

Kvale, S. (1996) *Inter Views: An Introduction to Qualitative Research Interviewing*, Thousand Oaks, CA: Sage.

Lakkala, M., Rahikainen, M. and Hakkarainen, K. (2001) 'Perspectives of CSCL in Europe: a review', *ITCOLE Project Deliverable 2.01*. Available online at: www.euro-cscl.org/site/itcole/D2_1_review_of_cscl.pdf, last accessed 2 December 2005.

Land, R. and Bayne, S. (2005) 'Screen or monitor? Issues of surveillance and disciplinary power in online learning environments', in Land, R. and Bayne, S. (eds), *Education in Cyberspace*, London: RoutledgeFalmer.

Landauer, T.K. (1995) *The Trouble with Computers*, Cambridge, MA: Academic Press.

Landow, G. (1992) *Hypertext: The Convergence of Contemporary Critical Theory and Technology*, Baltimore: Johns Hopkins University Press.

Landow, G. (1997) *Hypertext 2.0: The Convergence of Contemporary Critical Theory and Technology*, London: The Johns Hopkins University Press.

Lankshear, C. and Knoble, M. (2003) *New Literacies: Changing Knowledge and Classroom Learning*, Buckingham: Open University Press.

Lash, S. and Urry, J. (1994) *Economies of Signs and Space*, London: Sage.

Latour, B. (1999) *Pandora's Hope: Essays on the Reality of Science Studies*, London: Harvard University Press.

Laurillard, D. (1993) *Rethinking University Education*, 1st edn, London: Routledge.

Laurillard, D. (1994) 'How can learning technologies improve learning?' in Martin, J., Darby J., and Kjollerstrom, B. *Higher Education 1998 Transformed by Learning Technology*, CTISS Publications, University of Oxford.

Laurillard, D. (2002) *Can Technical Standards Unlock the Pedagogical Innovation Needed for E-learning?*, paper presented at the IMS Open Technical Forum, Sheffield, England, September 2002. Available online at: http//:www.imsglobal.org/otf/d102SeptSheffield.pdf, last accessed 26 April 2003.

Laurillard, D. (2003) 'Application and content development and deployment: the challenges of e-learning, why Open Source matters', *BECTA expert seminar series*. Available online at: http://www.becta.org.uk/etseminars/presentations/presentation.cfm?seminar_id=12andsection=7_1andpresentation_id=8andid=2608.

Laurillard, D. and McAndrew, P. (2003) 'Re-usable educational software: a basis for generic e-learning tasks, in Littlejohn, A. (ed.), *Reusing Online Resources: A sustainable Approach to E-learning*, London: Kogan Page.

Lave, J. and Wenger, E. (1991) *Situated Learning – Legitimate Peripheral Participation*, Cambridge: Cambridge University Press.

Lawless, C. and Kirkwood, A. (1974) 'Training the educational technologist', *British Journal of Educational Technology*, 1(7), 54–60.

Lawless, S., Wade, V. and Conlan, O. (2005) 'Dynamic Contextual eLearning – Dynamic Content Discovery, Capture and Learning Object Generation from Open Corpus Sources', in Richards, G. (ed.), *Proceedings of World Conference on E-learning in Corporate, Government, Healthcare, and Higher Education 2005*, 2158–65. Chesapeake, VA: AACE.

Lay, S. and Sclater, N. (2001) 'Question and test interoperability: an update on national and international developments', in Danson, M. and Eabry, C. (eds), *5th International CAA Conference*, Loughborough: Loughborough University.

Lea, M. and Street, B. (1998) 'Student writing in higher education: an academic literacies approach', *Studies in Higher Education*, 23(2), 157–72.

Lea, M. and Stierer, B. (2000) *Student Writing in Higher Education: New Contexts*, Buckingham: Society for Research into Higher Education and Open University Press.

Lea, M.R. and Nicoll, K. (eds) (2002) *Distributed Learning: Social and Cultural Approaches to Practice*, London: RoutledgeFalmer/Open University.

Lehtinen, E. (2003) 'Computer-supported collaborative learning', in De Corte, E., Verschaffel, L., Entwistle, N. and van Merrienböer, J. (eds), *Unravelling Basic Components and Dimensions of Powerful Learning Environments*, 35–53, Advances in Learning and Instruction Series, Oxford: Pergamon.

Lehtinen, E., Hakkarinen, K., Lipponen, L., Rahikainen, M. and Muukkonen, H. (1999) *Computer Supported Collaborative Learning: A Review of Research and Development*, The Netherlands, University of Nijmegen, Department of Educational Sciences (The J.H.G.I Giesbers Reports on Education, 10). Available online at: http://etu.utu.fi/papers/clnet/ clnetreport.html, last accessed 2 December 2005.

Levene, M. and Loizou, G. (2003) 'Computing the entropy of user navigation in the web', *International Journal of Information Technology and Decision Making*, 2, 459–76.

Levine, P. and Scollon, R. (eds) (2004) *Discourse and Technology*, Washington, DC: Georgetown University Press.

Levy, P. (2003) 'A methodological framework for practice-based research in networked learning', *Instructional Science*, 3, 87–109.

Lewin, K. (1952) *Field Theory in Social Science: Selected Theoretical Papers*, London: Tavistock.

Lewis, R. (1997) 'An activity theory framework to explore distributed communities', *Journal of Computer Assisted Learning*, 13, 210–18.

Liber, O. and Olivier, B. (2003) 'Learning technology interoperability standards', in Littlejohn, A. (ed.), *Reusing Online Resources: A Sustainable Approach to E-learning*, 146–55, London: Kogan Page.

Light, P., Nesbitt, E., Light, V. and White, S. (2000) 'Variety is the spice of life: student use of CMC in the context of campus based study', *Computers and Education*, 34, 257–67.

Lilley, M. and Barker, T. (2003) 'An evaluation of a computer adaptive test in a UK university context', in Christie, J. (ed.), *7th International CAA Conference*, Loughborough: Loughborough University.

Lillis, T (2001) *Student Writing: Access, Regulation, Desire*, London: Routledge.

Linn, M.C. (1996) 'Key to the information highway', *Communications of the ACM*, 39(4), 34–5.

Lisewski, B. and Joyce, P. (2003) 'Examining the five-stage e-moderating model: designed and emergent practice in the learning technology profession', *ALT-J*, 11(1), 55–66.

List, D. (2001) *Screenreading*. Available online at: http://www.dennislist.net/scread.html, last accessed 30 March 2006.

Littlejohn, A. (2003) *Reusing Online Resources: A Sustainable Approach to E-learning*, Open and Flexible Learning Series, London and Sterling, VA: Kogan Page.

Littlejohn, A. (2004) 'Supporting sustainable e-learning', *ALT-J*, 11, 3.

Littlejohn, A. (2005) 'Key issues in the design and delivery of technology-enhanced learning', in Levy, P. and Roberts, S. (eds), *Developing the New Learning Environment: The Changing Role of the Academic Librarian*, 70–90, London: Facet.

Littlejohn, A. and Cameron, S. (1999) 'Supporting strategic cultural change: the Strathclyde Learning Technology Initiative as a model', *ALT-J*, 7(3), 64–74.

Littlejohn, A. and Peacock, S. (2003) 'From pioneers to partners: the changing voices of staff developers', in Seale, J. (ed.), *Learning Technology in Transition: From Individual Enthusiasm to Institutional Implementation*, 77–90, Lisse, Netherlands: Swets and Zeitlinger.

Littlejohn, A. and McGill, L. (2004) Report on the effectiveness of resources for e-learning, report for the JISC-commissioned research study on the effectiveness of resources, tools and support services used by practitioners in designing and delivering e-learning activities. Available online at http://www.elearning.ac.uk/resources/effectivefinal/view.

Littlejohn, A., McGill, L. and Falconer, I. (forthcoming) 'Characterising effective eLearning resources'.

Livingstone, D.W. (2000) *Exploring the Icebergs of Adult Learning: Findings of the First Canadian Survey of Informal Learning Practices* (NALL Working Paper #10–2000), Ontario Institute for Studies in Education, University of Toronto.

Longo, B. (2001) 'How a librarian can live nine lives in a knowledge-based economy', *Computers in Libraries*, 20(10). Available online at: http://www.infotoday.com/cilmag/nov01/longo.htm, last accessed 28 February 2006.

LTS (2005) 'Learning and Teaching Scotland – metadata taxonomies'. Available online at: http://www.ltscotland.org.uk/about/guidelines/metadatataxonomies.asp, last accessed 30 March 2006.

Lukasiak, J., Agostinho, S., Bennett, S., Harper, B., Lockyer, L. and Powley, D. (2005) 'Learning objects and learning designs: an integrated system for reusable, adaptive and shareable learning content', *ALT-J*, 13(2), 151–69.

Luke, R. (2002) 'Access*Ability:* enabling technology for life long learning. Integrating technology into learning and working', *Educational Technology and Society*, 5(1) 148–52.

Lyotard, J.-F. (1979) *The Postmodern Condition: a Report on Knowledge*, Manchester: Manchester University Press.

McAlpine, M. (2002a) *Principles of Assessment*, Luton: CAA Centre.

McAlpine, M. (2002b) *A Summary of Methods of Item Analysis*, Luton: CAA Centre.

McCalla, G.I. (1993) 'Tutorial dialogue', *Proceedings of International Conference on Computers in Education (ICCE)*, Taiwan, December 1993.

McConnell, D. (2000) *Implementing Computer Supported Cooperative Learning*, 2nd edn, London: Kogan Page.

McConnell, D. (2002) 'The experience of collaborative assessment in e-learning', *Studies in Continuing Education*, 24(1), 73–92.

McConnell, D. (2006) *E-learning Groups and Communities*, Maidenhead: SRHE/Open University Press.

McFarlane, A.E. (2007) 'Online communities of learning: lessons from the world of games and play', in Andrews, R. and Haythornthwaite, C. (eds), *Handbook of Elearning Research*, London: Sage.

McFarlane Report (1992) *Teaching and Learning in an Expanding Higher Education System*, Edinburgh: Committee of Scottish University Principals.

McFarlane, A., Sparrowhawk, A. and Heald, Y. (2002) *The Role of Games in Education*, research report to the DfES. Available online at: http://www.teem.org.uk

McKenna, C. (2002) 'What do we mean by electronic literacy?' in Rust, C. (ed.) *Proceedings of Improving Student Learning Conference*, OCSLD.

McKenna, C. (2005) 'Words, bridges and dialogue: issues of audience and addressivity in online communication', in Land, R. and Bayne, S. (eds), *Education in Cyberspace*, Abingdon: RoutledgeFalmer.

McLuhan, M. (1989) *The Medium is the Message*, New York: Simon and Schuster.

McMahon, A. (2000) 'The development of professional intuition', in Atkinson, T. and Claxton, G. (eds), *The Intuitive Practitioner: On the Value of Not Always Knowing What One is Doing*, 137–48, Buckingham: Open University Press.

McNaught, C. and Kennedy, P. (2000) 'Staff development at: RMIT: bottom-up work serviced by top-down investment and policy', *ALT-J*, 8(1), 4–18.

McNay (1995) 'From collegial acedemy to the corporate enterprise: the changing cultures of universities', in Schuller, T. (ed.), *The Changing University?*, Buckingham: Open University/SRHE.

McNiff, J. (1988) *Action Research: Principles and Practice*, London: Routledge.

McNiff, J., Lomax, P. and Whitehead, J. (1996) *You and Your Action Research Project*, London: Routledge.

Mallen, G. (2005) 'Reflections on Gordon Pask's adaptive teaching concepts and their relevance to modern knowledge systems', *Proceedings of the 5th Conference on Creativity and Cognition*, ACM. Available online at: http://delivery.acm.org/10.1145/

1060000/1056238/p86mallen.pdf?key1=1056238andkey2=4360091311andcoll=GUI
DEanddl=GUIDEandCFID=60191711andCFTOKEN=81769415, last accessed 20
November 2005.

Malone, T.W. (1981) 'What makes computer games fun?', *Byte*, 6, 258–77.

Malone, T.W. and Lepper, M.R. (1987) 'Making learning fun: a taxonomy of intrinsic
motivations for learning', in Snow, R. and Farr, M. (eds), *Aptitude, Learning and
Instruction. Volume 3: Conative and Affective Process Analysis,* 223–53, Hillsdale, NJ:
Lawrence Erlbaum Associates.

Marais, E., Minnaar, U. and Argles, D. (2005) 'Plagiarism in e-learning systems: identifying and solving the problem for practical assignments'. Submitted to 15th International
World Wide Web Conference, Edinburgh, Scotland. Available online at:
http://eprints.ecs.soton.ac.uk/11598/, last accessed 31 March 2006.

Martin, A. (2003) 'Towards e-literacy', in Martin, A. and Rader, H. (eds), *Information and
IT Literacy: Enabling Learning in the 21st Century,* 3–23, London: Facet.

Mason, R. (2001) 'E-learning: what have we learnt?', in Rust, C. (ed.), *Improving Student
Learning Using Learning Technology,* proceedings of the 2001 ninth International
Improving Student Learning Symposium, Herriot-Watt University, 27–34. Oxford:
Oxford Centre for Staff and Learning Development.

Mason, R. and Weller, R. (2000) 'Factors affecting students' satisfaction on a web course',
Australian Journal of Educational Technology, 16(2), 173–200. Available online at:
http://www.ascilite.org.au/ajet/ajet16/mason.html.

Mason, R. (2002) 'E-learning and the eUniversity', *ALT Policy Board,* Birmingham.

Maudet, N. and Moore, D.J. (2000) 'Dialogue games as dialogue models for interacting
with, and via computers', *Informal Logic,* 21, 219–243.

Mayes, J.T. (1995) 'Learning technology and groundhog day. Hypermedia at work: practice and theory', in Strang, W., Simpson, V.B. and Slater, D., *Higher Education,*
Canterbury: University of Kent Press.

Mayes, J.T. and Fowler, C.J.H. (1999) 'Learning technology and usability: a framework for
understanding courseware', *Interacting with Computers,* 11: 485–97.

Mayes, J.T., Dineen, F., Mckendee, J. and Lee, J. (2001) 'Learning from watching others
learn', in Steeples, C. and Jones, C. (eds), *Networked Learning: Perspectives and
Issues,* London: Springer.

Mayes, T. (2003) 'Vision and theoretical perspectives: Introduction to Part 1', in Littlejohn,
A. and Buckingham Shum, S. (eds), *Reusing Online Resources, Journal of Interactive
Media in Education* (Special Issue), 2003(1). Available online at: www-jime.open.
ac.uk/2003/1/.

Mayes, T. and de Freitas, S. (2004) 'Review of e-learning frameworks, models and theories', *JISC E-learning Models Desk Study.* Available online at: http://www.jisc.ac.uk/
epedagogy.

Melrose, M. (1996) 'Got a philosophical match? Does it matter?', in Zuber-Skerritt, O.
(ed.) *New Directions in Action Research,* 49–65. London: The Falmer Press.

Merrill, M. (2001) 'Components of instruction: towards a theoretical tool for instructional
design', *Instructional Science,* 29(4/5), 291–310.

Millard, D., Howard, Y., Bailey, C., Davis, H., Gibert, L., Jeyes, S., Price, J., Sclater, N.,
Sherratt, R., Tulloch, I., Wills, G. and Young, R. (2005) 'Mapping the e-learning assessment domain: concept maps for orientation and navigation', *Proceedings of e-Learn
2005,* Vancouver, Canada.

Millen, J. (1997) 'Par for the course: designing course outlines and feminist freedoms', *Curriculum Studies*, 5(1), 9–27.

Moore, G.A. (1991) *Crossing the Chasm*, New York: HarperBusiness.

Moore, G.A. (1995) *Inside the Tornado*, New York: HarperBusiness.

Morgan, G. (1986) *Images of Organisations*, 2nd edn, London: Sage Publications.

Mumford, E. (2003) 'Designing human systems, the ETHICS method'. Available online at: http://www.enid.u-net.com/C1book1.htm, last accessed 30 July 2003.

Mwanza, D. (2002) 'Conceptualising work activity for CAL systems design', *JCAL*, 18(1).

NAGCELL (1997) *Learning for the 21st Century*, National Advisory Group for Continuing Education and Lifelong Learning (NAGCELL). Available online at: http://www.niace.org.uk/Organisation/advocacy/Archive/kennedybriefing.htm, last accessed 24 July 2006.

Naismith, L., Sharples, M. and Ting, J. (2005) 'Evaluation of CAERUS: a context aware mobile guide', in van der Merwe, H. and Brown, T. (eds), *Mobile Technology: the Future of Learning in Your Hands*, mLearn 2005 Book of Abstracts, 4th World Conference on mLearning, Cape Town, 25–28 October 2005, 50.

Nardi, B. (ed.) (1996) *Context and Consciousness: Activity Theory and Human-computer Interaction*, Cambridge: MIT Press.

NCIHE (1997) 'National Committee of Inquiry into Higher Education – the Dearing Report', in *Higher Education in the Learning Society*, London: HMSO/NCIHE.

NDPCAL (1973) *National Development Programme in Computer Assisted Learning, final report of the director*, London: Council for Educational Technology.

Nelson, D.A. (1983) 'Report of a working party on computer facilities for teaching in universities', Computer Board Universities and Research Councils (*CBURC*), London: CBURC.

Nelson, T. (1982) *Literary Machines*, Sausalito, CA: Mindful Press.

Nicol, D. and Coen, M. (2003) 'A model for evaluating the institutional costs and benefits of ICT initiatives in teaching and learning in higher education', *ALT-J*, 11(2), 46–60.

Nielsen, J. (1990) *Hypertext and Hypermedia*, Boston, MA: Academic Press.

Oatley, K. and Nundy, S. (1996) 'Rethinking the role of emotions in education', in Olson, D. and Torrance, N. (eds), *The Handbook of Education and Human Development: New Models of Learning Teaching and Schooling*, Cambridge, MA: Blackwell.

OLF (2003) *iPALIO 2003*, London: The Open Learning Foundation.

Oliver, M. (2000) 'An introduction to the evaluation of learning technology', *Educational Technology and Society*, 3(4), 20–30. Available online at: http://ifets.gmd.de/periodical/vol_4_2000/intro.html, last accessed 11 October 2002.

Oliver, M. (2001) 'Evaluating online teaching and learning', *Information Services and Use*, 20(2/3), 83–94.

Oliver, M. (2002) 'What do learning technologists do?', *Innovations in Education and Training International*, 39(4), 245–52.

Oliver, M. (2003a) 'The development of an accreditation framework for learning technologists'. Available online at: http://www.ucl.ac.uk/epd/alt-accreditation/.

Oliver, M. (2003b) 'Curriculum design as an acquired social practice: a case study of UK Higher Education', Paper presented at the 84th Annual Meeting of the American Educational Research Association, Chicago.

Oliver, M. (2004) 'Metadata vs. educational culture: roles, power and standardisation', in Land, R. and Bayne, S. (eds), *Education in Cyberspace*, 112–38, London: RoutledgeFalmer.

Oliver, M. (2005) 'Supporting academics through institutional change: what will the impact of sustainable e-learning be on staff roles?' Available online at: http://heacademy.ac.uk/, last accessed 20 December 2005.

Oliver, M. and Conole, G. (1998) 'The evaluation of learning technology – an overview', in Oliver, M. (ed.), *Innovation in the Evaluation of Learning Technology*, 5–22. London: University of North London Press.

Oliver, M. and Conole, G. (2003) 'Evidence-based practice and e-learning in higher education: can we and should we?' *Research papers in education*, 18(4), 385–97.

Oliver, M. and Dempster, J. (2003) 'Strategic staff development for embedding e-learning practices in HE', in Blackwell, R. and Blackmore, P. (eds), *Towards Strategic Staff Development?*, Buckingham: SRHE/OU Press.

Oliver, M. and Harvey, J. (2002) 'What does "impact" mean in the evaluation of learning technology?', *Educational Technology and Society*, 5(3), 18–26. Available online at: http://ifets.ieee.org/periodical/vol_3_2002/oliver.html, last accessed 11 October 2002.

Oliver, M., MacBean, J., Conole, G. and Harvey, J. (2002) 'Using a toolkit to support the evaluation of learning', *Journal of Computer Assisted Learning*, 18(2), 199–208.

Oliver, M., Price, P., Boycheva, S., Dugstad Wake, J., Jones, C., Mjelstad, S., Kemp, B., Nikolov, R. and van der Meij, H. (2005) 'Empirical studies of the impact of technology-enhanced learning on roles and practices in higher education', *Kaleidoscope project report D30–03–01-F*.

Oliver, R. (2002) 'Winning the toss and electing to bat: maximising the opportunities of online learning', in Rust, C. (ed.), *Proceedings of the 9th Improving Student Learning Conference*, 35–44, Oxford: OCSLD.

Oliver, R. (2005) 'Quality assurance and e-learning: blue skies and pragmatism', *ALT-J*, 13(3) 173–87.

O'Malley, C. (ed.) (1995) *Computer Supported Collaborative Learning*, Berlin: Springer-Verlag.

Ong, W. (1982) *Orality and Literacy: The Technologizing of the Word*, New York: Routledge.

O'Reilly, M. and Morgan, C. (1999) 'Online assessment: creating communities and opportunities', in Brown, S., Race, P. and Bull, J. (eds), *Computer-assisted Assessment in Higher Education*, 149–161, London: Kogan Page.

O'Shea, T. and Scanlon, E. (1997) 'Virtual learning environmnents and the role of the teacher', report of a UNESCO/Open University International Colloquim. Available online at: http://iet.open.ac.uk/pp/e.scanlon/download/UNESCO.pdf.

Outtz, J.L. (1998) 'Testing medium, validity and test performance', in Hakel, M.D. (ed.) *Beyond Multiple Choice Evaluating Alternative to Traditional Testing for Selection*, New Jersey: Lawrence Erlbaum Associates.

Pakstas, A. and Komiya, R. (2002) *Virtual Reality Technologies for Future Telecommunications Systems*, Chippenham, UK: John Wiley and Sons.

Panitz, T. (2001) *The Case for Student-centred Instruction via Collaborative Learning Paradigms*. Available online at: http://home.capecod.net/~tpanitz/teds.articles/coop-benefits.htm, last accessed 16 November 2005.

Papert, S. (1980) *Mindstorms: Computers and Powerful Ideas*, New York: Basic Books.

Papert, S. and Harel, I. (1991) *Constructionism*, Norwood, NJ: Ablex.

Parlett, M. and Hamilton, D. (1972) *Evaluation as Illumination: A New Approach to the Study of Innovatory Programmes*, Occasional paper 9, Centre for Research in the Educational Sciences, University of Edinburgh.

Patton, M. (1997) *Utilization-focused Evaluation: The New Century Text*, London: Sage.

Pea, R. and Seely-Brown (1996) in Chaiklin, S. and Lave, J. (eds), *Understanding Practice: Perspectives on Activity in Context*, Cambridge: Cambridge University Press.

Peacock, J. (2005) 'Information literacy education in practice from developing the new learning environment: the changing role of the academic librarian', in Levy, P. and Roberts, S. (eds), *Developing the New Learning Environment: The Changing Role of the Academic Librarian*, 153–80, London: Facet Publishing.

Pearson, E.J. and Koppi, T. (2006 in press) 'Supporting staff in developing inclusive online learning', in Adams, M. and Brown, S. (eds), *Towards Inclusive Learning in Higher Education*, Oxford: Routledge Press.

Pelletier, C. (2005) 'New technologies, new identities: the university in the informational age', in Land, R. and Bayne, S. (eds), *Education in Cyberspace*, London: RoutledgeFalmer.

Piaget, J. (1971) *Structuralism*, London: Routledge and Kegan Paul.

Piaget, J. (1973) *The Child's Conception of the World*, London: Paladin.

Pilkington, R.M. and Parker-Jones, C. (1996) 'Interacting with computer-based simulations', *Computers and Education*, 3(3), 275–85.

Pollert, A. (1991) *Fairwell to Flexibility*, London: Basil Blackwell.

Polsani, P.R. (2003) 'Use and abuse of reusable learning objects', *Journal of Digital Information*, 3(4). Available online at: http://jodi.ecs.soton.ac.uk/Articles/v03/i04/Polsani/.

Popper, K. (1996) *The Myth of the Framework: In Defence of Science and Rationality*, London: Routledge.

Powell, N., Moore, D., Gray, J., Finlay, J. and Reaney, J. (2004) 'Dyslexia and learning programming', *Italics*, 13(2). Available online at: http://www.ics.ltsn.ac.uk/pub/italics/Vol3–2/dyslexia.pdf, last accessed 5 October 2005.

Preece, J. (2000) *Online Communities: Designing Usability, Supporting Sociability*, Chichester, UK: John Wiley and Sons.

Price, J. (unpublished work), 'Dealing with Plagiarism in Higher Education', PhD thesis, University of Southampton.

Price, S., Oliver, M., Fartunova, M., Jones, C., van der Meij, H., Mjelstad, S., Mohammad, F., Nikolov, R., Wake, J. and Wasson, B. (2005) 'Review of the impact of technology-enhanced learning on roles and practices in higher education', *Kaleidoscope project report D30–02–01-F*.

Rainger, P. (2003) *A Dyslexic Perspective on e-Content Accessibility*. Available online at: http://www.techdis.ac.uk/seven/papers/dyslexia-index.html, last accessed 5 October 2005.

Ranson, S. (1994) 'Markets or democracy for education', *British Journal of Educational Studies*, 42, 333–51.

Ravenscroft, A. (1997) 'Learning as Knowledge Refinement: A Computer-based Approach'. Unpublished PhD Thesis, Computer based Learning Unit, University of Leeds, UK.

Ravenscroft, A. (2001) 'Designing e-learning interactions in 21C: revisiting and re-thinking the role of theory', *European Journal of Education: Special Edition on On-line Learning*, 36(2), 133–56.

Ravenscroft, A. (2004a) 'From conditioning to learning communities: implications of fifty years of research in e-learning interaction design', *ALT-J*, 11(3), 4–18.

Ravenscroft, A. (2004b) 'Towards highly communicative eLearning communities: developing a socio-cultural framework for cognitive change'. To appear in Land, R. and Bayne, S. (eds) *Cyberspace Education*, Routledge, Ch 9, 130–45.

Ravenscroft, A. and Hartley, J.R. (1999) 'Learning as knowledge refinement: designing a dialectical pedagogy for conceptual change', in Lojoie, S. and Vivets, M. (eds), *Frontiers in Artificial Intelligence and Applications, Volume 50, Artifical Intelligence in Education, Open Learning Environments: New Computational Technologies to Support Learning, Exploration and Collaboration*, 155–62, Amsterdam: IOS Press.

Ravenscroft, A. and Pilkington, R.M. (2000) 'Investigation by design: developing dialogue models to support reasoning and conceptual change', *International Journal of Artificial Intelligence in Education*, 11, 273–98.

Ravenscroft, A. and McAlister, S. (2006) 'Digital games and learning in cyberspace: a dialogical approach', *E-learning Journal*, Special Issue of *Ideas in Cyberspace 2005 Symposium*, 3(1), 38–51.

Rehak, D.R. and Mason, R.D. (2003) 'Keeping the learning in learning objects', in Littlejohn, A (ed.) *Reusing Educational Resources for Networked Learning*, London: Kogan Page.

Rekkedal, T. (1994) *Research in Distance Education – Past, Present and Future*. Available online at: http://www.nettskolen.com/pub/artikkel.xsql?artid=139, last accessed 30 March 2006.

Rheingold, H. (2002) *Smart Mobs: The Next Social Revolution*, Cambridge, MA: Perseus.

Rieber, L. (2001) 'Designing learning environments that excite serious play', 1–10, *Proceedings of ASCILITE 2001*, Melbourne, Australia, December 2001.

Roberts, G. (2004) 'The new covert curriculum: a critical, actor-network approach to learning technology policy'. *Networked Learning 2004: proceedings of the 4th international conference held at the University of Lancaster, 5–7 April 2004*. Banks, S., Goodyear, P., Hodgson, V. *et al.*, University of Sheffield and University of Lancaster. Available online at: http://www.networkedlearningconference.org.uk/past/nlc2004/proceedings/individual_papers/roberts.htm, last accessed 8 September 2006.

Roberts, G. and Huggins, R. (2004) 'Pedagogical pragmatism: a new critical approach to the development of resources for learning'. *Networked Learning 2004: proceedings of the 4th international conference held at the University of Lancaster, 5–7 April 2004*. Banks, S., Goodyear, P., Hodgson, V. *et al.*, University of Sheffield and University of Lancaster. Available online at: http://www.shef.ac.uk/nlc2004/Proceedings/Individual_Papers/Roberts_Huggins.htm, last accessed 29 March 2006.

Roberts, G., Aalderink, W., Windesheim H., Cook, J., Feijen, M., Harvey, J., Lee, S., Wade, V.P. and all the participants in the seminar (2005) *Reflective Learning, Future Thinking: Digital Repositories, e-Portfolios, Informal Learning and Ubiquitous Computing*. ALT/SURF/ILTA Spring Conference Research Seminar Trinity College, Dublin, 1 April 2005. Available online at: http://www.alt.ac.uk/docs/ALT_SURF_ILTA_white_paper_2005.pdf, last accessed 30 November 2005.

Roberts, T.S. (2005) *Computer-supported Collaborative Learning in Higher Education*, Pennsylvania: Idea Group Publishing.

Rogers, E.M. (1995) *Diffusion of Innovations*, 4th edn, New York: The Free Press.

Rosson, M.B., Carroll, J.M. and Bellamy, R. (1990) 'Smalltalk scaffolding: a case study of minimalist instruction', *Proceedings of CHI '90*, 423–9, ACM Press.

Rowley, J. (2002) 'JISC user behaviour monitoring and evaluation framework', *Framework Report to 2002 (Higher Education) (Cycles 1–3)*. Available online at: www.jisc.ac.uk/uploaded_documents/cycle%201–3%20report.

Säljö, R. (1999) 'Learning as the use of tools: a socio-cultural perspective on the human-technology link', in Littlejohn, A. and Light, L. (eds), *Learning with Computers, Analysing Productive Interactive*, London: Routledge.

Salmon, G. (2000) *E-moderating: The Key to Teaching and Learning Online*, London: Kogan Page.

Salmon, G. (2002) *E-Tivities: The Key to Online Teaching, Training, and Learning*, London: Kogan-Page.

Salmon, G. (2005) 'Flying not flapping: a strategic framework for e-learning and pedagogical innovation in higher education institutions', *ALT-J*, 13(3), 201–18.

Salomon, G. (ed.) (1993) *Distributed Cognitions: Psychological and Educational Considerations*, Cambridge: Cambridge University Press.

Scanlon, E. (1998) 'Learning science', *On-line Studies in Science Education*, 30, 57–70.

Scardamalia, M. and Bereiter, C. (1996) 'Computer support for knowledge-building communities', in Kotchmann, T. (ed.), *CSCL: Theory and Practice of an Emerging Paradigm*, Mahwah, NJ: Lawrence Erlbaum Associates.

Sclater, N. (2003) *TOIA-COLA Assessment Metadata Application Profile v1.2*. Available online at: http://www.cetis.ac.uk/profiles/uklomcore/.

Sclater, N. (ed.) (2004) 'Item Banks Infrastructure Study (IBIS)', *Joint Information Systems Committee*. Available online at: http://www.toia.ac.uk/ibis.

Sclater, N. and Howie, K. (2003) 'User requirements of the ultimate online assessment engine', *Computers and Education*, 40, 285–306.

Sclater, N. and MacDonald, M. (2004) 'Putting interoperability to the test: building a large reusable assessment item bank', *ALT-J, Research in Learning Technology*, 12(3), 208–15.

Sclater, N., Low, B. and Barr, N. (2002) 'Interoperability with CAA: does it work in practice?', in Danson, M. (ed.), *6th Proceedings of the International Conference on Computer-Assisted Assessment*, 317–26, Loughborough: Loughborough University.

Scollon, R. (1998) *Mediated Discourse as Social Interaction*, London: Longman.

Scollon, R. (2001) *Mediated Discourse: The Nexus of Practice*, London: Routledge.

Scollon, R. (2003) 'The dialogist in a positivist world: theory in the social sciences and the humanities at the end of the twentieth century', *Social Semiotics*, 13(1), 71–88.

SCONUL (1999), 'Information skills in higher education', *SCONUL Position Paper*. Available online at: www.sconul.ac.uk/activities/inf_lit/papers/Seven_pillars.html, last accessed 30 March 2006.

SCORM (2004) *Shareable Content Object Reference Model*. Available online at: http://www.adlnet.org/scorm/history/2004/index.cfm.

Scott, B. (1996) *Obituary for Professor Gordon Pask*. Available online at: http://www2.venus.co.uk/gordonpask/gpaskobit.htm, last accessed 20 November 2005.

Scriven, M. (1972) 'Pros and cons about goal-free evaluation', evaluation comment, 3:1–7, in Thomas, L. (ed.) *Philosophical Redirection of Educational Research: The Seventy-First Yearbook of the National Society for the Study of Education*, Chicago: University of Chicago Press.

Seale, J. (ed.) (2003) *Learning Technology in Transition – From Individual Enthusiasm to Institutional Implementation*, The Netherlands: Swets and Zeitlinger.

Seale, J. (2006) *Disability and E-learning in Higher Education: Accessibility Research and Practice*, Oxford: Routledge.

Searle, J.R. (1969) *Speech Acts: An Essay in the Philosophy of Language*, Cambridge: Cambridge University Press.

Seaton, W.J. (1993) 'Computer-mediated communication and student self-directed learning', *Open Learning*, 8 June (2), 49–54.

Seely-Brown, J., Collins A., and Daguid P. (1989) 'Situated cognition and the culture of learning', *Educational Researcher*, January, 32–41.

Serving Maths (2005) 'Serving Maths: experiences from a JISC distributed e-learning project'. Available online at: http://www.oss-watch.ac.uk/events/2005–07–04/servingmaths.pdf, last accessed 30 March 2006.

Sharan, S. (ed.) (1990) *Cooperative Learning; Theory and Research*, New York: Praeger.

Sharpe, R., Beetham, H. and Ravenscroft, A. (2004). 'Active artifacts: representing our knowledge of learning and teaching, *Educational Developments*, 5.2, 16–21.

Sharpe, R., Benfield, G., Lessner, E. and de Cicco, E. (2005) 'Scoping study for the pedagogy strand of the JISC e-learning programme', *Final Report*. Available online at: http://www.jisc.ac.uk/uploaded_documents/scoping%20study%20final%20report%20v4.1.doc, last accessed 30 March 2006.

Sharples, M. (2003) 'Disruptive devices: mobile technology for conversational learning', *International Journal of Continuing Engineering Education and Lifelong Learning*, 12(5/6), 504–20.

Sheerman, B. (2005) 'Comment on the release of the House of Commons Education and Skills Committee (2005)', UK e-University Third Report of Session 2004–05, London: The Stationery Office.

Shetzer, H. and Warschauer, M. (2000) 'An electronic literacy approach to network-based language teaching', in Warschauer, M. and Kern, R. (eds), *Network-based Language Teaching: Concepts and Practice*, New York: Cambridge University Press.

Simon, H. (2001) 'Learning to research about learning', in Carver, S. and Klahr, D. (eds), *Cognition and Instruction: Twenty-five Years of Progress* (205–26). Mahwah, NJ: Lawrence Erlbaum Associates.

Simpson, O. (2005) 'E-learning, democracy and social exclusions: issues of access and retention in the United Kingdom', in Carr-Chellman, A.A. (ed.) *Global Perspectives on E-learning: Rhetoric and Reality*, London and New Delhi: Sage.

Skinner, B.F. (1950) 'Are theories of learning necessary?', *Psychological Review*, 57, 193–216.

Skinner, B.F. (1954) 'The science of learning and the art of teaching', *Harvard Educational Review*, 24(1), 86–97.

Slavin, R.E. (1990) *Cooperative Learning: Theory, Research and Practice*, Englewood Cliffs, NJ: Prentice Hall.

Smith, J. (2005) 'From flowers to palms: 40 years of policy for online learning', *ALT-J*, 13(2), 93–108.

Smith, J. and Oliver, M. (2000) 'Academic development: a framework for embedding learning technology', *International Journal of Academic Development*, 5(2), 129–37.

Smith, J. and Oliver, M. (2005) 'Exploring behaviour in the online environment: student perceptions of information literacy', *ALT-J, Research in Learning Technology*, 13(1) 49–65.

Social Science Research Unit (2003) *A Study of MLE Activity*. Available online at: http://www.mlestudy.ac.uk/, last accessed 29 July 2003.

SPAID (2005) *Storage and Packaging of Assessment Item Data Project website*. Available online at: http://www.jisc.ac.uk/index.cfm?name=toolkit_strath1.

SQA (2003) *Guidelines for Online Assessment in Further Education*, Glasgow: Scottish Qualifications Agency.

St Pierre, E. (2002) 'Science rejects postmodernism', *Educational Researcher*, 31(8), 25–7.

Stahl, G. (2003) 'Meaning and interpretation in collaboration', in Wason, B. Ludvigsen, S. and Hoppe, U. (eds), *Designing for Change in Networked Learning Environments: Proceedings of the International Conference on Computer Supported Collaborative Learning 2003*, Dordrecht: Kluwer Academic Publishers.

Stahl, G. (2004) 'Building collaborative knowing: elements of a social theory of learning', in Strijbos, J.-W., Kirschner, P. and Martens, R. (eds), *What We Know About CSCL: And Implementing It In Higher Education*, Boston, MA: Kluwer Academic Publishers.

Stake, R. (1980) 'Program evaluation, particularly responsive evaluation', in Dockrell, W. B. and Hamilton D. (eds) *Rethinking Educational Research*, London: Hodder and Stoughton.

Stake, R. (1994) 'Case studies', in Denzin, N. and Lincoln, Y. (eds), *The Handbook of Qualitative Research*, 236–47, London: Sage.

Stanton, D., Neale, H. and Bayon, V. (2002) 'Interfaces to support children's co-present collaboration: multiple mice and tangible technologies', *Computer Support for Collaborative Learning (CSCL) 2002*, 342–52, Boulder, CO: ACM Press, January 7–11.

Stephens, D. and Mascia, J. (1997) 'Results of a survey into the use of computer-assisted assessment in institutions of higher education in the UK'. Available online at: http://www.lboro.ac.uk/service/ltd/flicaa/downloads/survey.pdf, last accessed 26 May 2003.

Street, B. (1997) 'The implications of the New Literacy Studies for literacy education', *English in Education*, 31(3), 45–59.

Strijbos, J-W., Kirschner, P. and Martens, R. (eds) (2004) *What We Know About CSCL: And Implementing It In Higher Education*, Boston, MA: Kluwer Academic Publishers.

Sutherland, R. (1983) 'Connecting theory and practice: results from the teaching of LOGO', *Educational Studies in Mathematics*, 24, 95–113.

Taylor, J. (2004) *E-learning research consultation*. Available online at: http://kn.open.ac.uk/public/index.cfm?wpid=2843.

Taylor, P.V. (1993) *The Texts of Paulo Freire*, Buckingham: Open University Press.

Taylor, P. (1999) *Making Sense of Academic Life*, Buckingham: Open University Press.

Theng, Y.L. (1999) 'Lostness and digital libraries', *Proceedings of the 4th ACM Conference on Digital Libraries*, Poster Presentation, 250, ACM Press.

Thomas, P. and Carswell, L. (2000) 'Learning through collaboration in a distributed education environment', *Educational Technology and Society*, 3(3). Available online at: http://ifets.ieee.org/periodical/vol_3_2000/d12.html.

Thompson, T. (2005) 'Universal design and web accessibility: unexpected beneficiaries', *paper presented at: CSUN '05*, Los Angeles, 17–19 March 2005. Available online at: http://www.csun.edu/cod/conf/2005/proceedings/2392.htm, last accessed 5 October 2005.

Thomson, T. (1998) 'Beyond technology: successful work-based learning in the information society', in Eurlings, A. (ed.), *Bringing Information Technology to Education*, 186–99, Dordrecht: Kluwer.

Thorpe, M. (2002) 'From independent learning to collaborative learning: new communities of practice in open, distance and distributed learning', in Lea, M. and Nicoll, K. (eds), *Distributed Learning: Social and Cultural Approaches to Practice*, 131–51. London: RoutledgeFalmer.

Timmis, S. (2003) 'ELTI workshop: institutional audits to inform the embedding of learning technologies and promote cross boundary working in our institutions', *ALT-C 2003*, workshop, Sheffield. Available online at: http://www.shef.ac.uk/alt/abstracts/ 90work/1/ws3–211.htm, last accessed 29 March 2006.

Tolmie, A. and Boyle, J. (2000) 'Factors influencing the success of computer mediated communication (CMC) environments in university teaching: a review and case study', *Computers and Education*, 34, 119–40.

Topping, K. (1992) 'Cooperative learning and peer tutoring: an overview', *The Psychologist: Bulletin of the British Psychological Society*, 5, 151–61.

Traxler, J. (2005) 'Using mobile technologies to support learning in sub-Saharan Africa', in van der Merwe, H. and Brown, T. (eds), *Book of Abstracts*, 66, Cape Town: mLearn 2005.

Trehan, K. and Reynolds, M. (2002) 'Online collaborative assessment: power relations and "critical learning", in Steeples, C. and Jones, C., *Networked Learning: Perspectives and Issues*, London: Springer-Verlag.

Twining, P. and Evans, D. (2005) 'Should there be a future for Tablet PCs in schools?' *Journal of Interactive Media in Education*, 20. Available online at http://jime.open.ac. uk/2005/20/, last accessed 8 September 2006.

US National Commission on Library and Information Science (2003) *The Prague Declaration: Towards An Information Literate Society*. Available online at: www.nclis.gov/libinter/infolitconf&meet/postinfolitconf&meet/PragueDeclaration.pdf.

Usher, R. and Bryant, I. (1989) *Adult Education as Theory, Practice and Research: The Captive Triangle*, London: Routledge.

Vanderheiden, G. (1996) *Universal Design. What It Is and What It Isn't*. Available online at: http://trace.wisc.edu/docs/whats_ud/whats_ud.htm, last accessed 5 October 2005.

Vass, E. (2002) 'Friendship and collaborative creative writing in the primary classroom', *JCAL*, 18(1), March 2002.

Vass, E. (2004) *Children's Computer Supported Collaborative Writing*, PhD thesis, Open University.

Vaughan, T. (1998) *Multimedia: Making It Work*, Berkley, CA: McGraw Hill.

Vavoula, G. and Sharples, M. (2003) 'Putting order to episodic and semantic learning memories: the case for KleOS', in Harris, D., Duffy, V., Smith, M. and Staphanidis, C. (eds), *Proceedings of HCI 03 Conference, Volume 3*, 894–8, Crete, June 22–27, Lawrence Erlbaum Associates.

Virkus, S. (2003) 'Information literacy in Europe: a literature review', *Information Research: an International Electronic Journal*, 8(4). Available online at: http://informationr.net/ir/8–4/paper159.html.

Von Glaserfeld, E. (1993) 'Questions and answers about radical constructivism', in Tobin, K. (ed.), *The Practice of Constructivism in Science Education*, Hillsdale, NJ: Lawrence Erlbaum.

Vygotsky, L.S. (1962) *Thought and Language*, Cambridge, MA: MIT Press.

Vygotsky, L.S. (1978) *Mind in Society: The Development of Higher Psychological Processes*, Cambridge, MA: Harvard University Press.

Vygotsky, L.S. (1986) *Thought and Language*, Kozulin, A. (trans.), Cambridge, MA: MIT Press.

Vygotsky, L.S. and Cole, M. (1978) *Mind in Society: The Development of Higher Psychological Processes*, Cambridge, MA: Harvard University Press.

Warburton, W. and Conole, G. (2003) 'CAA in UK HEIs: the state of the art', in Christie, J. (ed.), *7th International CAA Conference*, Loughborough: University of Loughborough.

Ward, W.C., Frederiksen, N. and Carlson, S.B. (1980) 'Construct validity of free response and machine-scorable forms of a test', *Journal of Educational Measurement*, 7(1), 11–29.

Wasson, B., Ludvigsen, S. and Hoppe, U. (eds) (2003) *Designing for Change in Networked Learning Environments*, Proceedings of the International Conference on Computer Supported Collaborative Learning 2003, Dordrecht: Kluwer Academic Publishers.

Webber, S. and Johnston, B. (2004) 'Information literacy in the curriculum: selected findings from a phenomenographic study of UK conceptions of, and pedagogy for, information literacy', in Rust, C. (ed.), *Improving Student Learning: Diversity and Inclusivity: Proceedings of the 11th ISL Symposium*. Birmingham, 6–8 September 2004. Oxford: Oxford Brookes University.

Wegerif, R. (1998) 'The social dimensions of asynchronous learning', *Journal of Asynchronous Learning Networks*, 2(1), March 1998, ISSN 1092–8235.

Weiss, C. (1993). 'Where politics and evaluation research meet', *Evaluation Practice*, 14(1), 93–106.

Wellman, B., Quan-Haase, A., Boase, J., Chen, W., Hampton, K., Isla de Diaz, I. and Miyata, K. (2003) 'The social affordances of the internet for networked individualism', *JCMC*, 8(3). Available online at: http://jcmc.indiana.edu/issues.html, last accessed 7 November 2005.

Wenger, E. (1987) *Artificial Intelligence and Tutoring Systems. Computational and Cognitive Approaches to the Communication of Knowledge*, Los Altos, CA: Morgan Kaufman.

Wenger, E. (1998) *Communities-of-Practice: Learning, Meaning and Identity*, Cambridge: Cambridge University Press.

Wertsch, J. (1991) *Voices of the Mind. A Sociocultural Approach to Mediated Action*, Cambridge: Harvard University Press.

White, S. (forthcoming) *Higher Education and Learning Technologies: An Organisational Perspective*, PhD thesis, University of Southampton.

Wilcox, P., Petch, J. and Dexter, H. (2005) 'Towards an understanding of UKeU business processes within an e-learning lifecycle model', *Electronic Journal of E-learning*, 3(1). Available online at: http://www.ejel.org/volume-3/v3-i1/v3-i1-art8-wilcox.pdf, last accessed 30 March 2006.

Wiley, D.A. (2000) 'Connecting learning objects to instructional design theory: a definition, a metaphor, and a taxonomy', *The Instructional Use of Learning Objects*. Available online at http:/reusability.org/read, last accessed 24 July 2006.

Wiley, D. (2003) *Learning Objects: Difficulties and Opportunities*. Available online at: http://wiley.ed.usu.edu/docs/lo do.pdf, last accessed 26 April 2003.

Williams, D. (2005) 'Literacies and learning', in Levy, P. and Roberts, S. (eds), *Developing the New Learning Environment: The Changing Role of the Academic Librarian*, 49–69. London: Facet.

Wilson, S., Blinco, K. and Rehak, D. (2004) 'Service-oriented frameworks: modelling the infrastructure for the next generation of e-learning systems'. *A paper prepared on behalf of DEST (Australia), JISC-CETIS (UK), and Industry Canada*. Available online at: http://www.jisc.ac.uk/uploaded_documents/AltilabServiceOrientedFrameworks.pdf.

Wirski, R., Brownfield, G. and Oliver R. (2004) 'Exploring SCORM and the National Flexible Learning Toolboxes', in Atkinson, R., McBeath, C., Jonas-Dwyer, D. and Phillips, R. (eds), *Beyond the Comfort Zone: Proceedings of the 21st ASCILITE Conference*, Perth, Western Australia, 5–8 December: ASCILITE. Available online at: http://www.ascilite.org.au/conferences/perth04/procs/contents.html.

Witt, N.A.J. and McDermott, A.P. (2002) 'Achieving SENDA-compliance for web sites in further and higher education: an art or a science?', in Phipps, L., Sutherland, A. and Seale, J. (eds) *Access All Areas: Disability, Technology and Learning*, ALT/JISC/TechDis.

Wittgenstein, L. (2001) *Philosophical Investigations*, London: Blackwell.

Wolf, A. (2002) *Does Education Matter? Myths About Education and Growth*, London: Penguin.

Woods, D. and Giuliani, G. (2005) *Open Source for the Enterprise: Managing Risks, Reaping Rewards*, O'Reilly.

Woolley, D. (1994) *PLATO: the emergence of online community*. Available online at: http://www.thinkofit.com/plato/dwplato.htm, last accessed 24 March 2006.

Yates, S. (1997) 'Gender, identity and CMC', *Journal of Computer Assisted Learning*, 13 (4), 281–90.

Index

eBooks – at www.eBookstore.tandf.co.uk

A library at your fingertips!

eBooks are electronic versions of printed books. You can store them on your PC/laptop or browse them online.

They have advantages for anyone needing rapid access to a wide variety of published, copyright information.

eBooks can help your research by enabling you to bookmark chapters, annotate text and use instant searches to find specific words or phrases. Several eBook files would fit on even a small laptop or PDA.

NEW: Save money by eSubscribing: cheap, online access to any eBook for as long as you need it.

Annual subscription packages

We now offer special low-cost bulk subscriptions to packages of eBooks in certain subject areas. These are available to libraries or to individuals.

For more information please contact webmaster.ebooks@tandf.co.uk

We're continually developing the eBook concept, so keep up to date by visiting the website.

www.eBookstore.tandf.co.uk